A HISTORY

OIL,

OF THE

TAXES,

DEVITT FAMILY

and

AND THE

CATS

MALLET RANCH

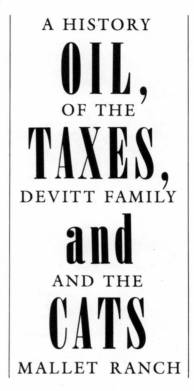

A HISTORY
OIL,
OF THE
TAXES,
DEVITT FAMILY
and
AND THE
CATS
MALLET RANCH

David J. Murrah

Texas Tech University Press

This book was set in Galliard and printed on acid-free paper that meets the guidelines for permanence and durability of the Committee on Production Guidelines for Book Longevity of the Council on Library Resources. ∞

Unless otherwise noted, all photographs which appear in this book were provided by Mrs. Helen Jones for preservation in the Southwest Collection at Texas Tech University.

Printed in the United States of America.

Library of Congress Cataloging-in-Publication Data
Murrah, David J.
    Oil, taxes, and cats : the saga of the DeVitt family and the Mallet Ranch / David Murrah
       p. cm.
    Includes bibliographical references and index.
    ISBN 0-89672-332-1 (cloth). — ISBN 0-89672-343-7 (special ed.)
    1. Mallet Ranch (Tex.)—History. 2. DeVitt family. I. Title.
F394.M294M87 1994
976.4'846—dc20

93-33654
CIP

94 95 96 97 98 99 00 01 02 / 9 8 7 6 5 4 3 2 1

Design by Barbara M. Whitehead

Endleaves: *Mallet Ranch Headquarters* by Mondel Rogers. Egg tempera, 34 inches by 69 inches, 1975. Courtesy Mondel Rogers, The Baker Gallery of Fine Art, and the Museum of Texas Tech University.

Texas Tech University Press
Lubbock, Texas 79409-1037 USA
1-800-832-4042

For my family—
my wife Ann, and children Jerel, Donna, Gene, and Elaine—
with heartfelt thanks for their
love and support.

CONTENTS

Preface

RANCHING has always been a revered facet of Texas history. Stories of trail drives, great round-ups, and life in the saddle have provided fascinating perspectives on cowboying and cattle. Yet often lost within the pages of cowboy lore is the fact that ranching was, and still is, a business. During the 1880s, some historic Texas ranches, such as the XIT, the Matador, the Pitchfork, and the Spur, were established and became the epitome of corporate big business for that day. For every major ranch, however, there were dozens of small ones whose owners were venture capitalists as well. These lesser-known cattlemen also moved onto the vast open ranges of West Texas to risk their investments in the face of open winter storms, drought, and long supply routes.

Most of the small ranchers did not survive the high risks. Some were pushed off the range by the large corporate ranches that acquired title to the land; others folded in the aftermath of the dry years of the late 1880s and early 1890s. Still others were forced out of business by a rapidly advancing farmers' frontier that was being driven by changing land laws that favored farm interests over those of cattlemen.

One survivor was the enterprising David Mantz DeVitt, a young newspaper reporter from New York who came to Texas in 1880 to seek his fortune. Although he had no practical experience in the livestock business, DeVitt, within a twenty-year period, parlayed a small investment into a 100,000-acre cattle operation located in the heart of the remote ranges of the Llano Estacado, now known as the western South Plains of Texas. DeVitt witnessed firsthand the rapid transition of the South Plains from open range ranching to enclosure. Through a partnership, he fashioned from the failure of others the Mallet Ranch, an enterprise that not only outlasted all the big ranches in the region, but continues to operate under the same family ownership.

Established in 1895, the Mallet Ranch will soon celebrate its one hundredth birthday, yet relatively few people know anything about it. Located in the southwestern quarter of Hockley County, the Mallet encompasses approximately fifty thousand acres of pastures and another five thousand acres of farm land. It is also dotted with more than one thousand oil wells, which have produced millions of barrels of oil from the Slaughter Field.

Although one might attribute the Mallet's longevity to the discovery of oil, the truth is that the Mallet was already four decades old when its first oil well came into production in 1938. By that time, most South Plains ranches had long ago broken up and disappeared under the plow. But the Mallet, with sandy soil pastures, scarred by the shallow depression of the always dry Sulphur Draw, did not attract prospective farmers during the 1920s when most of the region was being converted to agriculture. The Mallet remained primarily a cattle operation well into the Great Depression of the 1930s.

By the time oil was discovered on the Mallet, the ranch was remarkably intact, thereby allowing its owners to reap the rich harvest that oil brought to it. Moreover, because the Mallet land is primarily level, it is quite remarkable that most of it remained in grass during the irrigation boom of the 1950s instead of being converted to farms. The ranch still comprises one of the largest blocks of virgin high plains prairie still in existence.

Although the Mallet owes its preservation as a ranch partly to its remote location on the western South Plains, it is largely the unique personality of one of its principal owners, Miss Christine DeVitt, who in 1934 inherited a part of the ranch after the death of her father, ranch founder David M. DeVitt, that ensured its survival. Her insistence that her family hold onto the ranch, even during the depths of the Great Depression, ultimately brought the DeVitts' great wealth. Because much of that wealth is now invested in three charitable foundations, Miss DeVitt's 1934 decision to keep the ranch means that, today, millions of dollars are poured annually into worthwhile causes in Lubbock and the South Plains.

This book is primarily an effort to tell the story of the David M. DeVitt family, the majority owners of the Mallet Ranch. Its writing has been made possible by grants made to Texas Tech University by two of the DeVitt family foundations, The CH and the Helen Jones foundations, both located in Lubbock. I am particularly grateful to Louise Willson Arnold, President of the Helen Jones Foundation, and Nelda Thompson, Executive Director of The CH Foundation, for their vision in recognizing the need for this story to be told.

The telling would not have been possible without the wonderful cooperation of the surviving members of the DeVitt family, Mrs. Helen DeVitt Jones of Lubbock, and her daughter, Dorothy "Teddy" Secrest of Beverly Hills, California. Their gracious and timely donation of the records of the Mallet Ranch to Texas Tech University's Southwest Collection, as well as their personal interviews, opened venues of information never before available.

I am also indebted to a number of archivists and librarians in several institutions who provided critical information. Noteworthy to mention are the staffs of Texas Tech University Library, the Fort Worth Public Library, the Missouri State Archives, and the State Historical Society of Missouri. Helpful as well were the staffs of the Frederick, Maryland, Historical Society and of the Secretary of State's Registry Office in Hartford, Connecticut; Barbara Rust of the National Archives' Southwest Region Center in Fort Worth; Leon

Mitchell, of the Billy W. Sills Archives, Fort Worth Independent School District; and particularly Sara Hallier, Librarian for the Missouri Valley Special Collections, Kansas City Public Library.

More than twenty other individuals contributed immeasurably to this study through their gracious contribution of oral reminiscences about the Mallet Ranch and the DeVitt family. Carolyn Leatherwood of the Texas Tech University Development Office provided valuable information, and Nathaniel Birdsall helped with the research by reading countless pages of old newspapers on microfilm. Also, Gary Parker of Lubbock provided two file cabinets of Mallet records that had estrayed from the ranch's office. I am especially indebted to attorneys Don Graf and Rex Aycock, and staff members Susan Underwood, Becky Fairchild, and Mary Ann Wilkinson of the firm McClesky, Harriger, Brazill, and Graf for their help in making extensive legal materials available for my research.

Four other individuals also made major contributions to this work. Lauren Liljistrand, a Texas Tech graduate student in history, conducted extensive research and did the basic writing for the first two chapters. Dr. Bill Green of San Angelo spent many hours pouring through Tom Green County records and rare issues of the *San Angelo Standard Times*. Senior United States District Judge Halbert O. Woodward was of great assistance in locating a rich cache of information pertaining to a major court case involving Mr. DeVitt. My son Jerel Murrah of Fort Worth, who had the misfortune of officing next to the Fort Worth Public Library, willingly spent many hours reading microfilm and tracking other leads for me.

Finally, to those who covered my job while I took a leave of absence from Texas Tech, I owe a great deal of thanks, expecially to Dr. E. Dale Cluff, Director of Libraries, and all the staff of the Southwest Collection. To my wife Ann, who showed an incredible patience for tolerating my many late hours in my study at the computer, I am especially grateful.

David J. Murrah
Lubbock, Texas
December 1993

CHAPTER ONE

Quite a Number of Sheep

*I used to handle quite a number
of sheep, but . . . I do not think the
immediate outlook for the sheep
business is encouraging.*
David M. DeVitt, as quoted in *The
San Angelo Standard,* February 9,
1895.

ALTHOUGH the story of the Mallet Ranch
and its founders spans more than a century
of history, it centers primarily on only three
generations of the DeVitt family and begins in Maryland where
David Mantz DeVitt, founder of the Mallet Ranch, was born in 1856.

The DeVitt family probably settled first in Pennsylvania during
the 1700s. David B. DeVitt, David M. DeVitt's grandfather, was
born in Pennsylvania on November 28, 1791, and, as a young man,
moved to Frederick, Maryland, by the beginning of the War of 1812.
On August 25, 1814, the day after the British army sacked and burned
Washington, D.C., young DeVitt joined a Frederick militia company and began marching toward the nation's capital. Before it
could reach its destination, the company was dispatched to defend

Baltimore and served there until the Battle of Fort McHenry. There DeVitt must have witnessed personally the bombardment of the fort by British naval vessels, an engagement forever enshrined by another Frederick witness to the battle, Francis Scott Key, who penned his immortal "Star Spangled Banner" while watching from the deck of a British ship. A week after the battle, won by the Americans, DeVitt's militia company was discharged, and the young men of Frederick returned home triumphantly.[1]

After his militia service, David B. DeVitt settled in Frederick and learned the trade of coppersmithing. Frederick was a prosperous little community located forty miles northwest of Washington, D.C., near the National Road. A rich agricultural area, Frederick grew slowly but steadily, and young DeVitt prospered as well. In 1821, when he was thirty, he married Anna Mantz of Frederick.

Although David B. DeVitt was to enjoy a long life, tragedy became a hallmark for him and his descendants. His and Anna's first child, which was probably a girl, was born late in 1822, but died on December 8, 1823. Their second child, a boy whom they named David Mantz, was born sometime between 1823 and 1827. Anna DeVitt died on May 17, 1827, when she was twenty-seven years old.

In 1830, David B. DeVitt married Elizabeth Fout, with whom he would have six children. Yet as it had in his first marriage, tragedy struck early. DeVitt's first child by Elizabeth died at age two in 1833. The other five children, Amelia, Edward, Margaret, Phillip, and Anna, were born between 1833 and 1843.[2]

For his growing family, DeVitt built a large brick home in Frederick. Working as the principal engineer for the Independent Hose Company, as well as operating a small plumbing business of his own, DeVitt gained both prosperity and respect in Frederick. He served as a director of the Young Men's Bible Society in the 1820s and became an elder of the Presbyterian Church in 1830. He was also elected to the city's Common Council and served during most of the 1830s.[3]

Tragedy struck the DeVitt family once more. In the 1850s, David B. DeVitt's eldest son, David Mantz DeVitt married Elizabeth H. Pyfer of Baltimore and moved to Cleveland, Ohio. There, their first child, Phillip M. DeVitt, was born in 1854.[4] But in October 1855, David M. DeVitt was killed at age thirty in a carriage accident in Baltimore. Six months after her husband's death, on March 2, 1856, Elizabeth gave birth to a second son, whom she named David Mantz after her late husband.[5]

After the Civil War, Elizabeth DeVitt moved with her two young sons Phillip and David to Washington, D.C. By 1871, David, age fifteen, began to work as a page in the United States House of Representatives. This experience had a lasting impact on his life. Years later, in 1895, he told a reporter from the *Dallas News* about his experience. "I picked up a great many things there that have been of great service to me in after years," he recalled. "[A] boy of 12 or 15 years could go to no school that would be of greater benefit to him for a year or two than to become a page in the house or senate."[6]

His Washington experience probably put young David DeVitt in contact with the press, and by the late 1870s, he was trained for a career in journalism. From Washington, David moved to New York and began work as a reporter for the *Brooklyn Eagle*.

Meanwhile, his brother Phillip, who had married in 1876, set out the next year for Texas to make his career. Soon impressed with the opportunities in Texas, he apparently persuaded David to visit the Lone Star State. David wrote for his newspaper a glowing account of the booming cattle and sheep ranching ventures in the state and even convinced himself that Texas was his only future.[7] In 1880, David set out for Texas for good.

The DeVitt brothers soon found themselves in the sheep business. Attracted by profits that could be as much as 75 percent per year,[8] they established a sheep ranch in the heart of Texas, on the Edwards Plateau, approximately 150 miles northwest of Austin in McCulloch County, near Brady. Fort Concho, still an active military post, was only sixty miles to the west, but, as the nearest railhead was in Austin, the DeVitt brothers sold their wool and bought supplies there. "We lived in tents and subsisted on game, hard tack and sowbelly," David DeVitt reported several years later. "Game was plenty and we had all the deer, antelope and wild turkey shooting we wanted."

Within two years, the DeVitt brothers had increased their original flock of about fifteen hundred sheep to more than thirty-five hundred. But as their flocks grew, so did their troubles. Indians occasionally harassed them to steal horses. Prairie fires were always a threat. Cattlemen who moved into the area resented the presence of sheep and sheepmen. Because sheep needed to drift from range to range, sheepmen were soon restricted by the new barbed-wire fences being strung by cattlemen and farmers. Moreover, cattlemen resented how sheep clipped the grass at ground level and tried to drive sheep off their range. David DeVitt recalled later how cowboys would raid sheep ranches, scattering or slaughtering flocks and shooting at herders: "We always guarded our flock with Winchesters when we got wind of a raid, and every scrimmage was business from the word go."[9]

The DeVitts soon had enough. With much of West Texas opening up for utilization, they moved their operation farther west to Howard County, near Big Spring, in the heart of West Texas. Over a six-week period, the DeVitt brothers trailed their flocks to their new pastures, located primarily on open range about twenty miles east of Midland in Howard and Midland counties.

The DeVitt brothers liked the wide open spaces of isolated West Texas. This vast new country, which stretched west and north from the new railroad town of Abilene, was made accessible by the construction of the Texas Pacific Railroad across the region in 1881 and 1882. It offered both sheepmen and cattlemen new opportunities. The vast prairie was broken only by the shallow valleys of the Brazos, Colorado, and Pecos rivers. Only a decade before, the region had been home to huge bison herds and nomadic native American tribes, but military removal of the Comanches, Kiowas, and other Indians, coupled with the quick slaughter of the buffalo by hide seekers, left the region virtually vacant.

The first people to take advantage of the newly opened range were cattlemen from both North and South Texas who had observed the rich West Texas prairies while serving with military scouts during the Civil War or who had participated in the buffalo kill. These cattlemen included Charles Goodnight, C. C. Slaughter,

John B. Slaughter, William Hughes, Sam Lazarus, and J. Wright Mooar, all of whom would ultimately become legendary in ranching annals.

The DeVitt brothers' move into West Texas followed the first wave of ranchers by only a few years. Excellent rainfall meant lush grass, and the DeVitts were pleased with the rapid gain of their sheep on the rich grama and buffalo grasses that covered the rolling and level plains. Nevertheless, they soon found that they would have to drill wells and purchase windmills to provide water. Then each fall, they trailed their sheep southward into the rough breaks of the Devil's River for winter pasture. This land, David DeVitt recalled later, "[covers] 100 miles square and consists of canyons, valleys and low mountain ranges and is the richest stock land in the United States." One of its advantages, he noted, was that the grass in the area remained green all year and retained a lot of water, which made abundant watering places unnecessary.[10]

In addition to overseeing the operation of his ranch, David DeVitt found time to become involved in local politics and other matters. In 1882, he was elected to the first Commissioners Court after the organization of Howard County that year. The following year, he and Phillip moved their mother Elizabeth to Fort Worth. Concerned that her younger son had not yet wed, Elizabeth soon found a suitable mate for David.

Her choice was Florence Bailey, who was only seventeen when she moved to Fort Worth to find work as a servant girl. Orphaned at age five, Florence learned to be independent while struggling to make a life for herself. Recognizing Florence as someone who would stay in one place to maintain a family, Elizabeth DeVitt arranged for Florence and David to become acquainted, and the two were wed in 1884.[11]

David moved his new bride to the frontier ranch near Midland, and about a year later, on September 18, 1885, Florence gave birth to the first of their four children, a daughter whom they named Christine. In 1887, a second child, Harold, was born. With two small children, DeVitt decided to move his family to the bustling little community of San Angelo, near Fort Concho, where the children could attend school. The move was apparently made in 1889, and by 1890, the DeVitts had become prominent citizens of San Angelo.[12]

Moreover, David and Phillip began to branch out financially as they became involved in land and railroad speculation. First, they bought a half-interest in a large block of land on the east side of San Angelo. They also invested extensively in the proposed San Angelo, Abilene, Henrietta & Red River Railway Company. David DeVitt became the railroad's secretary-treasurer and spent a great deal of time traveling to promote it. David also boasted about his new home at every opportunity.[13]

Calling on his journalism experience and New York contacts, David DeVitt penned in 1890 a long article for his old newspaper, the *Brooklyn Eagle*, promoting the attributes of the raucous frontier community of San Angelo. "The wool marketed in this city last spring amounted to 2,000,000 pounds and 100,000 mutton went to Kansas City and Chicago," he noted. His adopted city, he boasted, had a number of civic improvements, including "electric lights, water works, [and] two ice factories." He pointed out also how fertile the land would be for farming, especially for growing cotton. Water was clean and relatively abundant, and, according to DeVitt, business was booming.[14]

But the prosperity of the 1880s in West Texas soon gave way to hard times. Recurring droughts, which began in the mid-1880s, coupled with extensive overgrazing of the range by cattle and sheep, reduced the once-lush West Texas prairies to stubble and weeds. The big sheep boom of the 1880s, which saw the number of Texas sheep nearly double, drove prices ultimately downward.[15]

Attracted to real estate and railroad speculation, Phillip DeVitt ended his ten-year partnership with his younger brother David in 1890 by selling his interest in the sheep ranch to Midland sheep rancher John Scharbauer for a total of $22,000. Apparently wanting to try his real estate skills in a bigger market, Phillip relocated his family to Fort Worth where he subsequently prospered in the development of the south half of the city. A Fort Worth street bears his name in tribute to his work.[16]

David DeVitt chose to cast his lot in West Texas, a choice that was subsequently to make a world of difference for his family. In his new partner, John Scharbauer, he found a mentor who would help him make the changes necessary to survive in tough times. Born in 1852, in Albany County, New York, the son of a German immigrant, John Scharbauer moved to Eastland, Texas, east of Abilene, in 1880, and began sheep ranching. In 1882, he moved to Abilene and expanded his operation through a partnership. In 1884, Scharbauer bought out his partner's interest and moved the flock to Mitchell County near Colorado City. Three years later, Scharbauer bought a ranch in Midland County near what is now Stanton, moved his sheep there, and made that ranch his headquarters.[7]

After the price of sheep began to drop, owing to continuing drought, DeVitt and Scharbauer began to dispose of their own sheep in 1892. DeVitt devoted more time to buying and selling sheep instead of raising them, handling as many as twenty thousand head annually. He soon gained a reputation in the Chicago livestock market "for handling stock of superior quality" and was hailed locally as "the great mutton manipulator of the West."[18]

DeVitt's success made him wealthy enough to consider moving to New York on a permanent basis. Although he frequently took his family to Chicago or New York when he was marketing sheep, he spent much of 1893 in the East, and his entire family attended the New York World's Fair in October of that year. Apparently enjoying city life, Florence persuaded David to let her and the family remain in New York City. In April 1894, the DeVitts leased their San Angelo home, apparently intending to make New York a permanent home, but their stay was short. By September, the DeVitts were back in Texas. From September 1894 until April 1895, they remained in Fort Worth visiting with family before returning to their home in San Angelo. Within less than a year, however, they would make a permanent move to Fort Worth.[19]

Despite his success brokering sheep, DeVitt became interested in moving into the cattle business. In October 1893, he purchased sixteen hundred head of stock cattle and placed them on leased pasture in Andrews County north of Midland. Likewise, Scharbauer began divesting his own ranch land of sheep in 1892. In fact, in 1892 and 1893, he shipped record numbers of sheep, approximately eighty-nine thousand, to market and began to look for cattle as well.[20]

By 1893, cattle were plentiful to buy, but good ranch land was hard to find. A series of droughts, which began in 1886 and peaked in 1893, had brought virtually to an end the big-range cattle industry. Collapsing cattle prices forced many of the large plains ranches into bankruptcy or selling their lands to farmers. Encouraged by declining prices for state-owned land and advancing railroads, farmers advanced hastily into West Texas, pushing ranchers farther west into the more isolated regions of the state. There was still money to be made in the cattle business. For the wise investor with money, the timing was right, and David DeVitt knew it. With Scharbauer's help, he was ready to jump into the cattle business and soon built his new venture on the ruins of another, the bankrupt Mallet Cattle Company of New Haven, Connecticut.

The Mallet Cattle Company had formed in January 1883 during the peak of the big cattle "bonanza" of the late 1870s and early 1880s. Attracted by the large profits reported in the eastern and foreign presses, capitalist venturers from as far away as Europe and Great Britain flocked to the Great Plains to acquire land and cattle. Two latecomers were Dwight P. Atwood and Roswell A. Neal of Hartford County, Connecticut, who bought one-sixth interest of a herd of cattle owned by George McWilliams and Thomas M. Peck of Colorado City, Texas, in January 1883. These cattle, many of which bore a brand resembling a mallet hammer, were located along the waters of Morgan Creek in eastern Mitchell County and western Howard County, about fifteen miles to the northwest of the new town of Colorado City.

Typical of such ventures, the new ranchers soon sought additional capital to fence and enlarge their range and attracted a number of other New England investors. In October 1884, Atwood and Neal joined with seven others in incorporating in Connecticut the Mallet Cattle Company and subsequently set the capitalization at two hundred thousand dollars.[21]

Dwight P. Atwood moved to Texas to manage the new ranch and established the Mallet headquarters about four miles north of the small community of Iatan, Texas, on the new Texas Pacific Railroad about fifteen miles west of Colorado City. Atwood subsequently fenced a large rectangular pasture three miles by five miles, comprising approximately ten thousand acres of state-owned public school land and railroad land. Soon the Mallet cattle had overgrazed the Mitchell County pasture. In 1886, The Mallet Cattle Company expanded into open range on the western South Plains in New Mexico and far West Texas. This part of the ranch, wedged between the Hat Ranch and the Four Lakes Ranch, encompassed 144 sections in Lea County, New Mexico, and Gaines and Yoakum counties, Texas, from present-day Lovington, New Mexico, to Plains, Texas.[22]

Comprised of more than ninety thousand acres, the western Mallet was so vast that the company chose simply to number its windmill sites rather than name them.[23] The Mallet's ranch house was one of the most notable ever built on the South Plains. John D. Earnest, the manager of the western Mallet, hired George Causey to design and build a magnificent five-room house which sat on one of the highest points in the area.[24]

By 1890 the Mallet Cattle Company owned more than six thousand head of cattle, but unfortunately for its New England owners, the herd was worth two-thirds less than it was six years before. With mounting feed bills, the company was soon heavily in debt, and as drought conditions worsened in the early 1890s, the investors were ready to sell out. In April, 1892, manager Atwood sold his milk cows and began to look for prospective buyers of Mallet cattle. Later that year, the Mallet Cattle Company reorganized in an effort to salvage its property, but continuing drought in 1892 and the Panic of 1893 forced it into bankruptcy.[25]

In 1893, the Mallet receivers began to sell the assets of the ranch. The manager of the western ranch, D. P. Earnest, bought the big pasture in Mitchell and Howard counties. Henry and M. Halff of San Antonio purchased the Texas range of the western Mallet, and converted it into a steer pasture of their Quien Sabe Ranch. Three other ranchers, Allen C. Lee, Jesse Heard, and Tom White, of Midland bought the New Mexico portion of the western Mallet and re-named it the High Lonesome Ranch.[26]

Another cattleman, Theodore Schuster of Fort Worth, acquired a remnant of the Mallet cattle as well as rights to its brand. Apparently a small operator, Schuster borrowed money from a Kansas City live-stock commission company and drove the herd to his own ranch in southwestern Hockley County, about twenty miles to the northeast of the Yoakum County western Mallet pasture. Schuster's K Ranch comprised a 150,000-acre pasture that stretched along the some-times waterless Sulphur Draw. Enclosed primarily by the fences of surrounding big ranches, Schuster's ranch included no deeded land. Most of the acreage had been previously given by the State of Texas to a number of counties scattered throughout the state. Schuster either used the land for free or obtained leases from some of the counties to maintain his occupancy.

Perhaps owing to continuing drought, as well as the national de-pression, Schuster soon found himself in trouble and began to look for a buyer for his range rights and the Mallet cattle. Because Schar-bauer had been leasing a block of land that lay nearby the K Ranch, he was already familiar with the K Ranch. Perhaps as a result, he and DeVitt in April 1895 purchased "improvements, wells, windmills, tanks, and fences" from Schuster and acquired the Mallet cattle from Schuster's mortgager.[27]

How much DeVitt and Scharbauer paid for the K Ranch range is unknown, but since the price did not include any deeded land, the purchase probably involved only a few thousand dollars. The cattle, however, which were primarily cows, cost ten dollars and fifty cents per head or forty-two thousand dollars.[28] Such a purchase was prob-ably David DeVitt's largest to date, and it put him in the cattle busi-ness in a big way. Moreover, he and Scharbauer now had a major stake in what had become the last cattle frontier of Texas.

Their new ranch on the Llano Estacado, or Staked Plains, soon became known as the Mallet, following the established custom of naming a ranch for its predominant brand. The new range offered the partnership something hard to find in 1895 Texas, a range un-spoiled by encroaching farmers. With national financial conditions improving, David DeVitt must have viewed his new enterprise on the isolated South Plains as a challenging promise, but never did he dream that the challenges would be as dramatic as those which lay ahead.

NOTES

1. Sallie A. Mallick and F. Edward Wright, *Frederick County Militia in the War of 1812* (Frederick, MD: Historical Society of Frederick County, Inc., 1992) 98, 354; T. J. C. Williams and Folger McKinsey, *History of Frederick County, Maryland,* Vol. 1 of 2 (Baltimore: Regional Publishing Company, 1979) 167; B. B. Paddock, ed., *History of Texas: Fort Worth and the Texas Northwest Edition,* vol. 4 of 4 (Chicago: The Lewis Publishing Company, 1922) 798. Miss Christine DeVitt always thought that she was in some way related to Francis Scott Key. A native of Frederick, Maryland, Francis Scott Key was a contemporary to Christine DeVitt's great-grandfather David B. DeVitt.

2. William R. Quynn, ed., *The Diary of Jacob Englebrecht, 1818-1878* vol. 1 of 3 (Frederick, MD: the Historical Society of Frederick County, Inc., 1976) 108, 251, 447, 582; Quynn, *The Diary of Jacob Englebrecht, 1818-1878* vol. 2 of 3, 79; Mary F. Hitselberger and John P. Dern, *Bridge in Time: The Complete 1850 Census of Frederick County, Maryland* (Redwood City, CA: Monocacy Book Company, 1978) 23.

3. *Ibid.,* 23, 457; Williams, *History of Frederick County, 1878,* vol. 1, 66, 298, 586, 631; Quynn, *The Diary of Jacob Maryland,* 450; Quynn, *The Diary of Jacob Englebrecht, 1818-Englebrecht, 1818-1878,* vol. 2, 97, 144, 149, 192, 196.

4. Paddock, *History of Texas,* p. 708. According to Paddock, Phillip DeVitt was born November 5, 1856, a date which would place his birth thirteen months after his father's death and several months after that of his younger brother. The correct date is 1854, as he was 83 when he died in 1937. See *Fort Worth Star Telegram,* September 21, 1937.

5. D. M. DeVitt's birthday is not recorded in the family papers or genealogical information in the Frederick Historical Society Library. However, in a letter to his daughter Helen, written March 8, 1923, DeVitt thanks

Helen for remembering his birthday and makes a passing reference to March 2. He was 78 when he died in March 6, 1934.

6. "Remembrances of a Page," *San Angelo Standard* (November 30, 1895), 1.

7. "Down in Texas," *San Angelo Standard*, 1.

8. Paul H. Carlson, *Texas Woollybacks: The Range Sheep and Goat Industry* (College Station: Texas A&M University Press, 1982), p. 3.

9. "Down in Texas, *San Angelo Standard*, 1.

10. *Ibid.*

11. Dorothy Gail Secrest to David Murrah and Lauren Liljistrand, personal interview, November 6, 1992; Cherry Duke, "DeVitts and Mallet Ranch Make their Mark in West Texas History," *Ranch Record* (Spring 1984), 1.

12. *San Angelo Standard*, July 19, 1890, p. 3; "Down in Texas,". Harold DeVitt's birth date is unknown. The June 20, 1891, *Standard* reported that "Dave DeVitt's four-year old son was kicked in the head by a mule . . ."

13. Duke, *Ranch Record*, 1; "Railroad News: Organization of the San Angelo, Abilene, Henrietta & Red River Railway Company—The Santa Fe Will Probably extend West from San Angelo," *San Angelo Standard* (October 25, 1890), 1; *San Angelo Standard* (7 June 1890) 3; "Personals," *San Angelo Standard* (22 August 1891) 1; *San Angelo Standard* (21 March 1891) 1; *San AngeloStandard*, November 1, 1890, p. 3, Deed Records, Book 4: 322-323, Tom Green County, Texas Deed Records, Book 2, 343-44, and Deed Records, Book 5, 1, Howard County, Texas.

14. "Down in Texas," *San Angelo Standard*, 1.

15. Carlson, *Texas Woollybacks*, p. 69.

16. Paddock, *History of Texas*, p. 708; *Texas Livestock Journal*, June 14, 1890; *Tarrant County Historic Resources Survey: Phase III, Fort Worth's South Side* (Fort Worth: Historic Preservation Council for Tarrant County, 1986), p. 140; Fort Worth City Directory, 1894-1924. Phillip DeVitt lived in Fort Worth until his death September 20, 1937, at the age of 83. His wife, Jessie, died August 12, 1912. See *Fort Worth Star Telegram*, September 21, 1937, and Deed Records, Book 200:558, Tom Green County, Texas.

17. James Cox, ed., *Historical and Biographical Record of the Cattle Industry and the Cattlemen of Texas and Adjacent Territory* (St. Louis: Woodward & Tiernan Printing Co., 1895), p. 432; Midland County Historical Society, *The Pioneer History of Midland County, Texas, 1880-1926* (Dallas: Taylor Publishing Company, 1984), p. 109.

18. *San Angelo Standard*, July 29, 1895, 3; December 8, 1894, 3.

19. *San Angelo Standard,* October 14, 1893, 3; April 21, 1894, 3; September 15, 1894, 3; April 13, 1895, 3; February 5, 1896, 2.

20. John H. Griffin, *Land of the High Sky* (Midland, Texas: The First National Bank of Midland, 1959), pp. 85-86; [Cox], *Cattle Industry of Texas,* 432; Midland County Historical Society, *Pioneer History of Midland County,* p. 110.

21. Bill of Sale, Book 1, pp. 146, 252-262, 269-299, 311-333, Records, Mitchell County, Colorado City, Texas; Records of Incorporation, Mallet Cattle Company, October 11, 1884, Records, Secretary of State, State of Connecticut, Hartford, Connecticut.

22. Eugene H. Price, *Open Range Ranching on the South Plains in the 1890s* (Clarendon, Texas: Clarendon Press, 1967), p. 54; Hinshaw, *Lea: New Mexico's Last Frontier,* p. 95.

23. Price, *Open Range Ranching,* pp. 56-57; Benton R. White, *The Forgotten Cattle King* (College Station: Texas A&M University Press, 1986), p. 40. According to Price, the Mallet Cattle Company's Horse Pasture was located along Sulphur Draw in Yoakum County near present-day Plains, Texas. Because the Mallet established by DeVitt was located on a different Sulphur Draw in Hockley County, some historians have mistakenly confused the two locations. See S. D. Myres, *The Permian Basin: Petroleum Empire of the Southwest,* Vol. II (El Paso: Permian Press, 1977), p. 222.

24. Price, *Open Range Ranching,* p. 56-57; Benton R. White, *The Forgotten Cattle King* (College Station: Texas A&M University Press, 1986), p. 40.

25. Bill of Sale, Book 2:114, Mitchell County Records; Mallet Cattle Company Annual Report, August 1890, Secretary of State Records, State of Connecticut; Deed Records, Book 6:22-29, Howard County, Texas.

26. *Ibid.*; Hinshaw, *Lea: New Mexico's Last Frontier,* 95-96; Price, *Open Range Ranching,* 54-55.

27. *San Angelo Standard,* April 13, 1895, p. 3; March 12, 1898, p. 2; D. M. DeVitt, deposition, pp. 238, 265-266, *Mallet Land and Cattle Company v. C. C. Slaughter,* Court of Civil Appeals Records, National Archives—Fort Worth Branch (hereinafter cited as *Mallet v Slaughter*).

28. *San Angelo Standard,* April 13, 1895, 3.

CHAPTER TWO

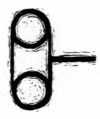

The Courthouse Was Open

*[C. C. Slaughter] said he was going
to take the land and use it any how
and that if I wanted to get any relief,
the Court house was over there open
to me.*
David M. DeVitt, January 30, 1904

IN mid-May 1895, David DeVitt set out from San
Angelo to visit his new ranch on the plains.
First stopping in Midland, he bought supplies
before setting out across the prairies toward his new ranch in Hockley County, more than one hundred miles away. After arriving on
the new Mallet Ranch, he stayed for more than a month, inspecting
the cattle, scattered waterings, and fences before returning home in
late June.[1]

The ranch was at first glimpse perhaps not what he expected. Described to him as well-watered and fenced, containing 150,000
acres,[2] the old K pasture was actually approximately 100,000 acres,
comprising most of the southwestern quarter of Hockley County
and about ten thousand additional acres in northern Terry County.
The pasture, created primarily by the construction of outside fences

by other ranches, extended from the west side of present-day Levelland south and west fifteen miles to the southwest corner of the
county. The only enclosure within the big pasture was a fence
around the Horse Pasture and ranch headquarters, which lay along
Sulphur Draw in the far southwest corner of the ranch.[3]

When DeVitt and Scharbauer acquired the ranch in 1895, most of
the land in the area was being used by ranchers for free, even though
the property belonged to a number of counties scattered throughout the state. In 1883, the Legislature deeded blocks of four leagues
each (17,712 acres) in Cochran and Hockley counties to approximately thirty unorganized counties as a reserve for each county
school fund. As a result, the counties were free to sell or lease their
land, but until the mid-1890s, there was little interest in the flat semi-
arid land of the South Plains. Primarily, their new ranch comprised
land belonging to Oldham, Edwards, Scurry, Rains, Maverick,
Kaufman, Baylor, Rusk, and Concho counties, and a two-by-ten-
mile strip of unsurveyed public domain.[4]

DeVitt soon realized that he and Scharbauer had purchased a vast
but isolated ranch. Although a few ranches had been operating in
the area for a few years, there was no permanent settlement within
the immediate area. To the north of the Mallet pasture was the
south fence of the three-million-acre XIT Ranch, which stretched
more than two hundred miles to the north. Also to the north and
west was the Diamond Ranch of Fort Worth entrepreneur Fount G.
Oxsheer, who had been ranching in the area since the mid-1880s.[5]
To the west was the remnant of the old St. Louis Cattle Company,
which was in the process of breaking up when DeVitt and Scharbauer purchased the Mallet. To the east lay the Nunn Ranch and
some smaller pastures. Thus, the Mallet, located virtually in the
heart of the treeless Llano Estacado more than one hundred miles
from any railroad, and fifty miles from the nearest town, was one of
the most isolated ranches on the South Plains. Access to the ranch
was sometimes difficult over nonexistent roads. The closest supply
store was fifty miles to the east in the little four-year-old village of
Lubbock.

The ranch's windmills were also widely scattered, and probably did not number more than six in the entire pasture. Some small scattered natural playa lakes provided water during rainy seasons; otherwise, cattle were forced to cross several miles from good grass to water.

Despite the disadvantages, DeVitt set out to improve his new plains ranch and cattle. Over the next two years, he and Scharbauer added windmills and tanks, and acquired grass leases from Kaufman, Edwards, and Rains counties to prevent others from getting the land. They also began to upgrade their herd. In December 1895, they culled from their herd the unwanted cows and a large herd of steers, which they drove to Amarillo and then shipped to Chicago.[6] In late 1896 or early 1897, they found a fine large herd of improved breed cattle in St. Charles, Louisiana, numbering approximately six thousand head, and had them shipped to the old Mallet pasture near Iatan on which DeVitt held a short-term lease.

This venture proved almost disastrous. The Louisiana cattle, accustomed to a warm climate, began to die in the February cold weather even before the train had reached its destination west of Colorado City. Because of the unusual nature of Texas cattlemen buying out-of-state stock, the story of DeVitt's and Scharbauer's troubles attracted wide attention. One newspaper report speculated that they would lose as much as half the herd.[7]

As veteran stock traders, both DeVitt and Scharbauer downplayed their losses at every opportunity. Scharbauer told the *Texas Stock and Farm Journal* in April that the cattle were doing "splendidly."[8] Then, in August the *Stock Journal* reported that DeVitt and Scharbauer had sold two thousand head of the Louisiana cattle for an above-market price of fifteen to nineteen dollars per head:

> These are the cattle . . . which came in for a large share of comment about that time. [It] was freely predicted by some croakers that their owners would be saved the trouble and expense of rounding them up in the spring for the reason that none of the cattle would survive the change from the land of orange blossoms to the rigors of Texas northers. But the "Or-

ange Blossoms," as the cattle have become quite popularly known, proved to be tougher than was supposed, and refused to turn up their toes to the daisies, being alike impervious to the blizzard's icy breath as well as that of public criticism. The change of diet from sea moss and swamp grass to the succulent curly mesquite above the quarantine line, agreed with the cattle amazingly, and they came out as sleek and fat as moles in the spring.[9]

The paper reported also that DeVitt and Scharbauer had driven the balance of the herd, numbering about three thousand head, to the Mallet Ranch in Hockley County, and that "it is their intention to cross them with imported Scotch Highland bulls, which will undoubtedly in time produce one of the finest herds in the state."[10]

With such favorable press, John Scharbauer decided it was a good time to sell out his share of the Mallet. By the fall of 1897, Scharbauer had moved to Fort Worth and had a large empire to manage. With ranches scattered throughout West Texas, banks in Midland and Pecos, and other business interests in Fort Worth, he no longer had time for the isolated Mallet. In mid-October 1897, he sold to his partner David DeVitt his entire interest in the Mallet land and six thousand head of cattle. The *Texas Live Stock Journal*, which rated the Mallet's as "one of the best-bred herds in the Panhandle," estimated that the transaction was worth as much as fifty-five thousand dollars.[11]

DeVitt was not quite willing, or perhaps not able, to go it alone. In November 1897, he found a new partner, F. W. Flato, Jr., of Kansas City, who purchased approximately one-half interest in the Mallet.[12] Flato was a product of one of the pioneer families in South Texas and the family community of Flatonia. In 1877, Flato began work for the Hunter & Evans Livestock Commission Company and soon became manager of its St. Louis office. In 1889, he became a stockholder and director of the company when it was reorganized as Evans-Snider-Buel Commission Co. In late 1892, he formed his own firm, the Drumm-Flato Commission Co. with Andrew Drumm and R. G. Head in 1893.[13]

Had Flato known what lay ahead for the Mallet, he may not have been willing to buy into the ranch. A formidable challenge lay ahead, one that could have been another factor in Scharbauer's decision to quit his South Plains partnership with DeVitt. In 1895, Scharbauer had purchased from famous Texas rancher Charles Goodnight two thousand head of improved Hereford cows and placed them on a leased pasture adjacent to the Mallet Ranch. Two years later, in January 1897, he sold the cattle to wealthy Dallas cattleman and banker Colonel C. C. Slaughter, who then moved the cattle to Fount Oxsheer's Diamond Ranch, which lay immediately north of the Mallet.[14] Scharbauer, recognizing Slaughter's growing interest in the big pasture country of the western South Plains, may have suspected that Slaughter was going to make a bid to put together a new ranch and knew he had the resources to do it. Rather than to get into a land fight with Slaughter, Scharbauer may have decided to let DeVitt fend for himself.

C. C. Slaughter was no stranger to West Texas and the Llano Estacado. Among the first cattlemen to push into the region, Slaughter had established his vast Long S Ranch along the headwaters of the Colorado River in Howard, Martin, Borden, and Dawson counties as early as 1876. In 1884, he expanded into the South Plains by acquiring the Running Water Ranch in Hale and Lamb counties west of present-day Plainview. With other acquisitions, he controlled more than 750,000 acres of West Texas land by 1895.[15]

However, because Slaughter had obtained nearly all of his ranch land from railroads, he owned only the alternate sections within each of his pastures; the remainder was reserved by the State of Texas for speculation and support of its public school fund. By the 1890s, farmers were pressing the state to sell the school land at an affordable price, and in 1895, the Legislature complied by passing the so-called Four-Section Act. This law provided that prospective settlers could purchase for fifty cents per acre up to four sections of state school land but were required to live on the land and make improvements. It also rescinded previous restrictions on settlement of land north of the Texas Pacific Railroad. As a result, "nesters" were soon camped on the public school land sections all over West Texas ranches, especially those of Colonel Slaughter's.[16]

Meanwhile, those counties that owned four-league blocks in Cochran and Hockley counties became amenable to selling their land. The pioneer South Plains rancher Fount G. Oxsheer, who had used the open ranges in the Mallet area for ten years, began consolidating his holdings by buying four-league tracts of county-owned school land in central Hockley County, between the XIT and the Mallet range. After Slaughter bought the Goodnight cattle from Scharbauer in January 1897, Oxsheer pastured them for a year on his Diamond Ranch in a partnership arrangement.[17] But by January 1898, Slaughter decided to put together his own ranch in the area and contracted with Oxsheer to make the necessary land purchases from the various counties. The contract called for Oxsheer to acquire for Slaughter from twenty to fifty leagues of land in Hockley and Cochran counties, including those owned by Concho, Baylor, Zavala, Maverick, Raines, Scurry, Edwards, and Kaufman counties. Since the list of leagues that Slaughter instructed Oxsheer to buy comprised virtually the entire Mallet pasture, it is obvious that Slaughter fully intended to squeeze David DeVitt off the South Plains.[18] To assist in the land acquisition, Oxsheer hired a Fort Worth land speculator W. E. Kaye to serve as a front for himself and Slaughter. In early 1898, Kaye and other agents went to work to buy the land for Slaughter but did so as secretly as possible.

DeVitt soon suspected that someone was working to gain title to a large block of land and decided that he should secure whatever pasture he could through leasing. In March 1898, he signed a lease for the 17,712 acres of Scurry County land; in April, he leased the Baylor County land, and in November, he acquired the small Atascosa County block in the far northeast corner of the ranch. In December, he learned from the Commissioners Court of Concho County that a man named R. S. Ferrell was trying to buy the Concho County block that DeVitt held under lease by transfer from Schuster. DeVitt was incensed because such action was in violation of an unwritten code, by which one rancher would honor another's range rights: "I hunted him up," DeVitt testified later, "and ask[ed] him what he was trying to buy the land in our pasture for up there, and he said that he did not know anything about it."[19] Ferrell did know, however, because he had made a deal with W. E. Kaye to allow Kaye to buy the land in Ferrell's name for Slaughter.

DeVitt then confronted Kaye about the purchase. Kaye said that he was buying the land for Ferrell. When DeVitt said that Ferrell did not have the money to buy such a large block of land, Kaye responded that Ferrell's uncle was putting up the money.[20]

DeVitt recognized the ruse created by Ferrell and Kaye and immediately went to Paint Rock to settle the matter with Concho County. Fortunately for DeVitt and Flato, their lease provided that they had preferential right to buy the land if it were ever offered for sale. DeVitt quickly negotiated a contract and bought the 4,228-acre block on January 3, 1899.[21]

The next confrontation was not as fortunate for DeVitt and the Mallet Ranch. In May 1899, five months after he had bought the Concho County land, he received notice from W. E. Kaye that Kaye had purchased more than 33,000 acres of the Mallet pasture, which consisted of the holdings of Maverick, Kaufman, and Edwards counties.[22] Only three months later, word came that R. S. Ferrell had purchased the entire 17,712-acre block of Zavala County's school land. Although DeVitt and Flato were only leasing 4,228 acres of the Zavala block, the acreage was contiguous to the main body of the Mallet Ranch.[23]

It was all stunning news to DeVitt, because he knew if he could not successfully fight this land grab, the Mallet would be split, leaving him and Flato with only fifty thousand acres, or one-third of their original ranch. But they had little choice about the fifteen thousand acres of Maverick and Kaufman county lands. Although they held leases, their contracts did not provide for preferential purchase. As a result, they lost the land when the Maverick County lease expired in December 1902.

What would happen in Edwards County was another matter. This seventeen-thousand-acre block was almost five miles square and comprised the entire northwest quadrant of the Mallet Ranch. Because it lay between Slaughter's land on the west and his newly acquired Maverick and Zavala lands on the east, it was a critical piece of property for both DeVitt and Slaughter. Its ownership was not to be settled without a fight.

DeVitt had secured his first lease on Edwards County in June 1896 and renewed it a year later. In June 1898, he negotiated a five-year lease. This time, he included in the contract a preferential purchase option that gave him first right to buy the land should the county opt to sell it.[24]

Meanwhile, Slaughter's agent, W. E. Kaye, knowing that Edwards County was a critical piece in Slaughter's land puzzle, opened his own negotiations with the Edwards County Commissioners Court. In March 1899, even though he was deaf, he negotiated and secured an agreement with the county that gave him the right to sell the county's school lands at eighty-five cents per acre. When the Edwards County judge pointed out to him that DeVitt and Flato's lease gave them a preferential right to purchase, Kaye responded that he believed DeVitt and Flato were insolvent and would soon default. Never questioning his story, the Edwards County commissioners awarded Kaye a sales contract, but stipulated that his contract was subject to that of DeVitt and Flato's.[25]

Kaye ignored the DeVitt and Flato option, and two months later, sold the entire Edwards County block to R. S. Ferrell for $17,712, or one dollar per acre, a transaction that gave Kaye a handsome commission of $2,656.80. Subsequently, on May 24, 1899, Ferrell sold and transferred title to the land to C. C. Slaughter, making only passing reference to the DeVitt and Flato option.[26]

Apparently, Kaye and Ferrell believed they could bluff DeVitt and Flato out of the Edwards County land. Indeed, in his letter to D. M. DeVitt, written May 23, 1899, the day before Ferrell conveyed the land to Slaughter, Kaye warned DeVitt, "I am not the only one wanting to buy lands within your pasture.... If you are disposed to use and occupy these lands for a few years and will not hinder nor work against me in the purchase of others, I will treat you as fairly as I have done the St. Louis Cattle Company."[27]

But DeVitt ignored Kaye's deceptive letter and wrote directly to County Judge James M. Hunter of Edwards County, reminding him of the DeVitt and Flato purchase option. Judge Hunter quickly assured him that the sale was contingent upon all the provisions of the DeVitt and Flato lease.[28]

Confident of the strength of their contract, David DeVitt decided to let the matter rest for awhile. His partner, F. W. Flato, could not. Like Scharbauer, he may not have been willing to challenge Slaughter and, apparently in personal financial trouble, he feared a long litigation. In November 1900, Flato made an effort to compromise with Slaughter. In a letter, he offered to consider a possible land trade, but Slaughter refused. Instead, Slaughter countered by demanding possession of all of the Edwards County land. Flato said no; "It would be simply out of the question to consider dividing the land as you suggest as it would ruin our ranche and practically destroy its value."[29]

Flato then proposed that Slaughter buy out his and DeVitt's entire interest, but Slaughter refused even to consider it. "This land was purchased for the purpose of making a solid ranch," Slaughter wrote in response, after his annual company meeting with his five sons. "Had you offered to buy their [the Slaughter Company's] 300,000 acres they might have taken it under consideration. Your proposition was so unsatisfactory they would not consider it."[30] Thus, with no hope of compromise, the scene was set for a courthouse fight and possibly a small-scale range war.

Late in 1900, DeVitt and Flato sued Slaughter over possession of Kaufman County land. Slaughter was confident that any court would see matters his way, and the initial decision proved him right. In February 1901, he obtained title to the Zavala County block and at the same time won the suit with DeVitt over the Kaufman County land.[31] With much glee he reported to his ranch manager and son George Slaughter:

With this deed in our hands, we will *at once* sue Mr. DeVitt for "Trespass to try title," and there is no court on this earth that will keep us from possession of the land. With Kaufman, Maverick, and Zavala Counties in our possession, where is DeVitt and Flato? They will be around soon for a compromise.

Mark what I say, Flato will be over here soon, wanting to compromise and telling us how much he has always loved the Slaughters.[32]

But David DeVitt was determined not to be bullied by Slaughter. In February 1902, he decided to exercise his lease option to buy the land in Edwards County, and went to Rock Springs personally to attend the regular monthly session of the Edwards County Commissioners Court. DeVitt met no opposition from the commissioners; in fact, they disavowed any knowledge of the sale to Kaye and accepted in principle DeVitt's offer of ninety cents per acre.[33]

However, the Edwards County commissioners failed to issue DeVitt and Flato a deed to the property. By this time, realizing that they had created a potential legal nightmare for themselves, as well as for both DeVitt and Slaughter, the commissioners decided to revoke both DeVitt and Slaughter's contracts and not sell the land. DeVitt kept up his pressure on Edwards County. In late May, he tendered an offer of one dollar per acre: "I regret that it looks like we are bound to have some controversy with the County over this matter," DeVitt wrote to the Edwards County Judge, "although I have reason to count on the friendly attitude of the County in this transaction."[34]

With the delay, the struggle shifted to Hockley County and became a war of words between the Slaughter and Mallet cowboys. Because DeVitt's lease had expired on June 1, 1903, Slaughter hired extra men in July to construct a fence and began drilling a new water well on the Edwards County land. In late August, before they could make much headway, DeVitt's foreman succeeded in getting an injunction in the Lubbock County Court to stop the action.[35]

By mid-October, Slaughter's attorney, G. G. Wright, who was also his son-in-law, had broken the injunction. On October 17, Slaughter cowboys once again rode into the Mallet pasture, resumed drilling the water well, started surveying a fence line, and drove the Mallet cattle off the Edwards County land.

By Sunday, October 18, both DeVitt and Colonel Slaughter had come to the scene of the pending fence fight, and on the next day, met face-to-face. Their conversation was brief: "I told him that we owned the land," DeVitt later testified, and "[Slaughter] claimed that he had bought the land from Ferrell and had paid his money. . . . He said he was going to take the land and use it anyhow and that if I wanted to get any relief the Court house was over there open to me."[36] DeVitt took Slaughter at his word, went directly to Lubbock the next day, and sought an injunction in the state district court. Meanwhile, on Saturday, October 24, Slaughter's foreman H. T. Boyd completed the fence that shut out the Mallet cattle from the Edwards County land, but later in the day found the new fence cut in several places. Two days later, he began rebuilding the fence, but before he could complete it, he was served with another injunction to stay off DeVitt's land.[37]

While attorneys maneuvered in the courthouse, DeVitt and Slaughter cowboys continued their stand-off. During November and December, Slaughter's fence was rebuilt, and then cut down at least five times. Cowboys on both sides began carrying guns. One Slaughter cowboy wore a blister on his leg from carrying a holstered gun for several weeks.[38]

In early November, it appeared that DeVitt and Flato had won the day. The Edwards County Commissioners Court, which had delayed issuing a deed to the partners because of threats of litigation from Slaughter, finally decided to give DeVitt and Flato a deed, but only after the partnership had agreed to hold the County blameless from any resulting litigation. DeVitt rushed to Rock Springs, negotiated the purchase of the land for one dollar per acre, and returned in seeming triumph to Fort Worth.[39] But Slaughter ignored the County's action and continued his efforts to take possession of the land.

The crisis worsened in late December. DeVitt and Flato won another temporary injunction against Slaughter in October. When Slaughter's cowboys arrived in Seymour to testify in the court hearing, the Baylor County sheriff arrested them for breaking the judge's injunction and put them in jail for one night![40] But the state district court subsequently dissolved the injunction on December 18. Once word reached the ranch, Slaughter's men began rebuilding the fence again. Meanwhile, DeVitt's foreman Hall Jarman set up a camp on December 21 at the Edwards County windmill in an effort to hold the land. Eight days later, on the 29th, he removed it, because, as he later testified, "the employees of C. C. Slaughter were menacing and making threats of violence against the employees of the Mallet Cattle Company so camped on the land, and I feared a personal encounter."[41]

But Jarman had a surprise in store for the Slaughter cowboys. On December 18, the day that the state district court dissolved the injunction, DeVitt and Flato filed papers in Jefferson City, Missouri, to incorporate under the laws of Missouri, and three days later, on December 21, the Secretary of State of Missouri issued articles of incorporation to the new Mallet Land and Cattle Company. On Christmas day, 1903, the Mallet filed suit in the United States Circuit Court against C. C. Slaughter "for an injunction to restrain the defendant, C. C. Slaughter, from trespassing upon the plaintiff's land . . . and to remove cloud from title to said land."[42]

By December 29, Mallet foreman Hall Jarman had the federal injunction in hand. He rode to the Edwards County windmill with three of his own men and there found Slaughter foreman H. T. Boyd. Jarman then read to Boyd the injunction. Boyd responded by saying that Jarman had no right to serve any papers from the United States Court. "I could not pay any attention to same," Boyd later testified, "as they had already deceived me once before and I did not have any confidence in them."[43]

Jarman then drove a herd of Mallet cattle to a gate in the new Slaughter fence. According to Jarman, Boyd blocked the gate with his buggy. "I asked Boyd if he intended preventing my putting the cattle through the gate . . . even if he had to use violence to do so," Jarman testified. "He answered in the affirmative. . . . Three other employees of C. C. Slaughter were [near], with guns."[44] Fearing an encounter, Jarman said he turned the cattle loose and returned to the Mallet headquarters.

The stand-off continued into January 1904. Instructing his men to defy the injunction, Slaughter's cowboys stayed camped on the Edwards County land until late January when it became apparent that a federal judge was going to cite Slaughter for contempt of court. On January 18, Slaughter ordered his cowboys to abandon their camp until the matter could be resolved in court.[45] Thus, peace finally returned to the Llano Estacado and the great Hockley County fence-cutting war of 1903 had ended, or so it seemed. In reality, the fight had merely shifted to the courthouse where a rough legal road lay ahead for DeVitt and Flato. To make matters worse, DeVitt would soon find himself with a new partner and, in effect, facing the battle alone.

NOTES

1. *San Angelo Standard*, May 18, 1895, 2; July 6, 1895, 3.

2. *Ibid.*, April 13, 1895.

3. D. M. DeVitt, Deposition, *Mallet v. Slaughter*.

4. *Ibid.*

5. Benton R. White, *The Forgotten Cattle King* (College Station: Texas A&M University Press, 1986), p. 53.

6. *San Angelo Standard*, December 21, 1895, 2-3.

7. *Ibid.*, February 6, 1897; 2; February 13, 1897, 2-3.

8. *Ibid.*, March 27, 1897, 2.

9. "Those Louisiana Cattle," *San Angelo Standard*, August 21, 1897, 2.

10. *Ibid.*

11. *San Angelo Standard*, October 23, 1897, p. 2.

12. F. W. Flato, Deposition, February 1904, *Mallet v. Slaughter*.

13. Cuthbert Powell, *Twenty Years of Kansas City's Livestock Trade and Traders* (Kansas City, MO: Pearl Printing Co., 1893), pp. 304-305; "Obituary," *The Cattleman* (December, 1941) 52.

14. C. C. Slaughter to George M. Slaughter, January 15, 1897, George M. Slaughter Papers, Southwest Collection, Texas Tech University.

15. See David J. Murrah, *C. C. Slaughter: Rancher, Banker, Baptist* (Austin: University of Texas Press, 1981), pp. 48-85.

16. *Ibid.*, pp. 54, 84-85.

17. White, *Forgotten Cattle King*, p. 61.

18. "Articles of Agreement between F. G. Oxsheer and C. C. Slaughter," January 3, 1898, *Mallet v. Slaughter*.

19. David M. DeVitt, Deposition, *Mallet v. Slaughter*.

20. *Ibid.*

21. Abstract of Title, Concho County School Land, Mallet Ranch Records, Southwest Collection, Texas Tech University (hereinafter cited as Mallet Records).

22. W. E. Kaye to D. M. DeVitt, May 23, 1899, D. M. DeVitt Deposition, *Mallet v. Slaughter.*

23. List of Lands Bought by C. C. Slaughter, Deposition, C. C. Slaughter, *Mallet v. Slaughter.*

24. D. M. DeVitt, Deposition, *Mallet v. Slaughter;* "Slaughter v. Mallet Land and Cattle Co.," *The Federal Reporter: Cases Argued and Determined in the Circuit Court of Appeals and Circuit and District Courts of the United States,* V. 141, April-May, 1906 (St. Paul: West Publishing Co., 1906), p. 283, hereinafter *The Federal Reporter.*

25. Judge James M. Hunter, Deposition, February 10, 1904, *Mallet v. Slaughter.*

26. *Ibid.,* 284.

27. W. E. Kaye to D. M. DeVitt, May 23, 1899. D. M. DeVitt, Deposition, *Mallet v. Slaughter.*

28. James M. Hunter to D. M. DeVitt, June 18, 1899, September 2, 1899, D. M. DeVitt, Deposition, *Mallet v. Slaughter.*

29. F. W. Flato to C. C. Slaughter, December 22, 1900, C. C. Slaughter Deposition, *Mallet v. Slaughter.*

30. C. C. Slaughter to F. W. Flato, January 5, 1901, C. C. Slaughter, Deposition, *Mallet v. Slaughter.*

31. C. C. Slaughter to George M. Slaughter, February 16, 1901, George M. Slaughter Papers.

32. C. C. Slaughter to George M. Slaughter, February 16, 1901, as cited in Murrah, *C. C. Slaughter,* p. 88.

33. D. M. DeVitt, Deposition, *Mallet v. Slaughter.*

34. D. M. DeVitt to S. A. Hough, June 2, 1903, pp. 403-404, *Mallet v. Slaughter.*

35. *Ibid.;* H. T. Boyd, Diary, August 31, 1903, in possession of H. T. Boyd, Jr., Shallowater, Texas. H. T. Boyd was foreman for the Slaughter Ranch. C. C. Slaughter, deposition, *Mallet v. Slaughter.* The court records for the August 1903 case have disappeared from the Archives of the Lubbock County Courthouse.

36. D. M. DeVitt, Deposition, *Mallet v. Slaughter; The Federal Reporter,* 285.

37. H. T. Boyd Diary, October 24, 1903.

38. Murrah, *C. C. Slaughter,* p. 89.

39. D. M. DeVitt, deposition, *Mallet v. Slaughter; Federal Reporter*, 285.

40. H. T. Boyd, Jr., to David Murrah, January 28, 1993, unrecorded interview.

41. Hall Jarman, Deposition, February 1904, *Mallet v. Slaughter*.

42. *Federal Reporter*, 283, 286, 289; C. C. Slaughter, Deposition, transcript, 457, *Mallet v. Slaughter*.

43. H. T. Boyd, Deposition, February 4, 1904, *Mallet v. Slaughter;* H. T. Boyd Diary, December 29, 1903.

44. Hall Jarman, Deposition, February 1904, *Mallet v. Slaughter*.

45. H. T. Boyd, Deposition, *Mallet v. Slaughter;* C. C. Slaughter to George M. Slaughter, January 28, 1904, George M. Slaughter Papers.

CHAPTER THREE

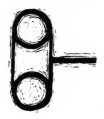

Christine's Chance at Mallet Ranch Life

It must have been in the summer time
that my sister [Christine] began to
have some chance at West Texas
ranch life—Mallet Ranch life, in
fact!
Helen DeVitt Jones, c. 1984.

U NDOUBTEDLY, DeVitt's and Flato's quick action in December 1903 to incorporate their holdings as the Mallet Land and Cattle Company saved the ranch for the two partners. By forcing their case into a new jurisdiction, they removed the Edwards County dispute from the Texas state courts, where C. C. Slaughter apparently held considerable influence, to the more impartial federal court.

DeVitt and Flato won the first round in the federal court. On May 31, 1904, United States Circuit Court Judge Edward R. Meeks ruled in their favor, granting them a permanent injunction and ordering Slaughter to pay court costs.[1] But the fight was far from over. Not accustomed to losing, Slaughter vowed to take the matter all the way to the United States Supreme Court. Moreover, he planned to challenge the overnight birth of the Mallet Land and Cattle Company, which had put the dispute in the federal court.

As the court battles took shape, Slaughter's attorney son-in-law set out to prove that the DeVitt and Flato partnership had incorporated only for the purpose of removing the case from the state court. Over the next year, he made a valiant effort to get DeVitt and Flato to admit that as their motive. But such was not to be the case.

During their lengthy testimony in the Edwards County land dispute, both DeVitt and Flato told the story of the incorporation of the Mallet Land and Cattle Company. David DeVitt testified that he and Flato had been contemplating such a move for more than a year so they might "get in a tangible form, and separated, our interest in the business in the form of collateral that we could use for private matters."[2] He had gone to Kansas City in September, five months before the December incorporation, and engaged a Kansas City law firm to begin preparing the charter. Moreover, he noted that F. W. Flato was anxious to get the incorporation because he was owed considerable debt and needed the stock for security.

DeVitt said that he delayed the filing of the charter because he did not want to upset the process of getting title to the Edwards County land. Once that was accomplished in mid-November, however, he had to remain in Texas to attend the court hearings over the requested injunction. The hearing finally got underway in Seymour on December 17, and, several hours before the judge dissolved the injunction on the afternoon on the 18th, DeVitt wired Flato to proceed with incorporation.[3] Before the end of the day, DeVitt and Flato's attorneys in Kansas City had the necessary documents ready to file. Three days later, on December 21, 1903, Missouri's Secretary of State issued a charter to the Mallet Land and Cattle Company, and DeVitt and Flato each conveyed their individual interest in the ranch to the new corporation.[4]

Apparently, Kansas courts in 1903 did not observe Christmas as a holiday, because DeVitt and Flato's attorneys on December 25, 1903, filed their suit against Slaughter in the United States Circuit Court, which in turn promptly issued a new injunction against Slaughter. Thus, within the period of a week, DeVitt and Flato had successfully incorporated and set in motion a process to resolve the dispute. Because of the haste and timing of the incorporation, Slaughter's attorney G. G. Wright pressed the issue in the federal court.

United States Circuit Court Judge Edward R. Meeks held a preliminary hearing in Lubbock in February 1904. Attorneys for both sides took extensive depositions from all parties involved, including DeVitt, Flato, Slaughter, and several of the Mallet and Slaughter cowboys. On May 31, after examining more than five hundred pages of testimony, Judge Meeks handed down his decision and ruled in favor of DeVitt and Flato. Moreover, he granted a permanent injunction against the Dallas rancher and banker, and ordered Slaughter to pay court costs.[5]

True to his word, Slaughter immediately appealed the decision to the United States Court of Civil Appeals in New Orleans. At the same time, he challenged the jurisdiction of the Circuit Court because of the hasty incorporation of the Mallet Land and Cattle Company. The appeal took more than a year to resolve, but by October 1905, the three judges of the Court of Appeals refused to overturn the decision of the lower court. The appeals court also declared that it could find no problem with the incorporation of the Mallet Land and Cattle Company and noted that the plaintiff failed to dispute any of DeVitt's and Flato's testimony concerning their reasons for incorporation.[6] The decisiveness of the appeals court's ruling apparently influenced Slaughter not to appeal the decision to the United States Supreme Court.

For Slaughter, the loss of the Edwards County block caused some inconvenience because it separated his Lazy S Ranch into two parts, divided by a five-mile strip of the Mallet Ranch. To move Slaughter cattle, his cowboys had to cross DeVitt land, creating a situation that probably hastened improved relations between the two ranches. The loss, however, made little difference in Slaughter's overall plans. He subsequently gained title to nearly 250,000 acres in Cochran and Hockley counties. In 1911, he turned the property over to his wife and nine children. But, ten years later, two years after Slaughter's death in 1919, the heirs divided the ranch among themselves and the Lazy S Ranch ceased to exist.[7]

For DeVitt, victory in Edwards County was a matter of life and death for the Mallet. Had he lost the fight, he probably would have sold his interests because the Edwards block represented approximately one-third of his deeded holdings. Many years later, after De-Vitt's death in 1934 and the discovery of oil on the Mallet, the winning of the Edwards County suit would mean millions of dollars to the DeVitt heirs and other Mallet owners.

The Edwards County land was not the only Mallet property in dispute. DeVitt and Slaughter had other clashes over parcels of land. Even though Slaughter had tried to buy the Scurry, Rains, and Baylor county blocks that DeVitt had under lease, the commissioners of each of those counties rejected Slaughter's generous offers, primarily because they resented the Dallas cattleman's already vast holdings. Although DeVitt subsequently lost the Baylor lease, which lay on the far eastern side of the ranch, he was able to hold onto the Scurry property and ultimately purchased it in 1914. Likewise, he kept the Rains County land leased until the 1920s, but apparently chose not to buy it.

Almost from its beginning in 1895, the shape and boundaries of the ranch were constantly changing. In 1896, DeVitt leased 24,930 acres of unsurveyed land that bordered the Mallet's southern pastures and were a part of a strip of land that would within a few years spawn a storm of controversy on the South Plains. He also leased nearly ten thousand acres of railroad and state school land that lay to the far south in Terry County.

The unsurveyed land that DeVitt leased was part of a two-mile-wide strip that ran east to west sixty miles across southern Hockley and Cochran counties. Because the surveyed land on the south had failed to meet with the surveyed land on the north, this strip remained unclaimed and part of the public domain until the late 1890s. For many years, area ranchers simply incorporated the strip into their pastures and used its grass for free.

David DeVitt may have been the first of the South Plains cattlemen actually to lease a part of the unsurveyed strip. In late July 1896, he obtained a lease from the state on approximately twenty miles of the strip that adjoined the Mallet's south side.[8] At the western end

34

of the strip lay the ranch's headquarters on a gentle slope of Sulphur Draw.

Because the demand for cheap land increased after 1900, the unsurveyed strip soon attracted the attention of prospective settlers. Jim Jarrott, a young Erath County lawyer and former state legislator, recognized that the vacancy could be colonized and subsequently applied to the Texas General Land Office to survey the strip so that he could assist settlers in proving their claims. In 1901, Jarrott moved his family to Lubbock, and from there spent much of the year staking the sections, including ten that lay within the bounds of D. M. DeVitt's lease.[9]

In early spring of 1902, Jarrott began moving families to the strip, and in April, each head of household claimed four sections under the Land Law of 1897, which provided that settlers who would live on public domain could purchase the land for as little as one dollar per acre. But some of the area's ranchers were angered by the intrusion, and one apparently decided to teach the prospective settlers a hard lesson.

In August 1902, after Jarrott located a number of families on the strip, including his own, the young lawyer was murdered by gunfire at an isolated windmill only three miles from the strip. If the assassin's intent was to scare the settlers off the strip, it did not work. "We became more intent and closely allied in our fight for survival," wrote Mary Blankenship, who with her husband had staked a claim. "The name Jim Jarrott became a legend among us, and his martyrdom served to spur us on. We were determined not to pull up stakes and retreat back to the East."[10]

The murder polarized the West Texas community. Farmers in the area blamed the ranchers, accusing them of hiring an assassin to murder Jarrott in order to frighten away the strip's settlers. The ranching community was appalled at the deed, and Lubbock's local gossip implied that Jarrott's wife, Mollie, may have been involved. The murder became the South Plains' major unsolved mystery; more than thirty years would pass before the killer would be identified. In 1933, Jarrott's widow, who had married Monroe G. Abernathy, learned that a professional killer, "Deacon" Jim Miller of

Oklahoma, had confessed to the killing before he was hanged in 1909 and said that he had been paid five hundred dollars to kill Jarrott. He never revealed who paid him, however, carrying his secret to the gallows.[11] Many speculated that the murder was authorized by a big rancher in the area. David DeVitt was never a suspect because his claim on the strip was protected from incursion by his 1896 lease and Jarrott did not intend to place settlers on Mallet land.

Because DeVitt's headquarters lay on the controversial strip, he needed to convert his lease to a deed. To do so, he would have to move his family from their comfortable home in Fort Worth to the isolation of the Mallet. The law required the settler to improve and live on the land at least six months of the year. When his lease expired in 1903, DeVitt moved his wife and family from Fort Worth to a small two-room house on a four-section claim, now known as Block X, in July 1903 to begin the three-year process of proving his claim.[12]

DeVitt had moved his family from San Angelo to Fort Worth in 1896. The move gave the DeVitt children, who had started school in San Angelo, better opportunity for education. Christine, who was twelve, and Harold, eleven, attended nearby public schools. When, Florence gave birth to a second daughter, Helen, on December 7, 1899, the new baby was excuse enough for a new house. By early 1900, the family had settled into a large and comfortable home on the south edge of Fort Worth.[13]

As in previous generations, a terrible tragedy struck the young DeVitt family. Harold, who was fourteen, was killed in a hunting accident, probably in the summer of 1901 while he was visiting his father's ranch.[14] Grief-stricken, Florence wanted another child and on May 16, 1902, gave birth to her second boy, who was named David Mantz, Jr.

When David DeVitt announced to his family in early 1903 that they would be moving from Fort Worth to the ranch for at least six months of the year, each member must have reacted differently. For Helen, only three years old, the train trip and long wagon ride from Big Spring to the ranch were among her earliest memories. For Christine, nearly eighteen, the return to a West Texas ranch must have been exciting. She had always enjoyed the ranch and a return to West Texas would give her the opportunity to improve her out-door skills and horseback riding.

For Florence, however, it was a different kind of venture. With a one-year-old baby boy and three-year-old girl to care for, Florence must have found it a considerable challenge to rear her young family so far removed from any town. Moreover, because of the Jarrott murder and the isolation, she must have been frightened for her family. The situation worsened because of her husband's long legal fight with Slaughter over the Edwards County land. The ongoing litigation in the fall and winter of 1903, coupled with his efforts to in-corporate and to sort out his business affairs with his partner F. W. Flato, kept him away from the ranch for more than six months. Nonetheless, the family remained at the ranch until January 1904.[15]

Florence must have kept busy cooking for the handful of cowboys employed by the ranch, but otherwise, life was lonely. Neighbors were virtually nonexistent. Although there were scattered ranch line camps, few, if any, other women lived on the ranches of the west-ern South Plains. In fact, only a handful of people lived in the entire four counties of Cochran, Hockley, Terry, and Yoakum. Only an occasional trip to Lubbock or Big Spring for supplies would give the family opportunity for social contact.

During the next two years, DeVitt proved his title to the land by dutifully moving his family back and forth from Fort Worth to the ranch, probably staying on the plains from mid-April through late September.[16] After 1905, Helen was ready to start school, and for the next several years, the DeVitt family made its home in Fort Worth on a permanent basis. Mr. DeVitt spent much of the year at the ranch, but Florence may have never visited it again. As Helen recalled many years later, she herself did not return to the ranch until she was grown and out of college, probably in 1925.[17] But apparently, Christine, and later, David, Jr., enjoyed going to the ranch in the summer and did so at every opportunity.

With his family resettled in Fort Worth, DeVitt devoted most of his time to the management of the Mallet. When they incorporated in December 1903, DeVitt and his partner F. W. Flato owned 5,544 head of cattle, including 2,300 three-year-old steers being wintered along the Powder River in Custer County, Montana. Using the Texas ranch as a cow-calf operation, the partners shipped their annual steer crops north to Montana for finishing. Indebtedness on these cattle totaled $43,390. Carrying both heavy business and personal indebtedness, Flato soon found himself in financial difficulty. By late 1904, he began to look for a way out of his seven-year partnership with DeVitt. During the year, he transferred to DeVitt 52 of his original 452 shares. With his remaining 400 shares, he negotiated an agreement with his longtime livestock commission partner, Andrew Drumm. For these shares, which Flato transferred to Drumm Commission Company, Drumm agreed to pay off Flato's $25,000 indebtedness and to transfer to Flato an $11,000 note that he held on cattle in Montana, as well as $23,000 of notes he held on Flato's brother, C. H. With consideration of the stock value and a cash payment to Flato of $2,500, the exchange made the entire deal worth $64,526.61 on paper.[18]

DeVitt must have been pleased with the arrangement because he had exchanged a flamboyant partner who was quick to draw on Mallet's reserves for a wealthy, experienced cattleman.

Andrew Drumm was nearly seventy-six years old when he acquired the Mallet stock. A native of Ohio, Drumm earned college degrees before joining the California gold rush in 1849 at age twenty. Subsequently, he began raising hogs to furnish to the mining camps, and by 1869 had sold his land and established one of the first meat packing companies in the area.[19] In the early 1870s, "Major" Drumm, as he was known, relocated to Texas and began trail driving cattle to the railheads in Kansas. He later became one of the first to move cattle onto the so-called Cherokee Strip and subsequently established the U Ranch on 100,000 to 150,000 acres near present-day Cherokee, Oklahoma.[20] About 1881, Drumm moved to Kansas City and in 1893, joined with F. W. Flato in establishing the Drumm-Flato Commission Company. Soon, Drumm-Flato became one of the largest livestock commission companies in the nation with offices in Kansas City, Chicago, and St. Louis. With Flato's continuing financial difficulty, Drumm in 1902 bought most of the company stock and changed its name to the Drumm Commission Company.[21]

When Major Drumm acquired Flato's Mallet stock, he became DeVitt's virtual silent partner and probably never saw his Texas holdings. DeVitt became the sole manager and decision maker. Although Mallet records are sketchy for the first thirty years of its operations, it is apparent from existing sources that DeVitt was a very successful manager, making the ranch productive and profitable. For example, sales for 1905 of 1,200 steers and 101 cows grossed $43,461; ranch expenses were probably less than $10,000, thus yielding a net profit of more than $30,000.

The ranch had debts to pay, though, and DeVitt continued to operate it conservatively. He employed the fewest men possible. Initially, he operated a cow-calf operation, but soon learned that a breeding ranch required more men and money to operate than would a steer ranch. Subsequently, he converted the ranch to primarily a steer operation. Annually, he bought approximately 1,000 to 1,200 head of yearling calves and held most of them for as many as four years, depending on the market. Thus, he would have an annual production of heavy grass-fed four-year-old steers, which he would ship by rail to markets in Kansas City, St. Joseph, Missouri, and Chicago.

Net profits climbed and fell with rainfall on the South Plains. Except for 1905, when the area received more than thirty inches of rain, annual moisture remained at an annual seasonal average, approximately eighteen inches, throughout the first decade of the twentieth century. Drought returned to the region in 1910, and Mallet Ranch expenses jumped to nearly $14,500. As the drought lingered, costs climbed nearly 50 percent by 1912, to $21,760, reflecting increased feed purchases.

Because of the drought, DeVitt sought additional grassland for his cattle and in 1911 was able to purchase from the Pennicks 638 acres that joined his personally owned Block X land on the west. The drought took its toll; expenses remained high and cattle sales low because of the lack of good grass. In 1914, even though good rainfall returned, with some areas receiving as much as thirty inches, the ranch's net income had shrunk to less than $18,000.[22]

Good rains continued throughout 1915, marking the first and the last time that the South Plains had ever received more than thirty inches in two successive years. Because of the outbreak of war in Europe, cattle prices began a steady rise that was to last through 1917, bringing to West Texas ranchers cattle profits similar to those in the glory days of the early 1880s. As his ranch received higher-than-average moisture in 1915, DeVitt carried over a large number of cattle, and at the end of the year showed an inventory of 1,500 three-year-old steers and 1,750 two-year-olds. His gross income for 1915 jumped to $156,773, the highest in the ranch's twenty-year history. DeVitt used $71,000 to restock the ranch, but netted approximately $70,000 profit for the year.[23]

Because of the high carry-over of cattle and the return of average rainfall, DeVitt had to sell off much of his stock to prevent overgrazing. Consequently, 1916 proved to be a record year for Mallet cattle sales, with receipts totaling nearly $163,000. After receiving some good late-summer and fall rains, DeVitt plowed much of the profit back into restockers.

Unfortunately, 1917 proved to be one of the driest years on record, with West Texas receiving less than nine inches in some areas, approximately half the annual average. From January through April, the Lubbock weather station collected slightly more than one inch of moisture. Summer rains were sporadic at best, and only a wet September, when three inches were recorded in Lubbock, prevented total disaster for area ranches. The 1917 drought was followed closely by a severe January 1918 winter storm that decimated herds of West Texas cattle already impoverished by the drought.

Despite the unfavorable conditions, the Mallet pulled through. Having discontinued his cow-calf operation, DeVitt was apparently able to weather the drought by simply shipping steers to market early if he did not have adequate grass. Other ranchers were not so lucky, as they were forced to reduce their breeding herds. The drought, which continued into the spring of 1918, coupled with winter weather losses, forced cattlemen to ship to market early; prices began a gradual decline that ultimately spelled disaster for many West Texas ranchers. Although the drought broke in the fall of 1918, declining prices, pushed down even further because of the end of World War I, probably forced DeVitt to throw more steers on the market than he had planned. Gross Mallet sales for 1918 were at a record $239,000, but, owing to the falling prices, DeVitt purchased only half the usual number of calves to restock the ranch.

Despite the drought and collapsing prices, DeVitt closed the decade of the war years as a very prosperous cattleman. He used the wartime profits to reduce the ranch's land indebtedness, improve the ranch's waterings, purchase more land, and to become a speculator in stocks. Much of DeVitt's effort also went into improving the steer operation. By 1920 he had fenced and cross-fenced the ranch into sixteen pastures watered by twenty-three windmills. Yearling calves, generally purchased and driven from ranches that lay to the south or southeast of the Mallet, would be placed first in the ranch's south pastures in Terry County near the headquarters on Sulphur Draw. As the cattle aged, they would be moved north on the ranch, and by the time they were ready for shipment to either market or northern ranches for finishing, the cattle would be at the extreme north end of the ranch, ready to drive to the railroad at Bovina. After the Santa Fe had built its branch line from Lubbock to Seagraves in 1916, DeVitt shipped Mallet cattle from Ropesville, approximately twenty miles east of the ranch headquarters. This locale served the ranch until 1925 when the Santa Fe extended another branch line west from Lubbock across central Hockley and Cochran counties to the New Mexico state line at Bledsoe. As a result, the new town of Whiteface, only two miles north of the Mallet's north fence, provided the ranch with its major shipping point for many years.

DeVitt did not commit all of his money to the cattle business. During the war years, he invested more than $12,000 in United States Liberty and Victory bonds. He also continued to acquire title to land in his own name, some to supplement the Mallet's pastures and some for speculation. By 1920, DeVitt personally owned 4,496 acres of ranch and farm land as well as city lots in Fort Worth, Abilene, and San Angelo, collectively valued at more than one hundred thousand dollars.

Like many other Texans, DeVitt also plunged into one of the waves of oil speculation that swept the country with the discovery of each new field. Most of his purchases of oil stock came in 1917 and 1919. In the fall of 1917, he bought five hundred dollars worth of stock in the Union Oil Company of Wichita, Kansas, as well as one hundred dollars worth of the Flint Hills Petroleum Company stock. Over a two-year period, he bought a thousand shares, at one dollar per share, of the Cowpunchers Oil Company, another Kansas corporation.

With the discovery of the Ranger, Texas, oil field in 1917, DeVitt was attracted to investments in royalty interests in north Texas. One 1919 lease proposal involved himself and twenty-eight other investors, including his old ranching partner John Scharbauer and a future partner J. Lee Johnson, both of Fort Worth.[24] By 1920, DeVitt had invested more than ten thousand dollars in oil stocks, of which nearly all proved to be worthless, except for twelve shares of the Texas Company, which later became Texaco, Inc.

Nonetheless, by 1920, with his controlling interest in the Mallet Land and Cattle Company, DeVitt was able to demonstrate to his financiers a net worth of more than six hundred thousand dollars. Although information is not available for his financial condition when he formed his original partnership in the Mallet with John Scharbauer in 1895, he likely had less than twenty-five thousand dollars at the time. DeVitt proved himself to be a prudent, if not shrewd cattleman, by improving his net worth more than twenty times during his first twenty-five years of running the Mallet. Although he would never live to realize it, his investment in land would likewise prove to be shrewd.

NOTES

1. Murrah, *C. C. Slaughter*, p. 89.
2. D. M. DeVitt, Deposition, *Mallet v. Slaughter*.
3. *Ibid.*
4. *Ibid.*; Articles of Incorporation, Mallet Land and Cattle Company, Archives, Secretary of State's Office, Jefferson, City, Missouri.
5. Murrah, *C. C. Slaughter*, p. 89.
6. *Federal Reporter*, 293.
7. Murrah, *C. C. Slaughter*, 134. For an extensive history of the Lazy S Ranch, see David Murrah, "Cattle Kingdom on Texas' Last Frontier: C. C. Slaughter's Lazy S Ranch" (MA Thesis, Texas Tech University, 1970).
8. Deed Records, Book 2, pp. 382-383, Hockley County, Texas.
9. Castro County Historical Commission, *Castro County, Texas, 1891–1981* (Dallas: Taylor Publishing Company, 1981), p. 476.
10. Connor, S. V., ed., *The West Is For Us: The Reminiscences of Mary A. Blankenship* (Lubbock: West Texas Museum Association, 1958), p. 43.
11. Jack Abernathy to M. G. Abernathy, March 23, 1933, letter, [photocopy], James W. Jarrott Reference File, Southwest Collection, Texas Tech University.
12. *General Laws of the State of Texas Passed at the Regular Session of the Twenty-Seventh Legislature* (Austin: Von Boeckmann, Schutze & Col, 1901), p. 295; R. D. Holt, "School Land Rushes in West Texas," West Texas Historical Association *Year Book*, X (1934), 42-57.
13. Deed, Mallet Records. The house was purchased for $3,300.
14. Dorothy Secrest to David Murrah, unrecorded interview, November 6, 1992.
15. D. M. DeVitt, deposition, *Mallet v. Slaughter*.
16. Florence A. DeVitt to Christine DeVitt, January 1905, Family correspondence, Mallet Records.

17. Helen D. Jones, Speech to Lubbock Women's Study Club, c. 1984, typescript, Mallet Records.

18. F. W. Flato, Note, 1904, Mallet Records.

19. Meade L. McClure, *Major Andrew Drumm 1829-1919* (n.p., 1919) 5-10; David E. Dexter, "Veteran K. C. Commission Man, Who Never Boasted Long Life Recipe and Has Lived as Conditions Dictated, Celebrates Birthday," *Kansas City Post* (6 February 1919); *Kansas City Star* (9 February 1939), Newspaper clippings, Kansas City Public Library.

20. "Monument Erected to Major Drumm," *The Cattleman* (August 1932) 7.

21. "Age No Bar to Stockman," *Kansas City Times* (14 April 1919); *Kansas City Star* (20 April 1919); McClure, *Major Andrew Drumm 1829-1919,* 10-11.

22. Statement of Account, 1914, Mallet Records.

23. Inventory, 1915, Mallet Records.

24. Worthless Stock File, Mallet Records.

CHAPTER FOUR

My Personal Attention

But I cannot run this ranch and give
it my personal attention which it
requires, and live a thousand or
fifteen hundred miles away. I would
like to be where you are and see you
and be able to take proper care of you.
I wish you would think about coming
back to Ft. Worth to live next Fall.
David M. DeVitt to Helen DeVitt,
March 8, 1923.

IN every respect, the Mallet Land and Cattle Company from its beginning made David DeVitt a good living. As general manager, DeVitt drew a salary in 1904 of $250 per month, or $3,000 annually, a generous amount by early 1900 ranch standards.[1] Cowboys at the same time generally made only $35 to $45 per month, and a ranch foreman only $75 to $100. By 1914, DeVitt had increased his pay as manager to $5,000 annually, and by 1922, to $7,500.

DeVitt enjoyed his success as a rancher, but he apparently led a double life in doing so. To his family, employees, and ranch neighbors, he was regarded as a tough, if not, miserly, individual. H. T. Boyd, C. C. Slaughter's foreman and the Mallet's closest neighbor, always referred to him as "Old Man DeVitt," even though the two were about the same age.[2] On the ranch, DeVitt was all business, keeping both his family and employees on limited resources. Away from the ranch, he played the wealthy cattleman, patronizing the fine hotels and clubs of cities he would visit, and bestowing expensive gifts and jewelry on numerous lady friends.

It is no wonder, then, that the DeVitt family began to drift apart as the children grew older. Christine finished high school in Fort Worth, where she mastered penmanship, and, according to Helen, received "first prize" recognition upon graduation. Christine also studied bookkeeping and, as Helen recalled, "enjoyed it more than any other course."[3] Unknown to Christine at the time, bookkeeping would be a skill on which she would rely heavily in future years.

Without much help from her husband, Florence DeVitt did her best to teach her daughters about the finer things of life; she insisted that Christine take piano lessons, perhaps in an effort to head off Christine's love for ranch life. Also, in 1903, shortly after the family had moved to the Mallet, Florence persuaded Mr. DeVitt to send Christine "back East" to finishing school, to the Hollins Institute, a few miles north of Roanoke, Virginia, near the Blue Ridge Mountains. A girls' school in the tradition of the old South, the Hollins Institute had been established in 1842; Christine remained there for two years and graduated in the spring of 1905.[4]

Christine then moved to St. Louis to attend Forest Park University to study music. There she found a teacher, friends, and a life that she never forgot: "This experience and these friends, my sister never stopped talking about all through life," Helen recalled after Christine's death. "It seems that every one there greatly admired and loved Dr. Kreiger who taught piano. But I also heard constantly [from Christine] about the young women in the dormitory and their experiences with the head of the college—the very, very strict Mrs. Cairns. I wonder if the others there recounted those tales for as long or as vividly as my sister did!"[5]

After her studies in St. Louis, Christine returned to Texas and joined her family in Fort Worth. At twenty, she had a decided advantage over most young women of her age; she had an education and could play the piano well enough to teach. As a result, Christine offered private piano lessons for a few years.

Christine also probably assumed a motherly role over her sister Helen, who was fourteen years younger than she. In 1914, when Helen was fifteen and ready for advanced schooling, Christine joined with her in enrolling in nearby Texas Christian University. Christine studied in the College of Arts and Sciences while Helen was in the College of Fine Arts. After a year, Helen apparently dropped out, but Christine continued. By the fall of 1916, she was listed in the University's catalog as a junior. Although she did not finish school, she did obtain a teaching certificate before her departure in 1917. Meanwhile, Helen reentered TCU in the fall of 1917 and remained for a year.[6]

Christine soon put her advanced education to work. In September 1917, she began teaching at the Fort Worth Riverside High School for the 1917-18 school term, and may have remained for the following year as well.[7] She then taught at DeZavalla Public School Number 8 for the full year of 1919-20 at a salary of one hundred dollars per month. She must have performed well as she was paid a 5-percent bonus for the year.[8]

By 1918, David, the youngest of the children, was sixteen and nearing the end of his public schooling. Determined to follow in his father's footsteps, David worked hard every summer to become a hand on the ranch. R. E. Turner, whose mother and father both worked on the Mallet in 1918, remembered David quite well, even though Turner was only four years old at the time. Turner vividly recalled how three of the older hands got into a water fight with David. "Those cowboys, " Turner remembered, "really loved to play tricks on that boy."[9]

Kate Boyd Keathley, whose father, former Slaughter foreman H. T. Boyd, owned the neighboring ranch to the DeVitts on the west, remembered David as an excellent hand and handsome cowboy. Because the Mallet cowboys helped the Boyds during roundup, David made annual visits to the Boyd Ranch. "He was tall, thin, reddish blond hair, and freckles," Kate Boyd Keathley recalled. "He was always jolly, laughing, full of fun, and very amiable. Everybody liked him."[10] By 1920, when he was eighteen, young David had become a regular hand on the Mallet Ranch.

By 1918, with David headed for the ranch, Christine working, and Helen ready to find another school, Florence DeVitt decided to leave Fort Worth and move, at least on a temporary basis, to California. Her move may have been prompted by several factors. There was already a strain on the DeVitt marriage, caused by Mr. DeVitt's long absences from home. Secondly, Helen was interested in attending school in California. Also, Mr. DeVitt, who had always dreamed of living in California, apparently encouraged Florence and Helen to head west. As a result, Florence and Helen settled in Berkeley, where Helen enrolled in the University of California.[11]

In 1921, Christine apparently ended her brief teaching career and left the family's old Fort Worth home to join her mother and sister in California. To make the trip, Christine chose an alternate route, one that Helen described as a "glorious and very scenic railway journey by a northerly route none of us had ever taken to California."[12] Whether Christine only intended to visit and then return to Fort Worth is unknown. Once there, she stayed. With Christine's reunion with her mother and Helen, the women apparently decided to move to Los Angeles, perhaps at the insistence of Mr. DeVitt, so that the family would be closer to West Texas. "Los Angeles was fairly nice in those years," Helen remembered. "Our little home [was] on Afton Place [in Hollywood], a few doors east of the famous Vine Street—not then such a thoroughfare as it became later."[13]

For the family's California living expenses, Mr. DeVitt sent his wife $150 per month. Helen, who had graduated from the University of California, enrolled in school in Hollywood. Much closer to her father than Christine, Helen would write long, newsy letters to him, and often teased him about his hard work and habits. In one letter, she told him that his friend Fred Ryan had been arrested in San Diego for driving while intoxicated and for violation of the Wright Prohibition Act: "It came out in the paper as a 'wild ride,'" she noted. "Two pints of liquor (some of that bootleg kind you had summer before last, I guess) were discovered in his car."[14]

Unlike Helen, Christine was perhaps as much estranged from her father as was her mother. Because of her tendency to procrastinate, she found it difficult to prepare for and make long trips back to Texas. Thus, Helen went alone to visit the ranch in the summer of 1925, her first trip to the Mallet since she was a small child. There she sought out female companionship from neighboring ranches. The nearest ranch was that of H. T. Boyd. In 1911, Boyd had left the Slaughter operation, and, in partnership with his brother Oscar, had established his own ranch immediately west of the Mallet. The Boyds had four children, Hiley, Kate, Nelle, and Johnanna. Kate Boyd was seventeen when Helen came riding over one day to see her. Even though Helen was nine years older, the age difference did not stop the young ladies from having a good visit. Helen spent the night; then, on the following day, Kate went with Helen to the Mallet and stayed the night there.[15]

On another occasion that summer, Helen visited the Zavala Ranch on the east side of the Mallet and brought the camp manager's wife back to her father's ranch for a visit. "I have certainly enjoyed having Mrs. Havens with me," Helen reported to her father. "We have such a nice time talking together; I hate to see her go back."[16]

Helen's 1925 ranch venture also carried her into Ropesville, where the Mallet cowboys were shipping cattle on the Santa Fe railroad. Among other things, she wrote to her father of her brother David's romantic interests: "There were several young ladies present this morning, and as they took 'dinner' with us, I think David rather enjoyed himself."[17]

Helen also had romantic interests of her own. Even though she was quite shy, she could not avoid the attention paid to her by Lee S. "Bill" Secrest, a handsome young man she met during her 1925 summer visit. Bill lived in the new county seat town of Morton, eighteen miles northwest of the Mallet Ranch. A self-taught civil engineer, he had grown up in Hamilton, Texas, where he was a star athlete on the high school baseball team. But, he soon got bored with school, dropped out, and began work.[18] In 1923, Secrest was employed by land promoter and founder of Morton, Morton J. Smith to survey and stake Smith's new townsite in Cochran County.[19]

Helen met Bill at a summer party held on the Mallet Ranch, and shortly afterwards, on September 30, 1925, they were married in Tahoka, by the County Judge of Lynn County, C. H. Cain.[20] Mr. DeVitt, who was probably away from the ranch shipping cattle to market, was not pleased. Helen, anxious to make a new life for herself, moved to Morton to live with Bill, but after she became pregnant in the spring of 1926, she returned to California to be with her mother until the baby was born. Bill remained in Morton to work. Their only child, Dorothy Gail, was born in Los Angeles on December 23, 1926.

Helen's marriage to Bill was not to survive its seventh year. Uncomfortable with living in Texas, Helen wanted to stay in California. Subsequently, Bill quit his job in Cochran County and moved with Helen to San Diego, where he apparently found work for awhile. In the summer of 1930, when Dorothy was three and a half, Bill must have lost his job in California. With Helen and Dorothy, he then moved back to Texas, first staying a few months in Lubbock. Subsequently, he went to work for the Fort Worth and Denver railroad, which was building a new line from Childress to Pampa. While Bill worked for the railroad, Helen and Dorothy lived in Fort Worth, where Dorothy began school.[21]

Unhappy being alone in Texas, Helen and Dorothy returned to San Diego in 1931, and later to Los Angeles where Mr. DeVitt bought a house for them. Bill remained in Texas, perhaps unwilling to return to California, and Helen obtained a divorce in Reno, Nevada, in December 1933.[22]

While Helen was struggling with her marriage, Christine remained in Hollywood with her mother Florence. When Helen married in September 1925, Christine, who was single, had just celebrated her fortieth birthday and probably resented her "old maid" status. Although she busied herself with teaching piano and attending cultural events, Christine's constant presence soon strained her relationship with her mother, who was only eighteen years older than she. A 1929 letter to Helen reflects Florence's growing impatience with her elder daughter:

Helen, I simply can't write a very connected letter at best, but Christine has been on the job since I took up this pen and the outpouring has not ceased one second. . . . I defy duty or the devil to live in the same quarters with Christine as mother and daughter or sister even and not loose control of their temper. I am not equal to that trial just yet . . . I wail—how much longer "Oh, Lord"—will I be enveloped in her coat tangles and her everlasting criticisms and suspicions of every simple, single slightest whispers, and even I can't survive it much longer. . . . I wonder why Christine wasn't cut out something like the rest of us.

The same letter offers insight into Christine's hopes and dreams:

[Christine] turned out in her new coat to view the "Shrine Parade" last evening as it was about the close of festivities and she couldn't persuade me to give up five dollars for a ticket to the show. Of course, she was elated when she struck a fine young woman with a "Cadillac Car" who allowed her and several others to step in and ride with her, a Texan at that. Then one of the party gave her a complimentary ticket for which she was intending to give up three dollars for, much against my advice. Anyway, she saw the floats and must tell each and every single small detail. I should be glad for (anyone else but myself would say) [the] poor girl that she came in for that much of what she craves.[23]

But there would soon come the day when Christine would see her dream fulfilled.

Christine, who in later years would become notorious for her procrastination, apparently developed the habit relatively early in life. Her mother once reported to Helen, "Now [Christine's] on the go for a hat; she never hits the town till four o'clock and then goes moseying round and never comes to the object for which she presumably started."[24]

The strain between Christine and her father is apparent in the same letter. Concerned that Mr. DeVitt was not going to provide for Christine in his will, Florence declared to Helen of her own intent to help her daughters. "David Jr. will take over the bulk of everything outside of what is left to the favored relatives," she noted to Helen. "In fact I have always felt that should I make over the little I've accumulated to you and she, that would entirely justify him D.M.D. in leaving all to D, Jr., and certainly leaving <u>Ch</u> [Christine] out entirely. Of course that would be a loop hole only He'd do it anyway in Christine's case only."[25]

While his wife and daughters dealt with their problems, the senior David DeVitt continued to pursue his first love, the Mallet Ranch. By 1921, he was sixty-five years old, and with his son David coming of an age to take on more responsibility for the ranch, it seemed apparent that DeVitt would be ready to retire. The 1920s seemed to offer new opportunities to make more money, and DeVitt was not one to let such an opportunity slip by. His silent partner Major Andrew Drumm had died in 1919, and the prospect of a more active partnership in the company left him unsettled as the new decade approached.

His first challenge was a new depression in cattle prices. By late 1920, beef produced for a wartime economy found few buyers and prices slumped to less than four cents per pound. Some Texas ranches, such as the Pitchfork, suspended cattle sales altogether, but DeVitt apparently was able to outmaneuver the market collapse by shipping his steers before the price hit bottom in November. Although he grossed more than $182,000 for the year, his net income totaled only $27,000 as expenses were nearly double those of previous years.

In 1921, the ranch fared even worse, showing a net loss for the year of nearly $17,000. Moreover, poor rainfall in 1922 only prolonged the tough times. Although DeVitt was able to trim the ranch's losses for the year to less than $9,000, it was only because he had cut the ranch's annual expenses by nearly $40,000 from what they had been in 1920. Also, he cut his own salary from $7,500 to $4,500.

The cattle depression and drought did not deter DeVitt from trying to take advantage of the cheap price for cows. Even though he

Phillip M. DeVitt, c. 1910. From B. B. Paddock, ed., Fort Worth and the Texas Northwest, *IV (Lewis Publishing, 1922)* .

David M. DeVitt, c. 1920.

MALLET CATTLE COMPANY.

Ranch on Colorado river and Morgan cr+ek.

D. P. ATWOOD, Manager. Postoffice Colorado City, Texas. This brand kept up. Also cattle in following marks and brands:

HOT on right side and some **A** on hip; mark, crop left, over half crop and underbit right.

PCK T on neck; mark, swallow fork left, over half crop right.

FOP A on jaw ; mark, swallow fork left.

2LP mark, swallow fork left, over slope right.

2 on hip and side; mark, swallow fork left. **TGE** on either side, **JIM** on opposite side; m rk, crop left sharp right.

on neck, **2** on side,

and **O** on hip; mark, crop left, crop and under half crop right.

O on hip and **LET** on side mark, same as above.

O on shoulder, hip and side ; mark, under slope left, crop right.

mark, crop left, crop and under half crop right.

Mallet Cattle Company brand advertisement, 1885.   From Texas Livestock Journal, *October 1885.*

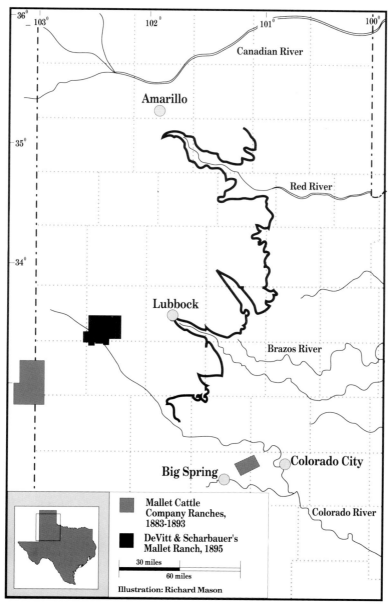

Locations of the original Mallet Cattle Company Ranch and DeVitt's Mallet Ranch.

Mallet Ranch headquarters, 1939, along Sulphur Draw in southwestern Hockley County. The site is virtually unchanged today. From O. R. Watkins, "A History of Hockley County" (master's thesis, Texas Technological College, 1941).

F. W. Flato, Jr., c. 1890. From Cuthbert Powell,
Twenty Years of Kansas City's Livestock Trade and
Traders *(Pearl Printing, 1893).*

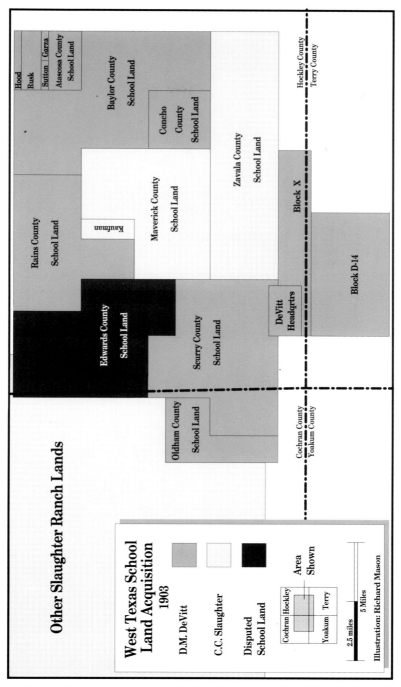

Mallet and Slaughter ranches, 1903, showing disputed Edwards County land.

Certificate of Incorporation, Mallet Land and Cattle Company, Inc., 1903.

Above. The only known picture of the DeVitt family, c. 1910, probably in New York City. Pictured are Florence DeVitt (left); her daughter Helen; son David; husband, David M. DeVitt; and daughter Christine. Right. Harold DeVitt, c. 1899. Harold was killed in a hunting accident in 1901.

Mallet Ranch headquarters, 1992. Photo by Artie Limmer.

Mallet headquarters, rear view, 1992. The left wing of the house was probably the original two-room structure occupied by the DeVitt family from 1903 to 1906. Photo by Artie Limmer.

Above.   Mallet Ranch bunkhouse, 1992. This box-and-strip structure may date from the 1890s. It is located immediately behind the main house at the ranch headquarters. Photo by Artie Limmer.
Right.   Major Andrew Drumm, 1890.   From George C. Berkemeier, Major Andrew Drumm, 1829-1919: An Adventurer Who Left a Living Memorial *(n.p., n.d.).*

DeZavalla School, c. 1920, Fort Worth, Texas, where the DeVitt children attended and Christine taught. Courtesy Fort Worth Public Library.

Helen DeVitt's class at the DeZavalla School in Fort Worth, 1907. Helen, who was eight years old, was probably in the second grade and is seated second from right on the front row, holding the sign.

Above. Mallet Ranch foreman George Green (left), and Mallet cowboys Aubrey Floyd and David DeVitt, Jr., c. 1925. The picture was taken during annual roundup at the Boyd Ranch, which bordered the Mallet on the west. Kate Boyd Keathley Collection, Southwest Collection, Texas Tech University. Right. Helen DeVitt, 1925, at the age of twenty-six.

Above Opposite.   Helen DeVitt Secrest and daughter Dorothy, c. 1929.
Below Opposite.   Dorothy Secrest and her father Bill Secrest, c. 1929.
Above.   Christine DeVitt (left), her mother Florence DeVitt, and
sister Helen Secrest, c. 1927.   This picture probably was taken shortly
after Helen's daughter Dorothy was born.

Above. Fred Brown, who currently leases the Mallet Ranch, displays an old Mallet branding iron he found in the headquarters barn. Photo by Artie Limmer. Left. W. D. Johnson, c. 1930. From H. I. Hester, ed., These Missouri Baptists *(Missouri Baptist Press, 1970).*

Above.   J. Lee Johnson, c. 1920.
From B. B. Paddock, ed., Fort
Worth and the Texas Northwest,
IV (Lewis Publishing, 1922).
Above Right.   David M. DeVitt,
1925.
Right.   Tom Jones, c. 1945.

Mallet headquarters barn, 1992. Photo by David J. Murrah.

Florence A. DeVitt, c. 1935.

had discontinued a Mallet cow-calf operation many years before, he was persuaded in 1922 by his longtime friend and employee Pat Ross to buy cow herds that had been thrown on the market by the depression. Ross, who had worked on the Mallet almost from its founding, persuaded his boss to form a partnership in 1915 on a herd of cows kept on pastures that they personally owned or leased in Terry County, south of the ranch.

The new venture involved the outright purchase of more than eleven hundred head of cattle, including one thousand cows and calves, and the leasing of additional pasture. Moreover, it was made possible by the breakup of the neighboring C. C. Slaughter Lazy S Ranch. After Slaughter's death in 1919, his wife and nine children could not agree on the operations of the vast ranch that surrounded DeVitt's property. In 1921, the Slaughters partitioned their 246,000-acre ranch into ten divisions and divided equally the livestock. But some of the Slaughters, including the youngest, Alex, of Dallas, had little interest in West Texas ranching. For his part, he had received the 17,000-acre Zavala pasture, which lay to the east of Mallet headquarters, and which at one time had been a part of the Mallet Ranch. Alex tried to operate the ranch for a year, but after losing money, decided to get out of the cattle business entirely. In late July, 1922, he sold to DeVitt and Ross 550 cows of the once vast Lazy S herd. These cattle were Herefords, descendants of the herd which had attracted Slaughter to the South Plains in 1897. DeVitt and Ross paid $55 per head for cows with calves, $40 for dry cows, and only $35 for two-year-old heifers.

The partners also leased from Slaughter 12,398 acres of the Zavala Ranch for twenty-seven cents per acre.[26] In June 1923, they added to their herd an additional 453 cows and heifers and eighty-eight steers. To finance the operation DeVitt and Ross borrowed more than $36,000 from the Union National Bank in Kansas City.

About the same time that DeVitt and Ross were putting together their deal for the Zavala Ranch, DeVitt was approached by another old friend, Ed Crocker, who wanted to form a partnership with him to buy another herd of Slaughter cattle, that of Carrie Slaughter Dean. Because the price seemed right, DeVitt agreed to the partnership, put into it $3,500 cash, and signed a joint note for $126,042. The partnership in turn leased 25,000 acres of the old Lazy S Ranch from Mrs. Dean, bought her cattle for $61,000, and purchased an additional herd from Lynn County rancher Cass Edwards. In all, DeVitt's new partnerships held apparently more than fifteen hundred head of cattle.[27]

Although DeVitt may have been pleased that his ranch had outlived that of his old nemesis Slaughter, the new ventures on Slaughter land were not rewarding. Cattle prices were slow to recover in the 1920s because many of the big ranches on the South Plains had begun to break up in the wake of a new wave of land colonization, forcing prices downward. For the first time since the early 1890s, D. M. DeVitt found himself facing major losses and feared that he might lose everything. In one of the few letters he wrote which are still extant, he bemoaned his situation to his daughter Helen:

> The simple fact is I am passing through the most fearful ordeal and experience in my business affairs I ever knew in all my life . . . I don't know if I will be able to live through it for my troubles are increasing instead of diminishing . . . . It has all come about being too trustful, and placing too much confidence in a man with whom I have had business dealings for twenty years.[28]

DeVitt's fears may have been justified, but he may have also over-dramatized his letter to Helen in order to discourage his wife Florence from buying a house in Los Angeles. The ruse did not work, as Florence bought a little home in Hollywood on July 25, 1923.

The old entrepreneur acted quickly to cut his cattle losses. First, he secured his notes in the Ross partnership by having Ross sign deeds of trust for Ross's part of the land and cattle, and later sent Ross to Fort Worth to borrow money from DeVitt's brother P. M. Also, DeVitt decided to end the Crocker partnership as soon as possible, and by the end of 1923 had succeeded in selling the cattle and the lease, thus cutting his personal loss to $5,500.

Meanwhile, as he was working his way in and out of losing partnerships, DeVitt turned to pursue another course, that of land colonization. By the early 1920s, all of the level plains located east, north, and south of Lubbock had been carved into 160-acre farms, and the region continued to grow rapidly. West of Lubbock, it was a different story. Most of the land was owned in solid blocks by big ranchers. The huge Spade Ranch, which stretched across nearly two counties for forty-eight miles in a long monolithic block, formed a formidable barrier to colonization west of Lubbock.[29]

As railroads began to penetrate the South Plains after 1907, land prices escalated, making colonization more attractive to the region's ranches. In 1908, C. C. Slaughter sold to farmers much of his Running Water Ranch in western Hale and Lamb counties after the railroad reached Plainview. In 1912, Austin cattleman and banker George W. Littlefield launched the sale of town lots and farms in and around his new city of Littlefield after the Santa Fe had stretched its mainline northwest from Lubbock.

Six years later, in 1918, the Spade Ranch donated to the Santa Fe eighty-five acres in southeastern Hockley County for a townsite along the railroad's branch line being constructed from Lubbock to Seagraves. Soon the little village of Ropesville offered not only easy cattle shipping for the Spade and Mallet ranches, but also offered prospective farmers rail access to markets and supplies. Residents in the Block X strip, proud of their new railroad and town, moved quickly to petition for the organization of Hockley County, which by 1920 boasted a population of 137. By 1921, the county had the required 150 residents and elected a county government, but, much to the chagrin of the supporters of the new town of Ropesville, voters chose to place the county seat in the county's center at the site of old Hockley City, which had been laid out many years before by C. W. Post, but never settled. Once Hockley City became the county seat, it was renamed Levelland and began to grow slowly. By 1924, both the Post Estate's Double U Ranch, which owned the Levelland townsite, and W. T. Coble's nearby Turkey Track Ranch prepared to put lands on the market for colonization.[30]

Meanwhile, to the west of the Mallet, Cochran County also began to open to settlers as members of the Slaughter clan disposed of their holdings. After the 1921 division of the Lazy S Ranch, the eldest

Slaughter daughter, Minnie Veal, decided to colonize 20,000 acres of her pasture that lay in northeastern Cochran County. She turned the project over to Morton J. Smith, a fast-talking West Texas cattleman who had lost his last dime in the cattle depression of 1919-1921. At a price of $20 per acre, land sold quickly, and by 1923, Cochran County supposedly had enough of a population to petition for a county government. Anxious to secure the county seat, Smith hastened to lay out a townsite, which he immodestly named Morton. Assisted by Bill Secrest, who would later marry Helen DeVitt, he chose a site in the northeastern part of the county in the center of Mrs. Veal's tract.[31]

Other county landowners had their own ideas about where the county seat should be. Slaughter heirs, headed by E. Dick Slaughter, laid out their own town, which they named Ligon, approximately four miles south of present-day Morton on Slaughter ranch land. A stormy election held in March 1923 resulted in Morton's being named the county seat, but E. Dick Slaughter succeeded in having the results set aside because of a questionable petition. Although a 1924 election finally produced a county government and once again designated Morton as the county seat, there was still turmoil ahead.

Cochran County quickly polarized into two factions in 1924. The newcomers, headed by Morton J. Smith, launched grand plans for a big courthouse and highways. The Slaughters and other ranchers, including H. T. Boyd and D. M. DeVitt, all of whom controlled most of the land in the county, feared being saddled with unnecessary taxes. After still another stormy and disputed general election in November 1924, Cochran County found itself with two sets of county officers, each claiming to be the legitimate government. At the first meeting of the Commissioners Court in January 1925, a Texas Ranger was on hand to keep the peace.

As feared by the ranchers, the Smith-led county commissioners immediately voted to build a $126,000 courthouse. The ranchers sued to stop it, but were overruled in state court. Then, D. M. DeVitt filed suit on behalf of the Mallet Company in federal district court in Amarillo and succeeded in getting an injunction that temporarily halted courthouse construction. By August 1925, however, the injunction was overturned and work proceeded on the courthouse, leaving the landowners with a sizable tax bill.[32]

The ranchers did not take the loss lightly. When the Santa Fe decided to build another branch line out of Lubbock in 1925, the Slaughter interests persuaded the railroad to build either through Morton or at least five miles from it. The Slaughters knew that the small landowners around Morton could not afford to pay the required railroad bonus and thus ensured that the line would cross the center of the county, bypassing Morton by seven miles. Consequently, the ranchers paid a substantial bonus to the Santa Fe; the Mallet's portion was $15,000. Subsequently, the construction of the railroad across central Hockley and Cochran counties heralded a boom for Levelland and the new town of Whiteface, located on the Cochran-Hockley county line. Demand for farmland increased dramatically, boosting land prices even higher.

By 1924, farmers had already bought most of the Littlefield lands in Lamb County, and real estate agents were clamoring for more. Late in 1923, W. E. Halsell, who had large holdings in western Lamb County, put his land on the market. It sold quickly for $25 per acre. Halsell's land agent, R. C. Hopping, then approached Isaac Ellwood in the summer of 1924, saying he was confident that he could market the Spade for $35 per acre. Ellwood agreed to the deal, knowing that a rail line would soon be built across the southern part of his Spade Ranch, further increasing demand for land. Within three months, by January 1925, Hopping and his partner Stanley Watson had sold 25,000 acres north of Anton, in southeastern Lamb County as 222 farms.[33]

Land colonization impacted the Mallet directly when in 1924 the company lost the last of its big county-owned leased pastures. Since 1897, DeVitt had maintained a lease on the Rains County block of approximately ten thousand acres in the northeastern part of the ranch. In 1924, owing to the rising land and railroad speculation that swept Hockley County, Rains County opted to sell its land, but, apparently, DeVitt chose not to pay a premium price for the block. As a result, the Mallet shrank to approximately 53,000 acres and assumed its modern shape.

Divided into twelve pastures, the ranch contained twenty-five windmills and nearly one hundred miles of fencing. Its pastures, named during the first few years of the Mallet's existence, bore exotic titles. Some, such as Sanctified and Leader, were probably named for bulls which originally serviced those particular pastures. Others, such as North and South Vat, and East and West Draw, reflected their geographic location. Still others, including Schuster, Ellington, Pennick, Copeland, and Dixon, were named for the original owners or users of the land.

The most colorful pasture names are attributed to accidents. The Hard Luck pasture received its name after a cowboy fell off the windmill located there. Short Finger pasture was so named because a well driller lost part of a finger. DeVitt apparently christened another pasture as Lucky Strike because water was found after only one attempt.[34]

Although he had his ranch shaped into a modern working ranch, DeVitt followed the land colonization developments with great interest. As early as 1922, the Mallet directors had approved a resolution instructing that "serious effort be made and diligently pressed to sell said land and this be done by selling first such portion of said land . . . which would least interfere with the conduct of the business of the company."[35] With the pending arrival of the railroad in Levelland in the summer of 1925, DeVitt decided it was time to make serious effort to colonize the ranch. Rather than offer the land wholesale to an agent, as did Mrs. Veal in Cochran County, DeVitt negotiated a tough contract with the firm of Hopping and Watson, the same agents who were handling sales for the Spade. The contract called for the sale of up to 44,000 acres of the Mallet for forty dollars or more per acre. To facilitate sales, the Mallet agreed to provide an office in Levelland and a 3-percent commission on all sales.[36]

Mallet land sales started slowly at first. On July 11, 1925, Wade A. Mastin bought the first Mallet land ever sold when he paid 10 percent, or $623, down on a 178.3-acre farm, which was Labor number 15 of League 46 of the Edwards County land, located four miles south of the new town of Whiteface along the Cochran-Hockley County line. Mastin's purchase price was thirty-five dollars per acre, with a fifteen-year payout.[37]

Two weeks later, the first train arrived in Levelland, and with it came more prospective land buyers. The Mallet had three buyers in September, two in October, and three in November. But after the fall harvest of 1925, prospective farmers flocked to the area, and the Mallet agents closed fourteen deals in December alone. One buyer was D. P. Atwood, the man who had founded the original Mallet Ranch more than forty years before.

On paper, the Mallet appeared to be on its way to making a fortune. After only a year and a half, its land sales totaled nearly $220,000 on the sale of only 5,741 acres. In reality, however, only $14,000 had actually been paid in; the balance remained to be paid. Moreover, the Mallet sales boom was short-lived. In 1926, the Spade opened much of its big pasture in eastern Hockley County for settlement, with land priced at thirty-five dollars per acre and interest at 6 percent. As a result, Mallet sales fell dramatically, with only thirteen deals closed for the entire year. As sales slowed, DeVitt's contractual arrangement with Hopping and Watson apparently ended. Apparently, young David DeVitt managed the sales office for the next two years.

It was also young David who drew the unpleasant task of handling foreclosures. Many new farmers on the land found themselves facing, but unable to pay, principal and interest payments of seven hundred dollars or more. Most turned the land back, but a few stayed on to become tenant farmers. With such reversals, land sales dwindled to nothing. The Mallet closed its land office in Levelland in early 1929 and moved the building to the ranch to be used as a residence at the Vat Camp.[38]

The Mallet's colonization experience taught D. M. DeVitt one thing, that ranching should be his sole business. After the land boom of 1925, he turned his attention once again to the cattle business, but he also found himself with new partners, W. D. and J. Lee Johnson. Both experienced cattlemen, the Johnson brothers intended to be anything but silent and fully expected the Mallet to pay handsome dividends. The challenge they subsequently presented to DeVitt and his heirs would last for decades.

NOTES

1. Minutes of Annual meeting, 1906, Mallet Records.

2. H. T. Boyd, Jr., to David Murrah and Lauren Liljistrand, June 15, 1992.

3. Helen D. Jones, Speech to Lubbock Women's Study Club, c. 1984, typescript, Mallet Records.

4. Florence DeVitt to Christine DeVitt, April 16, 1905, Family Correspondence, Mallet Records.

5. Helen D. Jones, Speech to Lubbock Women's Study Club, c. 1984, typescript, Mallet Records.

6. Compiled from Texas Christian University, *Bulletin, 1914-1918.*

7. *Public School Directory of Tarrant County, Texas, 1918-1919* (Fort Worth: n.p.), p. 12.

8. Payroll Records, Fort Worth Public Schools, 1919-1920, Billy W. Sills Center for Archives, Fort Worth Independent School District, Fort Worth, Texas.

9. R. E. Turner to David Murrah, September 23, 1992, unrecorded interview (notes in possession of author).

10. Kate Boyd Keathley to David Murrah, Interview, August 8, 1992.

11. Helen D. Jones, Speech to Lubbock Women's Study Club, c. 1984, typescript, Mallet Records.

12. *Ibid.*

13. *Ibid.*

14. Helen DeVitt to D. M. DeVitt, October 15, 1924, Mallet Records.

15. Kate Boyd Keathley to David Murrah, tape-recorded interview, August 8 1992.

16. Helen DeVitt to D. M. DeVitt, May 25, 1925, Family Correspondence, Mallet Records.

17. *Ibid.*

18. Dorothy Secrest to David Murrah, June 18, 1992, unrecorded interview.

19. Elvis E. Fleming, *Texas' Last Frontier: A History of Cochran County, Texas* (Morton, Texas: Cochran County Historical Society, 1965), p. 36.

20. The marriage license was issued for Lee S. Secrest and Helen DeVitt in Morton, in Cochran County. Since the county was organized in 1924, the license was only the fifteenth ever issued for the county at the time. Book 1, p. 9, Marriage Records, Cochran County, Texas.

21. Dorothy Secrest to David Murrah, June 1992; L. S. Secrest, Testimony, Question and Answer Record, *J. Lee Johnson vs. Christine DeVitt et al.*, October 28, 1941, p. 183, Mallet Records (hereinafter cited as *Johnson vs. DeVitt*).

22. Dorothy Secrest to David Murrah, June 1992; Helen Secrest to Florence DeVitt, June 6, 1932, Family Correspondence, Mallet Records. Bill Secrest later remarried and had two daughters by his second marriage. He died in Asheville, North Carolina, in 1968.

23. Florence A. DeVitt to Helen Secrest, June 7, 1929, Family Correspondence, DeVitt Records.

24. Florence A. DeVitt to Helen Secrest, c. 1929, Family Correspondence, Mallet Records.

25. *Ibid.*

26. DeVitt and Ross Contract, July 31, 1922, Mallet Records.

27. D. M. DeVitt to Helen DeVitt, March 8, 1923, Family Correspondence; DeVitt and Crocker Balance Sheet, Mallet Records. Although DeVitt makes no mention of Crocker in his letter, his references clearly point to the Crocker partnership.

28. D. M. DeVitt to Helen Secrest, March 8, 1923, Family Correspondence, Mallet Records.

29. Steve Kelton, *Renderbrook: A Century Under the Spade Brand* (Texas Christian University Press, 1989), p. 57. The Spade ran from Ropesville on the south in southeastern Hockley County 48 miles northward to the sandhills south of Olton in northern Lamb County.

30. Bill Billingsley, "Pasture Land to Promised Land," in *From the Heart of Hockley County* (Levelland: Hockley County Historical Commission, 1986), p. 201.

31. Fleming, *Texas' Last Frontier*, p. 26.

32. *Ibid.*, pp. 31-32.

33. Kelton, *Renderbrook*, pp. 115-118.

34. Howard Fowler to David Murrah and Lauren Liljistrand, June 18, 1992, tape-recorded interview.

35. Resolution, Annual Meeting of the Directors of the Mallet Land and Cattle Company, January 1922, Mallet Records.

36. Land Sales Contract, June 1925, Mallet Records.

37. Report of land sold, 1925-1926, Mallet Records.

38. David M. DeVitt, Jr., to D. M. DeVitt, June 24, 1929, Family Correspondence, Mallet Records.

CHAPTER FIVE

Under Sometimes Trying Situations

*So I can point with pride at my
record for the past 20 years in the
management of the Mallet Company
and in the results achieved, under
sometimes trying situations, which I
think will compare favorably with
that of any other cattle outfit in
Texas or elsewhere.*
David M. DeVitt to David A.
Murphy, August 14, 1933.

T O this day, few people, even those closely associated with West Texas ranching, have any
idea that 40 percent of the Mallet Ranch is
owned by descendants of W. D. and J. Lee Johnson. Their acquisition of the Mallet stock, which probably occurred in 1925, had a major impact on the future of the ranch.[1] Exactly how the Johnson
brothers acquired their four hundred shares of the Mallet stock is
not clear, but they brought with their ownership extensive experience in cattle raising, financing, and business management.

Products of the Texas frontier, the Johnson brothers had gained their business acumen on the prairies of West Texas. William Denver Johnson, born 10 October 1860 on his father's farm in Washington County, Texas, near Brenham, was the seventh of eleven children. In 1876, when he was only sixteen, he left home to move to Brown County, Texas, where he worked as a farmhand. Although he lacked formal education, he had always wanted to be a merchant. When the owner of the country store where he bought his supplies offered him a job in the store, he quickly accepted it.[2] Later, he moved to nearby Brownwood to work in a grocery store and at the Brownwood Post Office. The latter position, Johnson recalled many years afterwards, gave him valuable insight into human nature, knowledge that he would use extensively in the future. About 1883, he moved from Brownwood to the booming new town of Sweetwater, Texas, which owed its rapid growth to the construction of the Texas Pacific Railway through West Texas. There, he took a job in a general store, and, during the next four years, saved one thousand dollars. By 1887, he was ready to acquire his own store.

With a partner from the Sweetwater store, Johnson purchased a mercantile store in Pecos, in far West Texas. Johnson made money not only through his store but also in partnership with two of his brothers, who began to run cattle in 1887 on the open pastures along the Pecos River.[3] His older brother, F. W. "Woody" Johnson, had moved to Pecos in 1886 and began ranching about thirty miles northeast of the town. Later, W. D. and Woody were joined in the venture by their younger brother, Jesse Leon, or J. Lee, as he was later known.[4]

Soon the Johnson Brothers' W Ranch covered approximately one hundred miles (or twelve hundred sections) of land along the Pecos River in Loving, Ward, and Winkler counties, Texas. W. D. Johnson's primary work within the family business was financial management. Through his store in Pecos, W. D. also financed several other ranchers in the area.

In 1891, W. D. sold his store and, with his brother Woody, established the Pecos Valley State Bank. Primarily a cattle-loan operation, the Johnson brothers' business fared well. Meanwhile W. D. married Anna Kern of Houston, and the couple settled into a large home in Pecos. To give his growing family a better education (the Johnsons had four girls and one boy) and to put himself closer to the financial markets, W. D. sold his interest in the bank and moved to Kansas City, Missouri. There, he subsequently established the Western Cattle Loan Company.[5]

Despite his move, W. D. remained closely tied to Texas and the Southwest. With his brother Woody, he bought in 1903 approximately 126,000 acres of the XIT Ranch on the Texas South Plains near Bovina in southern Parmer and northern Bailey counties. He also operated a mercantile company in Bovina.[6] After three years, the Johnson brothers sold their ranch for a handsome profit. Part of their plains ranch was purchased by Michigan manufacturer Charles K. Warren, who in turn established what became the Muleshoe Ranch near the present town of Muleshoe.[7]

W. D. Johnson then launched out on his own. He acquired the famous Block Ranch in southeastern New Mexico and subsequently sold it for a $200,000 profit. He also ran cattle on Indian reservation land in northern Arizona for about fifteen years with the help of his friend Henry S. Boice. At times, the Arizona ranch would produce as many as fifteen thousand calves. To oversee his widespread ranching interests, Johnson made frequent trips to the Southwest, as many as one a month from his home in Kansas City. While in the area, he called on ranchers and subsequently financed the notes of many small operators throughout the region. H. T. Boyd, DeVitt's ranch neighbor, obtained financing for his own ranch from Mr. Johnson in 1911, and the Boyd children recalled fondly the visits the stately Mr. Johnson would make in their home.[8]

Meanwhile, J. Lee Johnson had made a successful career for himself. In 1890, in Pecos, he married Dora Allison, the widow of the famous gunfighter Clay Allison, who had been killed in a wagon accident in 1887. Dora, who had two daughters by her previous marriage, gave birth to J. Lee Johnson, Jr., in 1891. Three other daughters were born to the union.[9] About 1897, J. Lee moved his family from Pecos to Fort Worth. In 1903, he established the Cicero Smith Lumber Company, which he expanded over the next two decades into one of the major retail lumber outlets in Texas. By the time he purchased Mallet stock, J. Lee Johnson had established twenty lumber yards throughout Texas and Oklahoma.

D. M. DeVitt, because of his extensive contacts in both Fort Worth and Kansas City, probably had known the Johnson brothers since the early 1900s. But it was not until the 1920s that W. D. became intimately involved in the business affairs of the Mallet Land and Cattle Company. Beginning in 1920, he served as a director, but held only one token share of Mallet stock. About the same time, however, he became president of the Fidelity Union Bank and Trust Company of Kansas City and may have been involved in loaning DeVitt more than one hundred thousand dollars for his ill-timed partnerships with Ed Crocker and Pat Ross. As president of the bank, Johnson had access to the financial statements DeVitt had prepared to secure the loans, statements that showed his net worth was approaching three-quarters of a million dollars, and that the Mallet was worth more than a million dollars.

As president of the bank, Johnson had access also to the holdings of the trust department of the bank, and among which were 400 shares of Mallet stock, placed in trust there by Major Andrew Drumm. When Drumm died in 1919, he left the bulk of his estate to the Drumm Institute, which was to be set up as a home for boys.[10] Marion L. McClure, who had been a long-time vice president of the Drumm Commission Company, served as the trustee representing Drumm's interest in the Mallet and also as a Mallet director. Moreover, at the time of the annual meeting of the directors in February 1925, McClure himself held twenty shares of Mallet stock.

As the Drumm Institute prepared to build its first building, McClure apparently decided to cash in the Mallet stock to raise funds. The stock carried a face value of $100 per share, totalling $40,000 for the Drumm shares, but was worth considerably more. Its book value was approximately $1,000 per share, but its earnings value in the 1920s was much less, averaging approximately four dollars per share per year.[11] McClure sold Drumm's four hundred shares to the Johnson brothers for an unknown amount.

Although the Johnson brothers had extensive ranching experience, they had become involved also in oil developments in West Texas, and perhaps were motivated to acquire the Mallet stock because of the oil potential. Although oil fever had plagued Texas since the Spindletop gusher at Beaumont i n 1901, the citizens of West Texas were at first not affected. But with the discovery of the Ranger Field in Eastland County i n 1917, followed by the Burkburnett boom near Wichita Falls in 1919, West Texas ranchers with vast land holdings began to follow the oil play with considerable interest, and, as exemplified by D. M. DeVitt's oil stock purchases in 1918 and 1919, many cattlemen soon got caught up in the oil speculation.

The real fever hit the region after the Borger field opened in the upper Panhandle in 1926 with a ten-thousand-barrel-a-day well.[12] That news was followed closely by discoveries in the Permian Basin at McCamey and Crane in 1926 and 1927.[13] At the same time came the discovery of the famous Yates field in Pecos County, which had single wells capable of producing more than two hundred thousand barrels a day.[14]

Because the Mallet lay on the north edge of what geologists later identified as the great Permian Basin, oil companies were quick to try to lease portions of the ranch.

Encouraged by his Johnson partners, DeVitt began to review lease proposals late in 1928. On October 20, he signed his first leases with Texas Pacific Coal and Oil Company of Fort Worth. The deal blocked approximately seventy-two hundred acres of the south part of the ranch, for which DeVitt obtained a signing bonus of two dollars per acre. His royalty reserve was the standard one-eighth.[15]

A week later, DeVitt closed a lease with Roxana Petroleum Company for several tracts scattered across the south side of the ranch for bonuses ranging from two to three dollars per acre. In December, he signed another lease with The Texas Company for twenty-three hundred acres in League 51 in the Scurry County tract immediately north of the headquarters, for three and four dollars per acre.

Little resulted from the 1928 oil fever, except for the bonus money. The oil companies drilled a few wildcat wells, but found no oil.

Moreover, as new discoveries in East Texas came into production, oil prices dropped dramatically and speculation in Hockley County waned. Oilmen awaited future systematic exploration, which delayed discovery for nearly ten years.

Meanwhile, limited rainfall on the South Plains in 1927 and 1928 kept Mallet profits to a minimum, and, as the Depression approached, cattle prices began a long slide downward. By the end of 1929, the Mallet was showing a loss of $14,000, but it would have been much greater had it not been for a $23,000 windfall of bonus money paid to the ranch by oil companies for leases executed in 1928 and 1929.

For D. M. DeVitt and his family, the Mallet's poor showing for 1929 was only a forerunner of things to come. Despite the potential for oil discovery, the future looked bleak as cattle and farm prices began to tumble after 1930. Moreover, a terrible tragedy was soon to claim the life of young David DeVitt, causing his father to finally lose faith in his beloved Mallet Ranch.

By 1929, young David DeVitt was approaching his twenty-seventh birthday, and his father made him the Mallet's assistant manager. Ready to assume the role of manager of his father's vast holdings, he presented himself well to all who knew him. Tall, handsome, and well-mannered, he moved at ease among hands on the ranch or amidst polite society in Lubbock.[16] Although he was very popular among the single ladies of Lubbock, he apparently decided it was time to settle down, and on June 4, 1929, he married Miss Williamae Louise "Billie" Shelton in Levelland.[17]

For his bride, David built an addition to the original two-room house where his parents had first lived on the ranch. A kitchen, living room with fireplace and bath were added, making the ranch home a comfortable place to live. Two months after their wedding, a Lubbock service station manager, who apparently looked after the DeVitt vehicles, visited the young couple on the ranch and reported his findings to Mr. DeVitt in California. "David and his bride seem to be as happy as a picture. . . the wife was dressed in an apron and had lunch ready to serve. Looked very inviting and homelike. She mentioned that she would like to go to California, and would also like to meet you."

Apparently acquainted with Mr. DeVitt's taste in women, the writer added, "Rather think you will like her too, she is a blond you know."[18]

Young Billie soon got her wish about going to California and meeting Mr. DeVitt. In July 1930, David's father purchased for the couple a large business building on Santa Monica Street in Los Angeles. The building included several upstairs apartments, and the lower floor was leased out as an open-air market. Apparently, his plan for his son and wife was that they could commute between California and the ranch and would have a place to live at both ends.

Meanwhile, young David assumed a growing role in the management of Mallet Ranch affairs. With the senior DeVitt slowed by leg problems, David took care of day-to-day matters at the headquarters. Yet David's compensation of two hundred and fifty dollars per month raised the ire of W. D. Johnson's brother, J. Lee Johnson, Sr., of Fort Worth. Concerned about the deepening national depression, J. Lee wrote a strong letter of protest to D. M. DeVitt in July of 1930. "I now demand that you cease paying said salary to your son and charging the same to the Mallet Company," he stormed. "If you want to put your boy on a pension, you will have to pay the pension unaided by minority stockholders. I also demand that you cut your salary to $3,000.00 per anum, beginning at once." In closing, Johnson threatened that if his demands were not met, he would "apply for a receiver for the Mallet Company." Although he never did, the legal strategy was one that his son J. Lee Johnson, Jr., would use successfully more than a decade later.

D. M. DeVitt did not take Johnson's threat lightly. On August 1, 1930, he wrote to his attorney David A. Murphy in Kansas City of his concern. "As you can imagine, I am harrassed and overwhelmed with worries in connection with the welfare of the Company," he noted. "Mr. Johnson's letter simply adds a hundred fold to my cares and worries."

Fate intervened to end the Johnson threat, but the result was tragic. In October 1930, David and Billie were back on the ranch in time for the fall roundup. He helped the ranch hands load cattle in a truck, and then set out for Lubbock. According to the Levelland newspaper, on Friday evening, October 24th, he and Billie left Levelland after sundown, driving in his Buick sedan. About six miles east of Levelland, he struck a truck. "He was driving rapidly," reported the paper, "and ran into a truck and trailer," apparently crashing into the truck from behind. "[The truck driver] saw that an accident was eminent, and turned his truck into the bar pit. The car struck just behind the cab with such force that the front and left side of the car was torn away."[19]

At first, observers thought David was dead, but after seeing him gasp for breath, they loaded him and Billie into a passing car and rushed them to Levelland. Billie was only slightly injured, but David, according to the *Lubbock Avalanche*, had "suffered a fractured skull, a compound fracture of the left arm, and several lacerations on his face."[20] After receiving emergency treatment in Levelland, David was rushed to a Lubbock hospital, but he never regained consciousness. At 8:30 the following Sunday morning, he died, with his father apparently at his side.

On the following Monday afternoon, the family held a small funeral service in the home of the Mallet's bookkeeper, L. B. Wright. The service was conducted by the Reverend R. C. Campbell, pastor of the First Baptist Church of Lubbock. Burial followed at the Lubbock cemetery. Among the pallbearers were D. M. DeVitt's business associates, including France Baker and Sam Arnett of the Citizens National Bank; rancher George Boles; and Mallet employees, foreman George Green and E. M." Wadkie" Fowler. Tom Jones, who would later marry Helen, was also a pallbearer.

The loss of his second son was overwhelming to the family, and particularly to Mr. DeVitt. Nearly seventy-five years old, he was never the same after David's death. Without a son to carry on the management of the ranch, he must have felt it futile to try to hold on to the Mallet, as he could not imagine his wife or daughters having any interest or the ability to manage it. As the Depression deepened, and as oil wells proved to be dry holes, he ultimately became convinced that his only recourse was to sell the Mallet Land and Cattle Company in its entirety.

Worsening national conditions did not improve DeVitt's outlook for the Mallet. Even though ranch income fell, state, county, and school district taxes continued to rise. Because of its large size, the Mallet paid taxes to four counties and four school districts, Clauene, Cobleland, Levelland, and Sundown. Its tax bill for 1931 amounted to nearly $16,000. Cattle sales for the year amounted to only $42,907, yielding for that year after taxes and expenses a net loss of more than $76,000. Consequently, the Mallet directors slashed expenses, reducing D. M. DeVitt's $10,000 salary in half.

The next year, 1932, was even worse. With cattle prices hitting record lows, DeVitt, encouraged by higher than average rainfall for the year, decided to hold his steers off the market. At the Mallet's annual meeting of stockholders, held in January 1933, DeVitt reported on his unpleasant dealings with the ranch's land purchasers and tenant farmers. Out of the original thirty-seven purchasers, only twelve were still trying to keep up their payments. Apparently pressured by the Johnsons to collect, DeVitt read to the stockholders a letter he had sent to one farmer who was two years behind. "We have reached the point that we expect you to do something," he wrote to the recalcitrant farmer, "that would be satisfactory to the Mallet Company at once." He reported that the farmer called the letter "threatening," but he did remit five of his past-due notes. DeVitt told the Johnsons that it was not easy to put people off the land, and that he had had to use the sheriff on occasion.[21] Rents collected for the year amounted to only $1,149.01. He also reported that he had engaged J. A. Stroud of Levelland to watch over the farms and collect the rents, and that he would pay Stroud a 15-percent commission. DeVitt also must have reported to the other stockholders that he had decided to sell the ranch if a suitable buyer could be found. He may have made the decision independently, based upon the ranch's losses, the dimming prospect of oil, and the loss of his son. By 1932, however, he had also come under the influence of a man who very much wanted to see DeVitt sell the ranch. The man

was Tom Jones of Lubbock, a real estate agent who was subsequently to exert a great deal of influence over Mallet affairs.

William Thomas Jones was born February 5, 1892, in Georgetown,
Texas. His father, W. T. Jones was a prominent physician in the area,
and his mother, Ollie Snyder, was a member of a family who was to
achieve great fame in the ranching business in West Texas. Educated
at Southwestern University in Georgetown and at Vanderbilt, Jones
was a handsome man, nearly six feet tall. In 1924, Tom moved to
Lubbock to take advantage of the boom in land sales.[22]

Jones was a good storyteller and was also rather fond of good
whiskey. DeVitt, who also enjoyed occasional libations, became
Jones's friend soon after the latter arrived in Lubbock. Like DeVitt,
Jones lived in the Lubbock Hotel when he was in town; in later years
they both lived in the new Hilton Hotel in downtown Lubbock.

In March 1932, Jones finally persuaded DeVitt to let him try to sell
the ranch, and they signed a contract. The deal was relatively simple:
if Jones could find a buyer who would pay at least ten dollars per
acre, or $520,000, DeVitt would pay Jones a 5-percent commission;
the ranch had to be sold in its entirety, and the contract was to termi-
nate within six months. The contract made no mention of mineral
reservation.

Jones could find no takers. In July 1932, he renewed the contract
for an additional three months, but still there was no movement. In
1933, however, he renewed the contract again; this time, Jones
thought he had found the right buyer.[23]

The prospect was Amarillo rancher and oilman J. A. Whittenburg, who had come into a fortune through the discovery of large
oil and gas fields under the family ranch. Whittenburg also had family ties to the Coble farm and ranch interests that lay north of the
Mallet. Tom Jones courted Mr. Whittenburg heavily; on two successive Sundays in April 1933, he went from Lubbock to Amarillo trying to interest Whittenburg in the ranch, then followed the visits
with a gushy letter: "The people that buy and pay for good bodies of
land in a new country always reap the benefits far beyond their
greatest hopes," Jones noted. Jones's letter offered a picture-per-
fect description of the Mallet Ranch:

52,0000 acres all level, good loam land. Runs up to two miles of Railroad and shipping pens. Fenced into 12 separate pastures with 25 waterings all in First Class condition, and does not require any expenses for improvements. 99% all good farming land for feeds and cotton. The quality of this ranch is so good that the best cattlemen in this section say it will run 6,000 cattle; however, it never has been overstocked by present owner.[24]

Two weeks later, D. M. DeVitt paid his own call on Mr. Whittenburg and later confirmed by telegram that he was "ready to show [Whittenburg] my ranch and land and price you same on inspection by you."[25] From Amarillo DeVitt went on to Kansas City, but stayed in close contact with Tom Jones. "Have you sold the Mallet Land yet?" he wrote to Tom in late May. Just to show that he was not totally concerned with just business, he happily noted, "Lots of good shows and pretty girls in town. Wish you were here to enjoy them."

Although little of DeVitt's correspondence has been preserved, there remains enough for the years 1933 and early 1934 to allow tracing of his movements during the balance of his last year of life. In December 1932, after a two-month confinement for illness in a Lubbock hospital, he began a slow recovery in Lubbock, but by June 1933, DeVitt was able to travel to Kansas City to oversee the sale of Mallet cattle. From Kansas City, DeVitt took the train to California in mid-June 1933 and took up summer residence at his favorite spot, the Alexandria Hotel. Soon after his arrival, he called Helen at her home and spent his first day in town with her.

While in California, where he stayed for three months, DeVitt stayed in close touch with Tom Jones by letter and telegram. "You had better come on out and get a little taste of Heaven," he wrote, soon after his arrival. "You might see a few of the beautiful 'movie' stars. They tell me some of them forget to put on their silk stockings in the a.m. and go bare legged on the streets, quite 'shocking.'" And, he warned Tom that if he made the trip, he might not want to go back to Texas. "I confess I like it here a little better than Lubbock

myself," he noted. Then, the next day he wired, "Anxious to sell
Mallet Land. Wake up and get busy."[26]

DeVitt also persuaded Jones to go out to the ranch and check
things over for him. Tom was more than happy to oblige. On a Sunday morning, Tom arrived at the ranch early, and with foreman
George Green toured the entire ranch. Jones wrote DeVitt a long
but positive report: "Went to the wells and they are full of water at
the tanks and cattle are doing fine. . . . Mr. Green . . . took pride in
showing me the Barns full of feed."

Jones also described the cow herd located in the Pennick, Dixon,
and Copeland pastures on the south side of the ranch. The cows
were in "splendid condition," he noted. In the entire report, he
noted only two negatives; "I found [Mr. Cadill, a Mallet farmer]
very blue and the farming land not planted . . . and they stand pa-
tiently waiting for rain," he noted. He also reported that a seventeen year-old boy, who had sneaked on to the ranch to swim, was
drowned in the Hard Luck pasture tank. "I do not like to write this
kind of news, but believe from what George tells me that you had
this Well named properly when you called it Hard Luck."

Jones's report provoked a terse response from DeVitt about
George Green, who had failed to mention the drowning in his reports to DeVitt: "Mr. Green can ride a horse and can round up a
bunch of cattle," DeVitt replied, "but he is sadly deficient in some
things." He also chided Jones about not being able to sell the ranch
by noting that he had heard that G. G. Wright, C. C. Slaughter's
son-in-law, had sold the nearby Wright Ranch for cash. "Why haven't you written me about that?"[27]

DeVitt soon turned to another old friend, Sam Arnett, president
of the Citizens National Bank of Lubbock, to help him while he was
away from the ranch and designated him to be the Mallet's assistant
manager. Apparently, DeVitt had known Arnett from the 1880s.
Both had ranched near Colorado City where Arnett had managed
his family's ranch after his father, Dick Arnett, became manager of
the Ellwoods' Renderbrook Ranch. Then, in 1905, he became a
neighbor to DeVitt when he and the Ellwoods acquired the Lake
Tomb-Nunn Ranch, which lay to the east of the Mallet. By 1931,

Arnett, in partnership with the Ellwoods, had acquired the Citizens National Bank of Lubbock.[28] Arnett would subsequently play a large role in the affairs of the Mallet Ranch.

With Arnett monitoring Mallet interests, DeVitt found his summer vacation to be quite enjoyable. In every letter back to Texas, he noted the abundance of "beautiful blondes" in the Golden State. To Tom, he reported how he had recently had lunch with a "beautiful blonde lady about 25 years old," and that he and the young lady "soon got well acquainted." Moreover, he reported to Sam Arnett that he had a "blonde" taking him out to the beach for sun baths.[29]

While in California, DeVitt got a nibble on the ranch from another source who wanted to buy only the Edwards County land for ten dollars per acre, but DeVitt refused the offer: "Wish to sell all the Mallet Land instead of parceling it out," he wired to Tom Jones.[30]

By mid-August, DeVitt was still enjoying the blondes and the beaches in California. Perhaps concerned that his partners, the Johnsons, might think he was neglecting Mallet business, he wrote to his attorney in Kansas City, David A. Murphy: "I am in . . . far away California [but] I am not neglecting the Mallet Company business and am still 'on the job' and receiving the munificent sum of $3,000.00 per annum."

He wryly noted to Murphy that his salary, which had been as much as $10,000, had been cut by the Mallet directors three times in three years, "which does not make me happy." He added, with a derisive flair:

> I recall that my "big-hearted" stockholders, the Johnsons', think I am too liberally rewarded as it is. But, nevertheless, and notwithstanding, we have a homely saying in Texas that "the proof of the pudding is the chewing of the bag." So I can *point with pride* at my record for the past 20 years in the management of the Mallet Company and in the results achieved, under sometimes trying situations, which I think will compare favorably with that of any other cattle outfit in Texas or elsewhere.[31]

DeVitt planned to end his California vacation in mid-August, but health problems forced him to delay his trip.[32] Finally, on the eleventh of September, he took a train to Texas, stopped briefly in Lubbock, then went on to Kansas to supervise shipment of finished steers to market. For a number of years, he had been sending his three- and four-year-old steers to the Flint Hills of east central Kansas, near Elmdale, where they would graze the rich grass before going to market. Chagrined that his August shipment had brought as little as three and one-fourth cents per pound, he decided that he should be on hand himself to deal with the cattle buyers in Kansas City.[33] From Kansas, DeVitt instructed Tom Jones to delay offering the ranch for sale. "Am on a deal for Mallet land with Kansas parties," he wired. Meanwhile, Jones continued his subtle pressure on DeVitt to let him continue marketing the Mallet. He wrote DeVitt that, because of recent rains, the ranch looked beautiful, which in turn would inspire higher school taxes: "I am confident should an equalization Board go out on an inspection trip now, " Jones noted, "that they would raise the taxes to beat Hell and put two or three more stories on the School Buildings they already have."[34]

Apparently, nothing materialized from DeVitt's Kansas prospect. When he returned to Lubbock in October, he made an appointment to see Mr. Whittenburg in Amarillo, but an attack of asthma prevented his visit. Nonetheless, in a long letter, he priced the ranch to Whittenburg for ten dollars per acre cash, and described it as "95% tillable and fit for the plow. . . . Last year [Hockley County] produced and shipped 5,500 bales of cotton and the land is hardly scratched."[35]DeVitt's offer to Whittenburg was his last attempt to sell the ranch. Tom, however, had another scheme and tried to get DeVitt to buy still another ranch in New Mexico, the Four Lakes Ranch, which could be purchased for only $60,000: "Why don't you sell the farming land you have in Hockley," he suggested, "and let the Honest Farmers have this wonderful body of land and put your cattle in a country where they won't be harassed by farmers, high taxes, danger of prairie fires, and other hazards that the cowman always encounters when civilization begins to encroach upon his life long holdings instead." And, with words that were to ring hollow in the very near future, he added, "I feel and believe if we don't sell your ranch by Thanksgiving that it will be many years before we even get another prospect. Hockley County has great plans for the future, but they are not for you and yours or me and mine."[36]

Meanwhile, Miss Christine DeVitt came to Lubbock to pay her father a visit, perhaps her first in Texas for many years. But Mr. DeVitt left promptly for California. On October 9, while on the train, he wrote a quick note to Tom Jones to "take Christine out to the Mallet Ranch some day next week." Tom replied that he would try, although he apparently found her enjoying all the comforts of Lubbock's Hilton Hotel: "Miss Christine stated emphatically that she would not go to the ranch until the following Sunday," Jones noted in his reply.[37]

After arriving in Los Angeles, DeVitt apparently decided to take another approach to selling the ranch and wired Jones to "not price Mallet land to anyone including Whittenburg."[38] Instead, he pursued the possibility of a big oil lease. "Please don't give anyone my address or whereabouts," he telegraphed from Los Angles on October 17. From there, he went by train to Fort Worth where he spent considerable time trying to lease to oil companies approximately 30,000 acres of the ranch that had not been leased previously. His best prospect seemed to be Stanolind Oil Company, but the firm turned him down in November 1933.[39] Ironically, within a few years, the same company would control much of the Mallet's oil production.

While in Fort Worth, DeVitt tried also unsuccessfully to persuade his Lubbock banker and friend Sam Arnett to join him there for the cattlemen's convention. "Plenty of blondes and brunettes for your entertainment," he cajoled. "Very refreshing after a long dry spell. Plenty of liquid refreshments also not to forget horse racing."[40] But the entertainment may have proved too much for the old man. His health continued to fail. While in Fort Worth, he became sick again and found himself confined by a doctor to his hotel. Finally, by late November, he was well enough to travel to Kansas City, but checked immediately into a hospital there and stayed for nearly a month.[41] Before leaving Kansas City, DeVitt reported to his partner W. D. Johnson that Whittenburg was no longer interested in buying the ranch, and then wrote to Johnson's brother J. Lee in Fort Worth, indicating that he would accept twelve dollars per acre if J. Lee's son-in-law Earl North could sell it.[42] He tried to interest a Kansas City firm in listing the ranch as well.

Finally strong enough to travel again, DeVitt left Kansas City in early January 1934 and made his way to one of the most remote spots in Texas, a small health spa named Hot Springs, on the Rio Grande, directly across from Boquillas, Mexico, in what is now Big Bend National Park. There, where an entrepreneur had built a hotel near a flowing hot spring in the river, DeVitt tried to recover from his ailments (he suffered from varicose veins, asthma, and probably congestive heart failure). He spent three weeks in what he termed "almost solitude, but not quite."[43]

In late January, apparently rested and refreshed, DeVitt headed on to California, and once again teased his straight-laced banker friend Sam Arnett to join him in some fun. "When are you coming out to Los Angeles to inspire the Blondes and Brunettes?" he wrote. "Believe it or not, there are a lot of them here, well worth your inspection. Will hope to introduce you to my new Beer Hall, which I can sell you some stock in, and some of the Blondes and Brunettes will go along with the stock."[44]

His recovery did not last long. By early February, he became weaker, and his daughter Helen persuaded him to stay with her and Dorothy at their little home on Sweetzer Avenue in Los Angeles. DeVitt reported to Tom that his ankles had been bothering him but that he hoped to be back in Lubbock by the first of March. Meanwhile, the Johnsons became concerned again that no one was looking after the ranch and contacted DeVitt's Kansas City attorney, David Murphy. Murphy did his best to defend his client:

> I told [W. D. Johnson] that Mr. Sam Arnett was looking after matters for you on the ground and that you were keeping in daily touch with matters through correspondence and telegrams. . . . He seemed considerably worked up. . . . I judge that the Johnsons are getting ready for their usual expression of dissatisfaction at the company management.[45]

Murphy's letter was apparently his last to D. M. DeVitt. On March 2, DeVitt must have quietly celebrated his seventy-eighth birthday with Helen and Dorothy, but four days later, he died of heart disease while in Helen's home in Los Angeles. Much like the way he ran his life, DeVitt slipped away quietly. Because he kept his business to himself or in far-off Kansas City, the size of his holdings were relatively unknown to most residents of the South Plains. Indeed, in his obituary, the *Lubbock Avalanche* could describe him only as a "pioneer West Texas cattleman," who, according to old-time rancher R. C. Burns, "had been considered wealthy."[46]

DeVitt was buried in Los Angeles. Tom Jones, unable to attend the funeral, wrote to Miss Christine DeVitt expressing his grief as a eulogy for his friend:

> For ten years I have counted [your father] and known him to be my Friend and the acquaintanceship that I had with him will always have its influence on my life. I knew him as one of the best traveled and best informed men that I have ever known. He had one of the finest of Minds and was highly educated in the better things of life. I am confident that he was one of the highest types of the Anglo-Saxon race that can be found today. He never seemed the same after David's death and in the loss of both David and your Father I have seen two of my best friends pass away.[47]

D. M. DeVitt was justifiably proud of what he had accomplished with his establishment and development of the Mallet Ranch. During his thirty-nine-year management of the business, he had parlayed his original $25,000 investment into a million-dollar corporation. His consistent and continued effort to get undisputed title to his land paid off well in his lifetime. With his conservative management and strategy, which converted the Mallet into a steer operation, he made the ranch produce sizable profits. Unlike virtually all of its neighboring ranches on the western South Plains, which had gone out of business in the early 1920s, the Mallet withstood both drought and market depression. Moreover, unknown to DeVitt, he had preserved for his family a future treasure unimaginable for his day.

DeVitt also left some family matters undone. His will, first filed in 1926, expressed his intent for future management of his estate: "the stock of the corporation [should] be kept intact so that it can be voted . . . as a unit. I therefore earnestly request that no part . . . be sold . . . unless all of it is sold at one time."[48]

His intent was that the estate be held in trust until Helen turned thirty. DeVitt also named his son, David DeVitt, Jr., the principal trustee. Apparently, DeVitt felt sure that his wife and children would follow the lead of his only male heir. But David's untimely death in 1930 prevented that scenario.

In January 1931, DeVitt revised his will, naming his attorney David Murphy and banker Sam Arnett co-executors and co-trustees, with the trust to extend until Helen's thirty-fifth birthday, in 1937. When DeVitt died in 1934, only three years remained on the trust that he had established. Had he known what the future held, he probably would have established irrevocable lifetime trusts for all of his survivors.

Instead, his widow, Florence, and daughters Christine and Helen were soon to assume responsibility for a business they knew almost nothing about. In fact, the only ones in Lubbock who knew much about DeVitt's business were Tom Jones and banker Sam Arnett. Both would certainly play critical roles in the future of the DeVitt heirs and the Mallet Land and Cattle Company.

NOTES

1. W. D. Johnson Testimony, *Johnson vs. DeVitt*, Mallet Records. In his statement, Johnson said he became a stockholder in 1924, but he may have held only one share at the time.

2. Unsigned typescript, Pecos Museum, Pecos, Texas, 1-2; *Kansas City Star* (6 October 1940) [1], Pecos Museum; Alton Hughes, *Pecos: A History of the Pioneer West* (Seagraves, TX: Pioneer Book Publishers, 1978), p. 275.

3. W. D. Johnson Testimony, *Johnson vs. DeVitt*.

4. *Kansas City Star,* October 6, 1940; "W. D. Johnson is Dead," *The Kansas City Times,* April 14, 1951, 3.

5. Hughes, *Pecos,* 275-76; *Kansas City Star,* [2].

6. H. T. Boyd, Jr., to David Murrah and Lauren Liljistrand, May 22, 1992, tape-recorded interview.

7. See David J. Murrah, "From Corset Stays to Cattle Ranching: Charles K. Warren and the Muleshoe Ranch," *West Texas Historical Association Year Book,* LI, 1975, pp. 3-12.

8. H. T. Boyd, Jr., May 22, 1992; Kate Boyd Keathley to David Murrah, August 8, 1992, tape-recorded interview.

9. Dora's daughters were Pattie, who married Ed P. Byars of Fort Worth, and Clay Pearl, who married J. Lloyd Parker of Houston. Lee and Dora's children were J. Lee, Floy, who married E. L. North of Houston, Katherine, and Mary Louise. B. B. Paddock, ed., *Fort Worth and the Texas Northwest* (Chicago, Lewis Publishing Co., 1914), Vol.3, pp. 314-315.

10. "Age No Bar to Stockman," *Kansas City Times* (14 April 1919); *Kansas City Star* (20 April 1919); McClure, *Major Andrew Drumm 1829-1919,* 10-11.

11. The Drumm Institute opened its new $50,000 building for boys in 1929, and continues to operate in Kansas City to this day. George C. Berke-

meier, *Major Andrew Drumm, 1828-1919: An Adventurer Who Left a Living Memorial* (Topeka: H. M. Ives and Sons, 1976), p. 24.

12. Seth S. McKay and Odie B. Faulk, *Texas After Spindletop* (Austin: Steck-Vaughn, 1965), pp. 100-1-2.

13. Roger and Diana Olien, *Oil Boom: Social Change in Five Texas Towns* (Lincoln: University of Nebraska Press, 1982), pp. 14-15.

14. Richard B. Moore, "The Impact of the Oil Industry in West Texas," Ph.D. Dissertation, Texas Technological College, 1965, p. 26.

15. Lease file, Mallet Records.

16. Kate Boyd Keathley, August 8, 1992.

17. Marriage Records, Hockley County, Texas, Vol. I., p. 152.

18. D. H. Mansell to D. M. DeVitt, August 1, 1929, Family Correspondence, Mallet Records.

19. *Hockley County Herald*, October 31, 1930, p. 1.

20. *Lubbock Avalanche Journal*, Oct. 27, 1930.

21. D. M. DeVitt, note on copy of letter, D. M. DeVitt to A. G. Maxwell, November 1932, D. M. DeVitt Correspondence, Mallet Records (Hereinafter, all D. M. DeVitt correspondence is found in the DeVitt Correspondence, Mallet Records, as cited in this note.).

22. Senate Resolution No. 14, Texas State Senate, January 19, 1955, Mallet Records.

23. Contract between Tom Jones and Mallet Land and Cattle Company, Mallet Records.

24. Tom Jones to J. A. Whittenburg, April 22, 1933, D. M. DeVitt Correspondence, Mallet Records.

25. D. M. DeVitt to J. A. Whittenburg, May 5, 1933.

26. D. M. DeVitt to Tom Jones, May 26, June 18, June 19, 1933.

27. Tom Jones to D. M. DeVitt, June 19, June 20, 1933.

28. Sam Arnett, Testimony, *Johnson vs. DeVitt*; Steve Kelton, *Renderbrook*, pp. 38, 66-68.

29. D. M. DeVitt to Tom Jones, June 19, 1933; Sam Arnett to D. M. DeVitt. July 22, 1933.

30. D. M. DeVitt to Tom Jones, July 29, 1933.

31. D. M. DeVitt to David A. Murphy, August 14, 1933.

32. D. M. DeVitt to Sam Arnett, September 1, 1933.

33. D. M. DeVitt to David A. Murphy, August 14, 1933.

34. Tom Jones to D. M. DeVitt. September 19, 1933.

35. D. M. DeVitt to J. A. Whittenburg, October 7, 1933.

36. Tom Jones to D. M. DeVitt, October 13, 1933.

37. Tom Jones to D. M. DeVitt, October 12, 1933.

38. D. M. DeVitt to Tom Jones, October 12, 1933.

39. W. J. Nolte to D. M. DeVitt, November 17, 1933.

40. D. M. DeVitt to Sam Arnett, November 10, 1933.

41. D. M. DeVitt to Sam Arnett, November 24, 1933; to P. A. Dietz, January 8, 1934.

42. D. M. DeVitt to J. Lee Johnson, January 9, 1934.

43. D. M. DeVitt to Tom Jones, January 1934.

44. D. M. Devitt to Sam Arnett, January 1934.

45. David A. Murphy to D. M. DeVitt, February 21, 1934.

46. *Lubbock Avalanche Journal*, March 7, 1934.

47. Tom Jones to Christine DeVitt, March 8, 1934, Family Correspondence, Mallet Records. The fate of Billie DeVitt, the widow of David DeVitt, Jr., is unknown. In 1934, she was living in Odessa, Texas, but, according to a passing reference in a letter from David Murphy to J. E. Vickers, dated September 17, 1943, she was deceased.

48. Will, May 8, 1926, Mallet Records.

CHAPTER SIX

Dividing the Pie

We have got to act for ourselves and
take the consequences. There's no one
alive that isn't going to take out of us
all they can possibly get. . . . The Pie
will dry up . . . until what—there is
nothing but mould and we will be
welcome to that.
Florence A. DeVitt,
February 17, 1935.

BECAUSE David M. DeVitt had been such a private individual, his death caught both his family and business associates by surprise. Florence, who was sixty-seven at the time of his death, was hardly in a position to see after his affairs, particularly from her little home in California. But, with Miss Christine, it was a different matter. At age forty-nine, she was ready to fulfill her dreams as a wealthy Texan driving a big car. She lost no time in trying to assert her influence in the affairs of her father's estate, and made her way to Lubbock almost immediately. DeVitt's will had provided that Sam Arnett of Lubbock and David Murphy of Kansas City were to be co-executors, and Christine believed that most of the decision-making would take place in Lubbock.

Meanwhile, the Mallet Ranch continued to operate as a business. W. D. Johnson assumed the presidency and engaged Sam Arnett, who was already serving as co-executor of the DeVitt Estate, to become the active manager. But Florence DeVitt was determined to make sure that everything was handled right, and she turned to Los Angeles attorney Ralph G. Lindstrom for advice and possible handling of her interests in the estate.

Lindstrom apparently went directly to Lubbock, examined the will, visited with the executors, and reported to Mrs. DeVitt that all seemed to be in order, except for one thing: he was concerned about "the rather constant criticism" he received from Miss Christine while he was in Lubbock:

> Particularly it is going to be unfortunate if by her attitude of distrust of others, myself included, Miss Christine brings about either doubts on your part as to my work for you. . . . There is so much fineness in Miss Christine underneath this unfortunate habit of criticism.[1]

Miss Christine's opposition to Lindstrom's handling of her mother's interest in the estate may have stemmed from his proposed 25-percent fee. Regardless, her criticism and "attitude of distrust" set the tone for not only the settlement of the estate, but also the management of the Mallet for years to come.

Although Arnett and Murphy later persuaded Mrs. DeVitt to drop Lindstrom, Christine proved to be more difficult. She challenged their every move. When the executors proposed selling the ranch, Miss Christine refused to consider it. When they negotiated in January 1935 a new oil lease on DeVitt personal property (not Mallet Company property), she refused to sign it.[2] Even her mother was chagrined at Christine's bullheadedness about the lease. Florence wrote to Christine who was in Lubbock:

> The taxes will come out of us you know, and you also know that if we undertake to hold on to that ranch, we will be pau-

perized before [a year from] next April and who will wail the loudest, and be *really worse* off than *your self*. . . . You'd better have a small competence even, if it's sure, than hold out for bigger stakes you will most surely never get. You'd better listen to plain common sense reasoning.[3]

The major decision that the DeVitt women needed to make was whether to sell the Mallet. Apparently, all interests supported the idea of selling the ranch except Miss Christine. Florence, like Christine, had little trust in the lawyers and bankers who were dithering over her husband's estate; she was ready to sell out, fearing the worst from the Johnson stockholders. "We have got to *act* for ourselves and take the consequences," she wrote to Christine. "There's no one alive that isn't going to take out of us all they can possibly get. . . . The *Pie* will dry up . . . until what—there is nothing but *mould* and we will be welcome to that." But she also knew that if she agreed to sell the ranch without Christine's blessing, she would never hear the end of it: "I'm for selling, but not without your consent," she confessed to Christine, "for I'm just as well to be a poor dog, a pauper, as to be deviled out of my life by your refusings and abuses as I've suffered thru the past years. I can't stand up under it any longer."[4]

Her mother's strong words still did not budge Miss Christine. David Murphy went to Lubbock in late February 1935 to see whether he could persuade Christine to change her mind about leasing or possibly selling the ranch. Apparently, Christine had been insisting that executors' asking price for the ranch sale at ten dollars per acre was too low. But Murphy argued that her father had wanted to sell the ranch before his death and would have been willing to take ten dollars per acre for it; he pointed out that the price was agreeable to the Johnsons, and that he "did not know of a closer trader than Mr. W. D. Johnson." He noted also that "the ranch business was a hazardous business and that because of my interest in Mr. DeVitt's family, I would like to see them get their money out of this ranch and into Government securities, so that they would always know what their income would be and so that they would not be taking any risk at all."[5]

When Christine would not be won over, Murphy expressed his unhappiness with her in a letter to Mrs. DeVitt:

It is difficult to tell upon what Miss Christine bases her refusal. . . . She seems to think that a larger bonus and a larger annual rental may be obtained later. . . . So far as the sale of the ranch is concerned, Miss Christine seems to have less reason for withholding her consent than she has even for withholding her consent to the oil leases. . . . I have a very high regard for Miss Christine, but I really feel that she is unduly suspicious of everybody, and I think perhaps that is probably at the bottom of the stand she is taking.[6]

Murphy's assessment was probably correct, but if Christine was suspicious by nature, she was also consistent, and faithful to her own philosophy. Many years (and millions of dollars of income) later, in 1948, she explained her stubbornness this way: "I have followed what I have read is a policy of considerable force, and that is, do not make decisions hastily, don't ever let anyone scare you into making a trade of any kind in any great hurry. You should deliberate and take time."[7]

Indeed, on her copy of Murphy's letter to her mother, Christine made notes that confirm her 1935 adherence to such a philosophy. In his letter, Murphy had noted that he and Arnett "had the power to vote the stock . . . authorizing the sale of the ranch," but that they would not do so without "at least your consent and Mrs. Secrest's consent." He also indicated to Florence that he had told Christine that they "would feel bound to act upon the wishes of the majority of the stock." Christine interpreted his statement as a threat and noted to herself in the margin, "[Murphy] is determined to sell it in spite of my protests and objection if he can possibly fool and scare Mrs. DeVitt and Helen into giving their consent."[8]

Christine apparently gave in on the oil lease in question, but she never consented to selling the ranch, and Murphy and Arnett dropped the matter. Even though the executors paid an early distribution of funds to Mrs. DeVitt, Christine, and Helen in April 1935, Christine kept up her tirade against Murphy and Arnett and even protested the early payment. She told her mother that they had "deliberately withheld [the distribution] letter from me, although I was present in the bank . . .[and] they concealed from me the knowledge that they obtained my mother's and sister's signatures to this agreement."[9]

She berated Helen as well for wanting to sign a deed giving highway right-of-way to the State of Texas: "Don't ever sign a *deed* right-of-way," she emblazoned in red pencil across the face of Helen's copy of the contract. "The people who make out these deeds will put it over on you if they can and get a deed to your land through your ignorance if they can take advantage of you or anyone."[10]

Christine believed also that the executors were overcharging the estate for their services, and, despite assurances from her mother's California attorney that they were not, she still believed that Murphy and Arnett were cheating them. "I do wish you would tell Christine that I think she is unduly worried about this whole matter," Florence's attorney noted, "and that if she would stop worrying and worrying you, that you would be a lot better off and able to enjoy the part of the estate to which each of you will be entitled."[11]

His advice went unheeded by both Florence and Christine. By September, Christine was clamoring for her mother to hire a lawyer to challenge the federal government's estate tax, but Florence would not consent: "Hire another thief, yes, and fill his pockets with the last shred of money we've got, and lose, lose all," she complained to Christine. "Just as soon as our little dwindles down by paying taxes, right then Arnett and the Johnson Bros. will be on hand to take from all our holdings. We will not get a dime out of the cattle business."[12]

Christine also continued to hound the executors about their services. Arnett basically managed the ranch while he continued in his capacity as president of the Citizens National Bank of Lubbock. But Christine apparently wanted to run the ranch; for months she complained that Arnett and Murphy were dragging their feet on closing her father's estate. Then, when they set a closing date for May 1936, she complained that it was too hastily done.[13] And after closing, she demanded that the executors' accounts be audited, but sister Helen refused to go along. "It is just going to be throwing money to the dogs," she wrote Christine.[14]

When the estate finally was closed, Christine did not get her wish to be the ranch manager. Instead, W. D. Johnson became president of the Company and Sam Arnett continued to oversee ranch operations from Lubbock. Christine and Florence then challenged the executors' handling of the estate. In 1937, they hired Lubbock attorney J. E. Vickers, who questioned in court without success the executors' $10,000 fee and other payments from the estate.

While Christine carried on the fight in Lubbock, Florence continued to grow more bitter toward the whole situation. Clearly, as did Christine, Florence mistrusted men. "We will not only be skinned by the 'dozens of men,'" she once wrote, "but [we will] gradually pay out . . . of our own purses."[15] Florence ultimately saw the Johnson Brothers and Sam Arnett as the enemy. Once, after learning that the Mallet Company had paid a sizable bill to J. Lee Johnson's Cicero Smith Lumber Company, she noted, "The Fort Worth Johnson is going to grab out of that corp. as much as the K City Johnson does or know the reason why. The lumber bill attests to that deal."[16] In another letter, Florence complained that Sam Arnett was enjoying, at her expense, "a luxurious trip with all the pleasures and honors attached free as air" while Christine was left with the crumbs. "Defeatism again is our life—if not—our vulture."

Florence even directed her bitterness toward her favorite daughter Helen. Complaining that Helen might move into her neighborhood, Florence told Christine that, if Helen did so, she "would be forever present and always on hand to use me for her own convenience and profit. I've had my fill of it."[17] Subsequently, Florence's acridness became so evident that even Christine accused her of being a miser.

Still another letter to Christine, written in October 1938, reveals much about Florence's personality in her declining years:

You seem to have gotten much longer below the waist since I saw you last, but what woman doesn't when she gets older. Gee I hate to see the years creeping up on you. You have had such a wretched life, empty of anything. Of course, mine's been worse but there's no use talking of me; my days are numbered.[18]

Florence once acknowledged her personal bitterness in another letter to Christine; "I guess my horoscope was *hate*, for wherever I turn that sweet virtue seems to predominate." Such hate, she reasoned, stemmed from her hatred of her husband and from having no one.[19]

Florence's bitterness seemed to have little influence on Helen, who, according to Florence, lived in her own world: "She doesn't want to think about it or she does not want to share her thoughts or air them, prefers to keep herself to herself."[20] But with Christine, it was a different story. Apparently, she fed upon her mother's mistrust of men, even those who were doing their best to be of help. For example, Kansas City attorney David Murphy had watched carefully and consistently after Mr. DeVitt's interests in Kansas City, and, after DeVitt's death, tried to extend that courtesy to his heirs. But he subsequently bristled when he felt that Christine was accusing him of concealing Mallet decisions. "If I did not know you so well, and if I did not have the deepest interest in you and your welfare, I would resent the inference to be drawn from this statement," he scolded. "I think I have told you that I would be very unhappy if I was as suspicious as you are of everybody's motives."[21]

Florence joined Christine in mistrusting the evenhanded Murphy. When the attorney tried to persuade her and Christine to join Helen in allowing him to vote their stock in a single majority block, they refused. "I believe just what you said of him," Florence wrote to Christine, "that he will use all his devices to convince [Helen] that he is the one to hold that stock and vote it." Both Christine and Florence feared that Murphy would simply continue his support of Johnson's and Arnett's management of the Mallet, which they both opposed.[22] Finally tired of the struggle, Murphy surrendered his seat on the Mallet Board in favor of Christine at the June 1937 directors meeting.

In reality, by late fall of 1936, economic matters had begun to improve for the DeVitts and the nation as a whole. President Roosevelt's New Deal was beginning to impact the national economy. With rainfall on the South Plains in the summer and fall of 1935 having ended the disastrous 1934 drought, cattle prices began to climb upward. The Mallet directors voted to pay a 20-percent dividend in July 1936 and followed that with a second dividend of the same amount just three months later, in October. For the year, the ranch showed a $54,000 profit.

West Texas oil fever began to return as well. David Murphy gleefully reported to Florence in October 1936 that Gulf Oil had brought in a well two-and-a-half miles west of the ranch.[23] But as the Mallet stockholders began to talk of making new leases, Christine became more agitated at her lack of control of the ranch. In late November 1936, she fussed at her mother to do something, but Florence was at a loss to know what to do. "Last night's tirade over the ph[one] which cost you just ten dollars was disgraceful and what was accomplished?" Florence wrote to Christine. "If you want me to and can see or know or have a plan, I will come on out there [to Lubbock] and have some more of the delightful *hell* we always have, or I will go on to Kansas City and take the reins out of their hands or get on the board of directors."[24]

Mallet profits continued to climb as national conditions continued to improve and oil speculation increased. In 1937, the Mallet paid its first 50-percent dividend, followed by a 30-percent payment in 1938. Both years saw modest profits posted on the ranch's operation. Still, Florence continued her own tirade about the company's management. "We may as well call [the Mallet the] Johnson and Arnett ranch in which we will never share even in the small amount of land we are supposed to own," complained Florence in May 1938. And, in October, she continued on the same attack: "It's just too terrible to dwell on about the ranch and the way they, Mr. Arnett and Johnson, are gobbling the whole of that valuable property."[26]

For the ever-pessimistic Florence, even the possibility of new prosperity was too little too late. "I am longing to go some place before it is too late and indeed it isn't already," she wrote to Christine; "I've never had anything and now I can't use it."[27] But Christine, despite her complaints, was very much enjoying her new-found lifestyle as a West Texas business woman. Immediately after her father's death, she had taken up residence in Lubbock's Hilton Hotel, a place that would be her home for the next fourteen years. Moreover, although she could not drive, she acquired her father's big Buick car. After a few lessons on the ranch, she was soon cruising the streets of Lubbock. Her charges at a Lubbock service station reveal her driving habits, buying gas frequently, but rarely more than two gallons at a time.

Predictably, Florence was not pleased with Christine's new habits. "All your time is taken in dressing and speaking to people in the hotel, or on the streets and driving to and from to your meals," she berated. "Why don't you put your money where you can get a little interest to help out, even if a little, to pay your large expense account?"[28]

By the end of 1937, Christine considered herself very much a part of Lubbock and the South Plains. Ever since her arrival in the Hub City, she had been besieged by legal documents and attorneys regarding the settlement of her father's estate. Thus, it is no wonder that, for her 1937 Christmas greeting, she prepared a legal document to send to her friends, complete with a seal, which declared the following:

> I Christine DeVitt of the City of Lubbock in the County of Lubbock and State of Texas, being of sound and disposing mind and memory, a stout heart and slim purse, and being desirous of remembering bountifully and extravagantly, all whom it is my pleasure to remember this Holiday Season, do now graciously bestow and voluntarily bequeath to you all the riches of my good will, the fortune of my earnest desires, and the wealth of my love.

The document was witnessed by "Mary Christmas" and "Hap E. New Year."[29]

When business required Christine to go to Fort Worth or Kansas City, she found it difficult to get herself together to return to Lubbock. In late June 1937, she joined her mother and Helen in Kansas City for the annual meeting of the stockholders of the Mallet Land and Cattle Company, a meeting that she had succeeded in getting postponed twice. After the meeting, Florence and Helen made their way back to California, but Christine stayed on in Kansas City "for a few days." But, three months later, she was still there, which provoked her mother to write, "I am wondering too how long, oh Lord, it will take you to tear yourself away from KC and go back to Lubbock where you want to see first hand what is going on around the ranch." And, in the same letter, Florence hammered Christine for not paying a Lubbock street-paving bill: "Your excuse is that if we should sell this [property] this year the buyer could pay [the paving bill] knowing full well you have no idea of selling that [property] or anything else til Gabriel blows his horn, and not then even."[30]

In effect Florence's persistent bitterness, coupled with Christine's mistrust of the Mallet management, polarized the stockholders of the company, and the conflict could not have come at a worse time. Ten years of oil play on the western South Plains was showing promise of a big payoff. Since 1928, oil companies had been obtaining leases throughout the area, but the handful of wildcat wells that had been drilled proved to be dry holes. With the advent of the Depression, oil companies could no longer afford to support wildcat searches and thus dispatched seismograph crews to survey the unproven areas of the western South Plains. In April 1936, oil was discovered on the Bennett Ranch in southern Yoakum County, about ten miles to the south of the Mallet's southern pastures.[31]

After the completion of the Bennett well, the driller moved his rig into Cochran County, only two and a half miles west of the Mallet, onto the old H. T. Boyd Ranch, which had been acquired from Boyd by the Duggan Brothers. In October 1936, oil rose nearly to the top of the well hole, a phenomenon that set off, according to an El Paso newspaper, "a bombshell in oil play in the area. . . . Termed one of the most important strikes made in the region in several years, the . . . well is located in entirely 'wild' territory."[32]

But *wild* would soon be dropped from the description of the new fields. The Texas Company, later Texaco, had taken the lead in seismography, and by 1937 had determined that an oil trap might lie beneath the western part of Hockley County. As a result, the company obtained leases on approximately six thousand acres of the old Slaughter and Mallet ranches, as well as on land that farmers had purchased as a result of the breakup of the Slaughter Ranch. On the Guerry Farm east of the Mallet and one mile south of Sundown, Texaco began drilling a test well in April 1936. For nearly a year, drilling continued, ultimately to a depth of over 5,000 feet. After discovering oil saturation in the lime of the San Andres formation, Texaco then forced acid into the hole to permeate the tightly packed lime. As a result, the well began to produce more than five hundred barrels per day by April 1937. Located only two miles from the Mallet's east fence, the Texas Company No. 1 Bob Slaughter well gave the new field a name, that of Slaughter, and stirred the area into a new oil frenzy. Moreover, the Mallet lay directly between the two new strikes, with most of its acreage still unleased.

Florence DeVitt, in typical fashion, greeted the news of the close-by oil play with skepticism. When David Murphy wrote to her of the Duggan strike, he noted that it would "come close to proving up the entire ranch. I was very pleased at this news." But Florence wryly noted to Christine, "Yes, I do not doubt he has good, even better reason to be pleased than we have."

Drillers soon went to work on existing Mallet leases. Gulf began drilling almost immediately after the Duggan strike on its lease in the northeast corner of Section 6 of Block X, in the Schuster pasture east of the Mallet headquarters. The result was discouraging, however, and the well was plugged in July.

Although D. M. DeVitt and W. D. Johnson had signed dozens of leases before the oil strike, the Texas Company lease, signed in November 1935 by W. D. Johnson as Mallet president, was apparently one of those Christine had opposed earlier in the year. It was the seventh such lease that the Texas Company had obtained on the Mallet, and included only Labor 1 in League 52 and four labors in

League 49. Such careful spot leasing was the result of the company's expensive seismographic survey.

In May 1938, Texaco's investment paid off as the company brought in its first big strike on Mallet land. Located six miles southeast of the Duggan Field well in the Copeland pasture west of the headquarters, Texaco's Number 1-A Mallet gauged 734 barrels of oil, the first production of what would ultimately become nearly a billion barrels of oil from the Mallet.[33]

In August 1938, Texaco located another Mallet well two miles northwest of the Slaughter Field discovery well, sighted just inside the Mallet's east fence in the Schuster pasture, Labor 1 of League 52, Scurry County School Land. Completed December 7, 1938, the well came in producing 175 barrels per day. Moreover, the big producer proved that the newly discovered Slaughter and Duggan fields were parts of a huge San Andres deposit that stretched for many miles east to west across the Mallet Ranch. Subsequently known solely as the Slaughter Field, it would within five years be rated as the second largest field in Texas.[34]

The successive Slaughter and Mallet strikes launched a wave of drilling into the Slaughter Field. By the end of 1940, 101 wells had been drilled on Mallet land on existing leases. And, as the world edged toward war on two fronts, oil prices began to rise, creating new demands for oil lands. The Mallet Ranch was in an enviable position to cash in on the windfall, but there remained one problem—Miss Christine DeVitt—who was still was opposed to new leases. Subsequently, her opposition would throw the company into court, making the 1940s the stormiest decade in the history of the ranch.

NOTES

1. Ralph Lindstrom to Florence A. DeVitt, 3-29-34, Family Correspondence, Mallet Records. Hereinafter, unless otherwise noted, all personal DeVitt correspondence is from the Family Correspondence, Mallet Ranch Records.

2. David A. Murphy to Florence A. DeVitt, February 4, 1935.

3. Florence A. DeVitt to Christine DeVitt, February 17, 1935.

4. Florence A. DeVitt to Christine DeVitt, February 17, 1935.

5. David A. Murphy to Florence A. DeVitt, March 5, 1935.

6. *Ibid.*

7. Minutes, Special Meeting of the Directors, Mallet Land and Cattle Company, December 20, 1948, Mallet Records.

8. David A. Murphy to Florence A. DeVitt, May 5, 1935 (carbon copy).

9. Christine DeVitt notes, on letter David A. Murphy to Florence A. DeVitt, April 13, 1935.

10. Highway Department Contract, May 1935, Mallet Records. Unless otherwise noted, all future citations dealing with Mallet business are taken from the Mallet Ranch Records, Southwest Collection, Texas Tech University.

11. A. J. Verheyen to Florence A. DeVitt, May 14, 1935.

12. Florence A. DeVitt to Christine DeVitt, September 2, 1935.

13. George R. Bean to Christine DeVitt, April 28, 1936.

14. Helen Secrest to Christine DeVitt, June 8, 1936.

15. Florence A. DeVitt to Christine DeVitt, November 30, 1936.

16. Florence A. DeVitt to Christine DeVitt, March 19, 1937.

17. Florence A. DeVitt to Christine DeVitt, March 25, 1937.

18. Florence A. DeVitt to Christine DeVitt, October 26, 1938.

19. Florence A. DeVitt to Christine DeVitt, November 30, 1936.

20. Florence A. DeVitt to Christine DeVitt, March 25, 1937.

21. David A. Murphy to Christine DeVitt, January 27, 1937.

22. Florence A. DeVitt to Christine DeVitt, April 6, 1937.

23. David A. Murphy to Florence A. DeVitt, October 16, 1936.

24. Florence A. DeVitt to Christine DeVitt, November 20, 1936.

25. Florence A. DeVitt to Christine DeVitt, May 17, 1938.

26. Florence A. DeVitt to Christine DeVitt, October 26, 1938.

27. Florence A. DeVitt to Christine DeVitt, October 7, 1935.

28. Florence A. DeVitt to Christine DeVitt, October 19, 1936.

29. Christmas Greeting, 1937, Christine DeVitt File, Mallet Records.

30. Florence A. DeVitt to Christine DeVitt, September 29, 1937.

31. S. D. Myres, *Permian Basin: Petroleum Empire of the Southwest*, Vol. II (El Paso: Permian Press, 1977), p. 226.

32. *El Paso Times*, as cited in Myres, *Permian Basin: Petroleum Empire of the Southwest*, Vol. II (El Paso, Permian Press, 1977), p. 239.

33. Ruford F. Madera, "The Slaughter Field, Hockley County, Texas" (MS thesis, Texas Technological College, 1939), pp. 8, 14.

34. S. D. Myres, *The Permian Basin: Petroleum Empire of the Southwest*, Vol. II (El Paso: Permian Press, 1977), pp. 240-241.

CHAPTER SEVEN

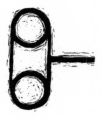

The Mallet Is Primarily Oil

Everyone now has to admit that the
Mallet Land property is primarily
an oil property. The more rapidly it
is developed for oil, the more rapidly
will the income from it be increased.
Mallet Company attorney
David A. Murphy
to Christine DeVitt,
December 11, 1940.

IN September 1939, Germany turned its modern war machine on neighboring Poland and within days, Europe had polarized for war. Repercussions of the outbreak, coupled with Japan's push toward domination of the rich oil fields of the Far East, sent shock waves through the United States. Oil prices, which had been as low as ten cents a barrel in the early 1930s, began to push upward.

Cattle prices also began to show recovery from the decade-long Depression, helped along by the return of normal rainfall to the South Plains following droughty years of the mid-1930s. On the Mallet, however, it was not back to the usual cattle business. A rising oil income, coupled with war fever, meant that the Mallet and its owners would soon come under the close scrutiny of the United States Internal Revenue Service. Moreover, the Mallet directors had to deal with its most formidable stockholder, Miss Christine DeVitt, who by 1940 had planted herself permanently in Lubbock so that she could be "on the ground" to know what was going on.

In June 1937, after the closing of her father's estate, Miss Christine was elected to the Board of Directors of the Mallet Land and Cattle Company and by 1940 had become vice president, replacing Sam Arnett, who had served as a director since the death of Mr. DeVitt. W. D. Johnson remained president. Although she had questioned the management of the company consistently since her father's death, by 1940 she was in a position to demand answers. When she got them, typically she wanted to postpone the decision making they necessitated. For example, she wanted to delay the company's decision to pay a 50-percent dividend for 1940, but Mallet attorney David Murphy persuaded her to change her mind. She had wanted to delay the laying of a pipeline on the ranch because she was upset over W. D. Johnson's handling of the arrangements with Magnolia Petroleum Company. She also opposed locating on the ranch a camp for pumping station workers.[1]

Her greatest concern, however, was over new oil leases for the ranch. For several months in 1940, W. D. Johnson had negotiated with the Canadian Texas Oil Company to lease a sizable portion of the northern end of the ranch, a proposal that involved more than seven thousand acres. For most of the Mallet directors, the lease was attractive; it was to pay a 25-percent royalty, and then a 12 ½-percent override after the cost of drilling had been paid. What it did not include was a cash bonus, and for that reason, Miss Christine objected.

Christine's concern was valid. Her personal income, along with those of her mother's and sister Helen's, in no way approached that of the Johnsons, who had extensive financial interests. She was less concerned about the income tax on a large cash bonus for leasing. Apparently, Johnson grudgingly agreed with her and indicated to Christine that she could handle the lease negotiations. David Murphy, who knew Christine quite well, warned her not to procrastinate on the matter.

Meanwhile, drilling proceeded rapidly, not only on Mallet leases, but on those that surrounded the ranch. In 1938, three wells were drilled on the Mallet. Four more were drilled in 1939, and another twenty-five by the end of 1940. Yet it was 1941 that brought the boom. By mid-year, more than one hundred new wells had been started, mostly by Texaco and Magnolia. Of greater concern to some of the Mallet owners was the development of twenty or more wells on the perimeter just outside of its undeveloped, unleased acreage. As the possibility of war became more real, particularly after Germany's invasion of France in May 1940, it became apparent that, if oil development on the Mallet was to reach its potential, action had to be taken right away.

Miss Christine was in no hurry. In January 1941, W. D. Johnson issued a call for the regular meeting of the stockholders so that a new oil policy could be formulated, but Christine refused to meet. Holding voting proxies from both her mother and Helen, Christine controlled voting interest in the company and thus could get her own way. Subsequently, she forced W. D. Johnson to set the 1941 annual meeting date thirteen different times from January to July. Finally, on July 31, the stockholders assembled in Kansas City. Although Christine attended the meeting, she steadfastly maintained later that W. D. Johnson had tricked her into attending.[2]

Helen attended the meeting also and at that time revoked her proxy with Christine. Apparently ready to make her own decisions rather than bow to Christine's preferences, Helen shifted her allegiance from her mother and sister to Johnson and Murphy and thus chartered a new course for the Mallet. As a result, she was elected a director, along with her ex-husband Bill Secrest, W. D. Johnson, and J. Lee Johnson, Jr., who had replaced his father on the Board after his death in 1937. Secrest, who had been divorced from Helen for nearly ten years, was apparently the choice of W. D. Johnson, who thought that Secrest's experience in engineering would be an asset to the company, and that Secrest would have some influence on Helen.

Christine protested the election, insisting that the directors be voted on individually, but the others refused. When she persisted, J. Lee Johnson, Jr. apparently rebuffed her, or as Christine later charged, "forcibly assaulted and seized [her] and threw her across the room, and forcibly attempted to prevent her from making any further protest."[3] The confrontation set the tone for not only the rest of the meeting but also for the next two years. Christine opposed unsuccessfully the election of W. D. Johnson as president, proposing instead that Johnson and Bill Secrest be made co-managers of the ranch. No other director supported the idea. Then, Helen nominated J. Lee Johnson, Jr., to replace Christine as vice-president.

Helen's shifting alliances also set into motion a chain of events that no one anticipated. For the remainder of the meeting, Christine opposed every action of the Board. She particularly opposed the election of Bill Secrest as assistant to the manager at a $5,000 salary. If he deserved that, she reasoned, then the Board should pay her and her mother the same amount, but no one else concurred.

The meeting stormed on for two days. At its end, the Mallet directors finished off Miss Christine, or so they thought, by removing her from its Oil Lease Committee.[4] Apparently tired of her refusal to meet and negotiate new leases, the other directors empowered Johnson to proceed with oil leasing. Almost immediately after the meeting, Johnson resumed negotiations with oil companies for new leases and was ready to present a proposal to the Board by August 25th.

Meanwhile, obviously concerned that certain Texas oil interests were trying to influence his new alliance with Helen Secrest, W. D. Johnson wrote on August 9 to Bill Secrest who was vacationing in Atlanta with his family:

> I am expecting you here [within two weeks] . . . I am afraid Helen is under control of Mast; she is staying at his house in Lubbock, but in a conversation with Lee Johnson yesterday afternoon, I got the information that she was in Dallas with Mast

and Mr. Morrow. . . . I wrote Mr. Arnett at Lubbock to please
see Helen and have a talk with her; he found out she was at
Mast's. Mast answered the phone, but he would not let Mr.
Arnett talk to her.

I hope you will come as soon as you can to look after Helen;
I am really anxious about her safety.[5]

Johnson was concerned also "that we are liable to be attacked by
Christine through some attorney" because of the action of the
Board at the July meeting. For that reason, he called for another
Board meeting on August 25. His concern was prophetic.

Taking a lesson from her father's use of the courts, Christine obtained a restraining order from a Kansas City judge by claiming that
the election of directors was illegal and that the assault by J. Lee
Johnson, Jr., had prevented her from exercising her rights. When
the other directors assembled to meet on the 25th, they were met by
a deputy sheriff of Jackson County, Missouri, with the order restraining their meeting. The Board had no choice but to adjourn.

One of the directors wasted little time in pursuing his own course
of action. On August 27, two days after receiving Christine's restraining order in Kansas City, J. Lee Johnson, Jr. filed a petition in
the 72nd District Court in Lubbock pleading that the court appoint
a receiver because of the deadlock among the Mallet directors,
which in turn was causing a loss of revenue. Judge Daniel A. Blair
immediately granted the request and appointed D. M. DeVitt's old
friend and banker Sam Arnett to be the receiver.

The days that followed became one of Lubbock's great legal cir-
cuses. On September 4, in an effort to persuade them to sign an
agreement supporting the receivership, W. D. and J. Lee Johnson
asked Florence and Helen to meet with them and their attorney, E.
L. Klett. Christine was apparently not invited. In the meeting, the
Johnsons outlined their frustration with Christine's delays and
stated how important it was that the leasing and drilling of the ranch
get under way. Then W. D. Johnson turned to Mrs. DeVitt and
asked what she thought about it. According to Helen, who had
carefully recorded the meeting for Christine's benefit, Florence re-

mained silent at first: "Then [Mama] said Well she hardly knew what to say—But she felt that the Johnsons had had the management for several years now, and that Christine was entitled to her turn at having the management."[6] W. D. Johnson then replied, "Mrs. DeVitt, she *has* had control of the board all along."

Helen reminded her mother that both she and Florence had given to Christine their proxies, which had, in effect, given Christine control of the company. Helen also pointed out to the group that the only thing Christine had done to find a manager was to offer it to Lubbock businessman L. S. Mast, who had turned her down.

Lee Johnson then told Mrs. DeVitt and Helen that he was there to "beg and plead with [them]" to sign the petition supporting receivership, but if they did not, "he would have no recourse except to appeal for protection of this company and his interests through the courts, which he would do no matter how much it would cost him." Helen also reported that Johnson said he had grounds to sue Christine for damages if the delay resulted in losses to himself.

Lee Johnson's comment did not set well with Christine when she read Helen's notes. In her own hand, written between Helen's lines, Christine responded for posterity's sake: "Just a dirty threat to my helpless mother and sister to high pressure them into signing the agreement and asking for the Receivership."

The Johnsons' tactic worked and won over Helen and Florence. As Helen reported to Christine, "By morning we were sick of the disorder of being around you and had no confidence in you whatsoever, so we went back to [the attorney's office]." Both Mrs. DeVitt and Helen signed the agreement just before the convening of the court's hearing on continuation of the receivership. Helen closed her report to Christine, "Don't count on me in your lawsuits."

When Judge Blair opened his hearing on the morning of September 5, he found all the stockholders in agreement except for Miss Christine. The hearing then proceeded. According to the *Lubbock Avalanche*, it "was enlivened by frequent admonishment of the court for order."[7] Among the witnesses was R. C. DeWoody, a Lubbock geologist, who stated that twenty-three offset wells producing near the Mallet Ranch borders were draining from the Mallet's resources. Still another witness stated that every day new leasing was delayed would lessen the Mallet's chances of getting drilling materials and supplies because the nation was moving toward rearmament. Apparently, at the end of the day, the testimony not only convinced Judge Blair, but Miss Christine as well, for, according to the *Avalanche*, her attorney J. E. Vickers "was able to announce that Miss DeVitt had joined the other defendants in adopting pleadings of the plaintiffs in asking that lease contracts be executed for drilling." With her objection removed, Judge Blair ordered that Arnett continue as receiver, but that leasing of the ranch for oil drilling must fall under the scrutiny of the court.

Arnett lost no time in trying to please both the court and the majority of the Mallet stockholders. With W. D. and Lee Johnson still in Lubbock, Arnett decided to pursue leasing quickly and immediately solicited a number of companies for proposals. On September 8, he signed a lease with oil man T. F. Morrow that covered fifteen labors and offered three-eighths royalty, but with no cash bonus. Two days later, Arnett completed negotiations with J. C. Hawkins of Dallas for the leasing of nearly seven thousand acres in a deal that would give the Mallet Company not only three-eighths royalty but also a $25,000 cash bonus and an additional bonus of $1,000 for each well completed, up to twenty-five wells.

Arnett's rapid action set off another legal landslide. Three days after the Hawkins lease was signed, Miss Christine filed an opposition; four days later, Florence DeVitt also filed her own opposition to the lease. Even W. D. Johnson joined in the opposition to the Morrow and Hawkins leases, alarmed that Arnett did not go through a sealed-bid process.

Just as quickly, Hawkins and Morrow pressed for confirmation of their leases. On October 28, Judge Blair tried the case without a jury. Eight attorneys were lined across the front of the courtroom, representing respectively the five stockholders, the two oil men, and the receiver. After long testimony from nearly all the principals, the court ruled against the oilmen Hawkins and Morrow and refused to confirm the leases.

But too much was at stake for Hawkins and Morrow. They promptly appealed Judge Blair's decision to the Court of Civil Appeals in Amarillo. There, on March 2, 1942, the court reversed Judge Blair's decision and ordered that the leases be confirmed and executed. Christine's attorney, J. E. Vickers, filed a motion for rehearing, but the request was denied on April 5. Similarly, W. D. Johnson filed his own appeal, charging that Arnett's hasty actions chilled bidding and stifled competition; however, the Court of Civil Appeals found no wrongdoing. With these setbacks, both Christine and W. D. Johnson appealed to the Texas Supreme Court, but the high court ruled that their cases were without merit.

Meanwhile, Helen Secrest took her own route in trying to settle the dispute among the stockholders. A Los Angeles attorney, R. W. Schoettler, proposed to her that the three DeVitt heirs pool their stock in a voting trust, and he would serve as their trustee. Among other things, he suggested also that they put him on the Board of Directors, move the corporation to Los Angeles, and take over the management of the company.[8]

To confirm Schoettler's plan, Helen wrote for advice to her father's old friend Tom Jones, who was at the time living in Austin. Delighted to help, Tom went promptly to Los Angeles to consult at length with Helen, her mother, and Schoettler. As a result, both Helen and Mrs. DeVitt signed the voting trust with Schoettler. "We know that you will be disappointed for our having entered into a voting trust agreement with Tom Jones and Roland Schoettler," Helen wrote to Christine, "[but] every time we have a decision to make we ask you for your ideas; we want you to help us, and we ask you to come out [to California], and we ask you for advice, but you always just tell us not to do anything, and it does not feel good here for you to always tell us to do nothing."[9]

Christine still refused to go along with the plan and apparently persuaded Helen to forego the trust. Unfortunately, there is no record of the 1942 stockholders' and directors' meetings. Helen apparently allowed David Murphy to vote her stock, and Christine found herself with a new ally in W. D. Johnson, who had sided with her on the issue of Arnett's leasing. The elder Johnson had disapproved of his nephew J. Lee Johnson's role in the leasing and thus found himself aligned with Christine on several issues. Miss Christine must have offered some compromise as well. As a result, she and W. D. joined forces to curtail Helen's influence. At the next election of officers, Christine's attorney J. E. Vickers and Mallet attorney David A. Murphy were both elected to the Board of Directors, replacing Helen Secrest and Bill Secrest. J. E. Vickers was elected president.

By midsummer 1942, the legal wrangling among the Mallet directors had run its course, but had left a trail of ill will, exhaustion, and great expense The rift that had developed between W. D. Johnson and his nephew, J. Lee Johnson, Jr., did little to restore harmony to the Mallet Board, but at least eased the dispute between the DeVitts and the Johnsons.

Moreoever, all the parties had simply grown tired of the fight, and not without reason. In May 1942, while preparing for one of the Mallet court cases, Christine's attorney, J. E. Vickers, spent nearly eighty-eight hours discussing legal matters with Miss Christine in his office. This amount of time, he reported in his statement, did not include countless hours with her on the telephone. During the ten months of the receivership fight from September to May, he reported that he spent 878 hours of work on the issue. When Christine stayed in Austin after the Supreme Court hearings in the summer of 1942, Vickers reported her absence from Lubbock to W. D. Johnson, adding wryly, "I am getting a much needed rest."[10]

By the end of 1942, despite the legal wrangling, the Mallet's economic picture was quite bright. With an income of nearly $350,000, $238,000 of which came from royalties, the Company stood ready to pay handsome dividends to its stockholders. Gradually, dissent among the owners declined, and by February 1943, Judge Blair was ready to end the receivership, provided that the directors could demonstrate that harmony did exist among them.[11] Only Lee Johnson opposed the termination.

For the annual meeting, held March 13, 1943, in Kansas City, all of the directors, including Miss Christine, put on their best faces. During the election of officers, when Vickers was reelected president and W. D. Johnson vice-president, the vote was unanimous, but Lee Johnson did not vote. Otherwise, the meeting proceeded smoothly, and the directors voted to declare a 100-percent dividend, or $100 per share.[12]

A transcript of the meeting reveals a very quiet Christine DeVitt, who apparently had adopted a tight-lipped policy in the interest of harmony. On one occasion, when she challenged another director's opinion, Tom Jones quickly reminded her, "They are putting down everything you say, Miss Christine," referring to the stenographer who was engaged to record the meeting.[13]

With the dispute apparently resolved, Judge Blair terminated Arnett's receivership March 15, 1943, and returned control of the ranch to the Mallet directors. But fences needed to be mended, both on the ranch, and among the Board members. Within weeks, Mr. Vickers was able to report to Mrs. DeVitt that Lee Johnson "is getting over his pout and now manifests an inclination to give us full cooperation in company matters."[14]

Miss DeVitt was still insistent, however, that she become a part of the active management of the Mallet company. Shortly after the termination of the receivership, she called W. D. Johnson and outlined her demand. "She said she wanted to be advised about everything," W. D. Johnson reported to her attorney and new company president J. E. Vickers, "and I told her we would do our best to advise her about everything she wanted to know about; she said she didn't want to have to ask, but that she wanted to be advised before anything was done without her asking for it."[15]

Johnson was obviously miffed at the demand. "If we cannot act on our own judgement and on our own responsibility, "he complained to Vickers, "then we can never make any progress." Yet, he moved toward compromise.

As a result, all were apparently in the spirit of agreement when the Board gathered on April 16, 1943 for its second meeting of the year. The directors designated Vickers and W. D. Johnson to be joint managers of the company, but also appointed both Christine DeVitt and Lee Johnson "to perform such duties as the President may assign to them." For such services, Vickers and W. D. Johnson were to receive salaries of $6,000 annually, and Miss DeVitt and Lee Johnson, $4,000.

Moreover, at Christine's insistence, the Board voted to move the company books to a permanent office in Lubbock and to employ a full-time bookkeeper, even though W. D. Johnson was adamantly opposed. From the date of the 1903 incorporation of the Mallet, the company books had been kept in Kansas City, primarily at the Drumm Commission Company office. About 1927, after the Johnsons had acquired the Drumm stock, Mr. DeVitt had moved the books to Lubbock where he employed a bookkeeper to look after the accounts.[16] Johnson was never pleased with the arrangement, and in 1931 persuaded DeVitt to return the books to Kansas City, where they remained until the establishment of the receivership, at which time the books were sent to Lubbock. Thus, in 1943, even though W. D. Johnson was eighty-three years old, he still watched carefully over his accounts and was opposed to the Mallet records being maintained in far-off Lubbock. But he relented; the move was made, and company president J. E. Vickers established an office on the second floor of the Lubbock National Bank.

Although the litigation proved quite costly, Christine had won out on two issues: she became salaried, and the corporate offices relocated to Lubbock. Nevertheless, the Mallet directors soon found themselves with still another problem—too much money. Mallet income for wartime 1943 exceeded all expectations. In 1942, the oil companies operating on Mallet leases had completed 147 wells. In 1943, with the legal disputes on the Hawkins and Morrow leases settled, an additional 139 wells came on line, for a grand total of 498 producing wells drilled since 1938. Royalty income for 1943 totaled more than a half-million dollars, and cattle income was over $260,000. Interestingly, administrative expense for the year, driven up by the cost of the receivership and related legal fees, was $32,018, whereas the cost of operating the entire ranch was only $22,770. For the year, the Mallet directors paid three dividends totaling 500 percent of stock value.

The new wealth also brought the Mallet owners high taxes, both personal and corporate. For 1942, the Company paid to the federal government nearly $135,000 in taxes. The next year it paid nearly twice as much. In addition, each stockholder faced a huge personal income tax. Because the Mallet had become a royalty receiver, with relatively little expense to charge against its income, company attorney David Murphy suggested in August 1942 to Miss Christine that the Mallet owners consider dissolution of the corporation as a means of avoiding double taxation. President Vickers passed the idea to Miss Devitt, but nothing came of the suggestion—at least for the time being.

Instead, despite wartime restrictions, the Mallet directors tried to make some changes in personnel and a few capital improvements on the ranch. They dismissed longtime foreman Wadkie Fowler in April 1943, replacing him with Charlie Middleton of Lubbock. They also ordered the construction of a one-room addition to the foreman's house and prepared the old DeVitt house for Helen's forthcoming visit that summer.

Meanwhile, Helen effected some changes of her own. On November 9, 1942, after a short courtship, she married her father's old friend Tom Jones. A few months later, she began pressuring her sister and the Johnsons to place him on the Mallet payroll. Initially, Christine opposed the move, fearing how it might impact her own salary, but Helen persisted. In August 1943, Helen wired from California a terse complaint to company president J. E. Vickers: "Mother and I would like to know why you do not give Tom a job?"

Although Vickers hastened to put Tom on the payroll, it took several months to work him into a permanent position. Because Mrs. DeVitt underwent surgery in California in December 1943, both Christine and Helen spent much of early 1944 at her bedside. Finally, in May, they joined the other Mallet directors and made a number of significant changes in the operation of the ranch and farm.

First, they fired longtime farm manager J. A. Stroud and replaced him with Helen's new husband, Tom Jones. Moreover, after years of foot-dragging, the Board bestowed upon Miss Christine the title of co-manager of the Mallet Land and Cattle Company. At the same time, the Board also qualified its action, over Christine's objection, by ruling that "only the President [Vickers] and Vice President [W.

D. Johnson] shall give orders or directions to employees of the ranch, or carry on any negotiations with any oil lessee."[17] The resolution in effect rendered Christine's power as co-manager worthless, much to her chagrin. But Miss DeVitt did gain some consolation at a follow-up meeting in June. She persuaded the Board to approve a resolution providing that no repairs or alterations could be made to the ranch without her consent and approval.

Miss DeVitt's historic insistence for holding out for the better deal did persuade the Board to negotiate a very favorable oil lease. The Board approved placing an additional one thousand acres of land into cultivation and awarded a major oil lease to Stanolind Petroleum that provided a three-eighths royalty, plus an additional one-sixteenth should the price of oil ever reach $1.50 per barrel. The latter provision, included to satisfy Miss DeVitt, would ultimately pay handsome rewards to the Mallet owners.

If the directors thought that 1943 had been a good year, the next year was even more remarkable. By the end of 1944, an additional 145 oil wells had been drilled, and total income was nearly one and a half million dollars. Once again, Vickers suggested that consideration be given to dissolving the corporation, and even demonstrated that Miss DeVitt's after-tax personal income would increase from $77,000 to $228,000 if the corporation were to be eliminated.[18]

Perhaps fearing that the owners could never operate as partners, there was even some talk among the directors of selling the ranch's royalties for twelve million dollars, provided that DeVitts could retain the surface, but no purchaser materialized.[19] Still the money rolled in—and out. Although the Mallet paid dividends totaling $600,000 for 1944, it also paid nearly $300,000 in school, county, and federal taxes. The future looked bright for not only the Mallet owners, but also for the coffers of the federal government and for every county and school district surrounding the ranch. Indeed, taxes would be the principal word in the Mallet's future.

NOTES

1. David A. Murphy to Christine DeVitt, December 11, 1940.
2. Minutes of the Board of Directors, Mallet Land and Cattle Company, December 17-18, 1947, p. 21, in possession of John Sones, May, Texas.
3. Petition to Circuit Court at Jackson County Missouri, August 1941, Mallet Records.
4. Minutes of the Board of Directors, July 31, August 1, 1941.
5. W. D. Johnson to L. S. Secrest, August 9, 1941.
6. Notes, undated, in envelope inscribed, "Helen's Version of happenings in 1941 Receivership."
7. *Lubbock Avalanche*, September 6, 1941.
8. R. W. Schoettler to Christine DeVitt, May 6, May 9, 1942.
9. "Dear Christine," undated letter, unsigned.
10. J. E. Vickers to W. D. Johnson, July 30, 1942.
11. Charles Crenshaw to David Murphy, February 8, 1943.
12. Minutes of the Annual Meeting, March 13, 1943.
13. Stenographic Report of the Minutes of Stockholders and meeting of Board of Directors of Mallet Land and Cattle Company, March 13, 1943, p. 53, in possession of John Sones, May, Texas. Interestingly, Mr. Sones found transcripts of the 1943 and 1947 Board meetings hidden in the wall of the Mallet Ranch headquarters, probably placed there by Christine DeVitt.
14. J. E. Vickers to Florence A. DeVitt, April 7, 1943.
15. W. D. Johnson to J. E. Vickers, March 22, 1943.
16. Transcript of Discussion Had Off the Record, Minutes of the Directors' Meeting, December 17-18, 1947.
17. Minutes of the Annual Meeting, Board of Directors, May 13, 1944.
18. J. E. Vickers to T. S. Cody, June 20, 1944.
19. Memo for Florence A. DeVitt, October 20, 1944.

CHAPTER EIGHT

Too Much Money

*I am impressing it on Miss DeVitt
that we are accumulating too much
money.*
A. L. Henderson to W. D. Johnson,
November 22, 1946.

A s World War II drew to its dramatic close in August 1945, Americans were ready to get back to normal as soon as possible. They also knew that there would be great adjustments as price controls would expire and taxes and wages adjusted to a postwar economy.

Although the war had been good for the Mallet owners financially, it had left the ranch's cattle operation sadly in disrepair. Despite an annual royalty income that by 1945 was approaching one and a half million dollars, the Mallet spent only a few thousand dollars on ranch improvements during the war. Its fences, windmills, houses, and barns had become dilapidated through the lean years of the Depression and the war. And because the ranch headquarters was located on DeVitt Estate property rather than on land owned by the Mallet Company, there had been an ongoing dispute between the

Board and Miss Christine over whether she or the corporation should bear the expense for repairs at the headquarters.

At war's end, the Mallet management worked hard to put its affairs in order. By mid-1945, President J. E. Vickers had resigned to return to his law practice. Taking advantage of the change in command, Helen's husband Tom Jones began playing a larger role in the management of the company, one that was much broader than his position of farm manager. Indeed, when the Mallet directors finally met in October for their 1945 annual meeting, they elected as their new president an old friend of Tom Jones, A. L. Henderson of Lubbock, to be the company president and office manager. Like Tom, Henderson had dealt in land sales as well as oil leasing for a number of years. Apparently, the Mallet directors, believing that they were getting an experienced oil land man, thought they had found the right man in Henderson. Luta P. Eaves, an experienced accountant and teacher at Texas Tech, became the bookkeeper under Henderson.

Initially, Henderson worked hard to make the Mallet office run and look like a big-time corporation. He set up permanent files and books, and, for a two-year period, kept the Mallet Company running relatively smoothly. Moreover, the Company finally settled the last of its legal bills from the costly receivership. Oil money continued to roll in from 675 producing wells. Such income made one stockholder very proud: "I don't think there is another corporation in the country that can make such an excellent showing."[1]

Unfortunately, three key people who had shared in the development of the ranch did not live to enjoy the enormity of its wealth. First, the Mallet lost its largest stockholder, Mrs. Florence A. DeVitt, when she died in California on November 30, 1945, with daughters Christine and Helen at her side. She was seventy-eight. In December 1943, Florence had undergone surgery at the Scripps-Howard Clinic in La Jolla, California, but never fully recovered. Although she remained ill, she insisted on living alone. In the fall of 1945, she did agree that she would move back to Texas, but only to Dallas. Helen bought a house for her in Dallas in November 1945, but Florence died before she could return to her native Texas.

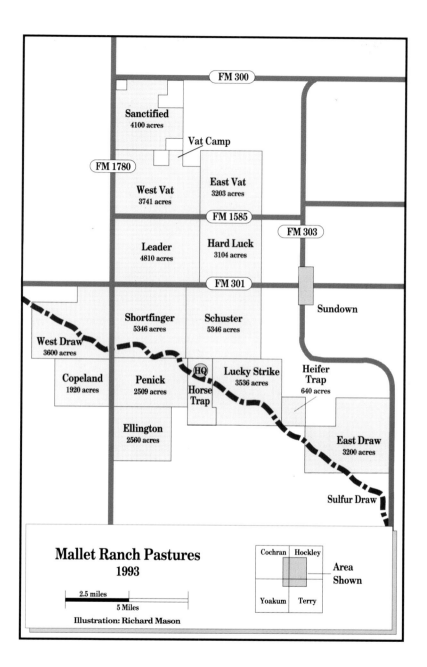

FM 300

Sanctified
4100 acres

Vat Camp

FM 1780

West Vat
3741 acres

East Vat
3203 acres

FM 1585

FM 303

Leader
4810 acres

Hard Luck
3104 acres

FM 301

Sundown

Shortfinger
5346 acres

Schuster
5346 acres

West Draw
3600 acres

HQ

Copeland
1920 acres

Penick
2509 acres

Horse
Trap

Lucky Strike
3536 acres

Heifer
Trap
640 acres

Ellington
2560 acres

East Draw
3200 acres

Sulfur Draw

Mallet Ranch Pastures
1993

2.5 miles

5 Miles

Illustration: Richard Mason

Cochran	Hockley	Area
Yoakum	Terry	Shown

Labeled "A heard in 'hard-luck' Pasture," this photo was taken by the author's aunt, Lena Bell Murrah, during a visit she made to the Mallet Ranch in 1934, and shows the effects of the drought on grass and cattle.

Lubbock's Hilton Hotel, constructed in 1929, served as a residence for many South Plains ranchers and business people, including David M. DeVitt and Tom Jones. Christine DeVitt also made it her home from 1935 until her eviction in 1948. Courtesy Southwest Collection, Texas Tech University.

Drilling a new oil well on the Mallet Ranch, 1962. Robert W. Gaston Collection, Southwest Collection, Texas Tech University.

Above. Mallet Ranch headquarters windmill and tank, 1939. From O. R. Watkins, "A History of Hockley County" (master's thesis, Texas Technological College, 1941).
Right. Mallet Ranch headquarters tank and windmill, 1992. Photo by Artie Limmer.

Miss Christine DeVitt inspects one of her many oil wells under the guidance of Amoco landman Robert Gaston, 1962. Robert W. Gaston Collection, Southwest Collection, Texas Tech University.

Helen DeVitt Jones (left), Tom Jones, and Christine DeVitt, c. 1944.

Former Mallet Ranch neighbor Hiley T. Boyd, Jr., inspects the huge cottonwood tree at the Mallet headquarters tank, 1992. Photo by Artie Limmer.

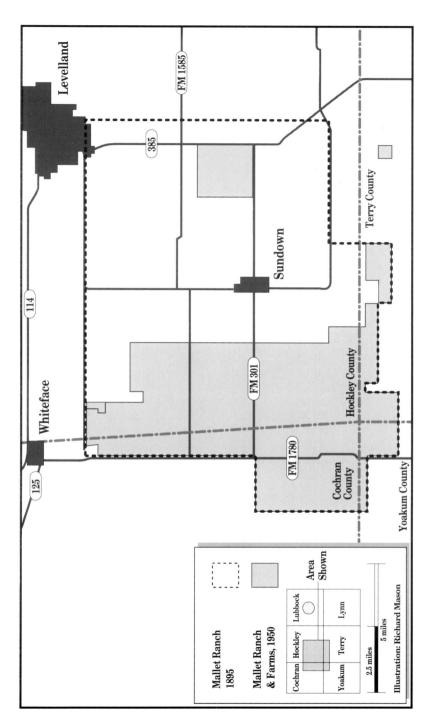

Mallet Ranch 1895

Mallet Ranch & Farms, 1950

Area Shown

Cochran	Hockley	Lubbock
Yoakum	Terry	Lynn

2.5 miles

5 miles

Illustration: Richard Mason

Levelland

FM 1585

385

114

Whiteface

125

Sundown

FM 301

FM 1780

Hockley County

Terry County

Cochran County

Yoakum County

Twin windmills and tank, Mallet Ranch, 1992. Photo by Artie Limmer.

Mallet headquarters windmill and cottonwood trees, c. 1970. This mill is no longer standing.

Mallet cattle, c. 1975, of the herd developed by Christine DeVitt and her foreman John Sones. Courtesy John Sones.

Mallet Ranch foreman John Sones and Miss Christine DeVitt, c. 1968. Courtesy John Sones.

Branding time at the Mallet, c. 1970. Courtesy John Sones.

Mallet Ranch foreman John Sones, 1976. Courtesy John Sones.

Left.   Dorothy "Teddy" Secrest, as a young teenager, c. 1939.
Below.   Dorothy Secrest, c. 1946, as a co-ed on the campus of the University of California at Berkeley.

*Right.   Helen DeVitt Jones, c.
1975.
Below.   Helen DeVitt Jones
and Tom Jones, c. 1953.*

Christine DeVitt (left), Dr. William Curry Holden, Helen DeVitt Jones, and Frances Holden, c. 1970. This picture was taken at the Pitchfork Ranch headquarters, 80 miles east of Lubbock, during planning stages for the Ranching Heritage Center at Texas Tech in Lubbock.

One of the Mallet farm houses, 1954.

D. Burns (left), Christine DeVitt, and Watt Matthews, 1969. As founding members of the Ranch Headquarters Association, later to be known as the Ranching Heritage Association, these three prominent West Texas ranchers played a crucial role in the establishment and development of Texas Tech's Ranching Heritage Center. D. Burns was the former manager of the vast Pitchfork Ranch, and Watt Matthews was co-owner and manager of the historic Lambshead Ranch.

Anne Snyder (left), Helen DeVitt Jones, and Dorothy Secrest, 1975, at the ground-breaking for the David M. DeVitt and Mallet Ranch Interpretation Center at the Ranching Heritage Center, a building funded primarily by gifts from Christine DeVitt.

Texas Tech University President Dr. Grover E. Murray breaks ground for the DeVitt Interpretation Center at the Ranching Heritage Center, 1975.

Diagram of the Mallet brand.

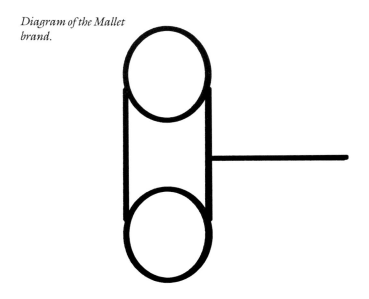

Christine DeVitt (seated) and her sister Helen DeVitt Jones celebrate Miss DeVitt's 96th birthday in September 1981. Miss DeVitt would not allow her hair to be cut for many years, but she consented for the occasion of her birthday and this photograph. Courtesy John Thompson.

Children in the Helen DeVitt Jones Cottage at The Villages in Topeka Kansas, one of Helen's long-time charities.

Dorothy Secrest Klein and her husband Theodore Klein, c. 1983.

Dorothy Secrest (left), Dr. W. C. Holden, and Helen DeVitt Jones, c. 1990.

Louise Arnold (left) and Helen DeVitt Jones, c. 1990.

Helen DeVitt Jones (seated), Dorothy Secrest, and author David Murrah, 1993, at a Texas Tech University reception given to honor Mrs. Jones for her generous support of Texas Tech. Courtesy News and Publications, Texas Tech University.

Helen DeVitt Jones (left) and her daughter Dorothy Secrest, c. 1991.

Christine DeVitt (left), Robert Gaston, and Anne Snyder, 1962, at an Amoco drilling rig. Robert W. Gaston Collection, southwest Collection, Texas Tech University.

Mallet cattle and the "twin windmills," 1962. This site was probably where the first ranch windmill was located. Robert W. Gaston Collection, Southwest Collection, Texas Tech University.

Florence's illness and death had an immediate impact upon the operation of the Mallet Land and Cattle Company. Essentially it meant that the Mallet had to postpone any consideration of dissolving the corporation. With Helen and Christine tied up in California for more than two years with their mother's illness and death, trying to work their way through California's complicated estate tax structure, the sisters had little time or inclination to deal with the complexity of dissolution. It meant also that controlling interest in the Mallet Company passed to two persons instead of three. Helen and Christine inherited equally their mother's stock, giving each of them approximately 26 ½ percent interest in the company. The Johnsons knew that if the two sisters could ever agree on how the Company should be run, their combined 53 percent interest would enable them to do as they pleased.

Moreover, the Johnson side, already weakened by a rift between W. D. and his nephew Lee Johnson, suffered its own setback when W. D. became critically ill in May 1947. Until he was eighty-seven, Johnson had continued to work in his office daily, managing his extensive holdings, which included not only the Mallet, but also three other ranches in the Permian Basin and far West Texas, as well as one in New Mexico and two farms in Missouri. A stroke left him virtually confined to his home, and by July 1947, a friend noted that "he seems to have lost his old interest in coming to the office and handling the business."[2] As Johnson's health continued to fail, the Fidelity Union Bank in Kansas assumed guardianship of his affairs. On April 13, 1951, at the age of ninety, Mr. Johnson died at his home in Kansas City. West Texas had lost another link with its frontier heritage.[3]

Still another death signaled the close of an era. Kansas City attorney David A. Murphy died on July 6, 1946. An old friend of David DeVitt, and longtime Mallet attorney, Murphy had been probably the most stabilizing factor through the Mallet's crisis years of the late 1930s and early 1940s. His correspondence with the DeVitt family reveals his valiant effort to protect its interests. After his death, his son John Murphy assumed the role of company attorney.

A self-made man, Johnson had not only parlayed a store clerk's salary into a fortune, but also assisted dozens of West Texas cattlemen financially for more than fifty years. Survived by his wife, a son, and four daughters, Johnson left to his family a carefully-planned legacy that continues to work for his descendants to this day.

With W. D. Johnson's stroke in 1947 and subsequent death, Lee Johnson of Fort Worth assumed an increasingly larger role in the operations of the Mallet. According to company policy, large purchases required the signature approval of two of the three designated co-managers. With W. D. Johnson incapacitated, only Miss Christine and Lee Johnson could conduct business and sign Mallet checks. Almost immediately, the two were once again at odds on several issues.

Their first disagreement was over the purchase of new bulls to build a new cow herd. Since the end of the war, the Mallet had been restocking with cows, and by June 1947, with more than three hundred cows on the ranch, was ready for additional bulls. Foreman Gradon Swanner, Tom Jones, and Lee Johnson had located twelve prime Hereford bulls near Fort Worth and placed an order for them, but Miss Christine refused to sign the check. A. L. Henderson tried to reason with her, but gave up and fired off a note to Johnson. "We haven't convinced Miss DeVitt we need any bulls," he noted. "Cows should have calves without any Bulls."[4] Henderson then asked Tom Jones to write to Christine "and explain to her" why the ranch needed more bulls. Apparently, Tom's nature lesson was successful as the Mallet purchased twenty-eight new bulls in August 1947, all registered Herefords.

Another dispute dealt with a dividend payment. As he had done in 1941, Lee Johnson once again grew weary of awaiting decisions from Miss Christine. When he had pressed her to approve payment of a large dividend in 1947, Christine wanted to delay it until her mother's estate was closed. The estate settlement dragged on, and by August, Johnson was ready to take action. "I am pleading with you in all seriousness, Miss Christine, to authorize the payment of this dividend," Johnson wrote; "however I want to state that in the event you again ignore my pleadings that such action on your part will force the Johnson *minority* stockholder to take such legal action as will be necessary."[5] To Helen, he complained, "Christine seems to have gained the idea that her judgment . . . is far superior to any and all minority Mallet stockholders. . . . I am demanding at least fifteen hundred Dollars per share to be paid within three weeks."[6] Johnson's threat did not go unheeded. Mindful that Lee had forced the receivership in 1941, Christine finally called Johnson and agreed to a dividend payment, noting sarcastically that the reason for her delay was that "she had no men of brains to seek sound business advice from."

Hard feelings between Miss Christine and Lee Johnson continued into the annual directors meeting held in December 1947, a meeting that had been postponed several times from its originally scheduled January date. For years, Miss DeVitt had wanted the books of the company audited for the period in the 1920s and 1930s when W. D. Johnson had kept them in Kansas City. At the Board's December 1947 meeting, she brought up the issue again, stating that Johnson's books "ought to be audited while Mr. Johnson is living in case there is something we don't understand about it."[7] Lee Johnson took offense to Christine's request. "Regardless of the opinions of those present," he said, "W. D. Johnson is incapacitated at this time. It would be impossible to ask him any questions regarding anything you might bring up."

"Well, I am very sorry to hear that," Miss DeVitt responded, but continued to press the issue by recalling how W. D. Johnson had always insisted that he audit D. M. DeVitt's books. "Mr. Johnson called for the books and audited them to satisfy himself for awhile, but after Mr. Johnson took charge, they weren't audited and weren't called for an audit by a vote at the meeting at all."[8]

Finally, Lee Johnson said sharply, "If you pass that resolution I will instruct that those records be destroyed before you can get them. That is how deeply I resent your resolution." When Christine tried to protest, he continued, "You shoot your best shot and I will shoot mine and I will destroy every damn one of them. I won't let that [audit] take place with W. D. Johnson incapacitated. I not only think it is out of order, I think it is deliberately mean to be brought up."

Somewhat taken aback, Miss Christine offered a vague apology. "I didn't dream I was going to make you angry," she said. "I didn't dream it was a tender point with you, I didn't know that."[9] At that point, the chairman of the meeting was able to steer the conversation to other points, and the issue probably never came up again. Apparently Miss DeVitt's motive in pressing for the audit had more to do with her long-harbored ill feelings toward W. D. Johnson's attitude about her father's bookkeeping than it did with questioning W. D. Johnson's integrity. But the debate ensured that Johnson's records would be lost to historians.

Miss Christine used the meeting also to make her strongest case ever for attaining equal status as a co-manager. Tired of a title in name only, she belabored the point for hours. "I want to know everything that goes on in the business, even a good many small things," she declared, "and I don't want the knowledge to be kept from me. I want to know about it even if my comment isn't asked for. I want to know about it in advance, not after it takes place."[10] Despite the stormy meeting, the directors found themselves closing out their most successful year to date. The Mallet Ranch had 695 producing oil wells by the end of 1947. Although oil production on the Mallet began to level off, oil prices edged steadily upward after the war and by 1947 had topped $2.50 per barrel. The ranch's daily allowable production had reached nearly 18,000 barrels, producing for the year 1947 an oil income approaching two million dollars. Federal taxes for the year amounted, however, to $456,000.

High taxes, coupled with the recurring feud between Miss DeVitt and Lee Johnson, may have prompted Mallet owners to move toward final dissolution of the company. Weary of postponements and argumentative meetings, the directors were primed to accept change. Moreover, rapidly rising oil prices in 1947 and early 1948 drove the company's royalty income upward to $250,000 per month. The corporation would face a tax bill of nearly a million dollars for the year.

Meanwhile, because of Mrs. DeVitt's death, both Christine and Helen were faced with paying a tremendously high California inheritance tax bill as well as federal taxes. Helen alone owed more than $900,000 in taxes in the spring of 1949. As a result, they began to give some thought to selling their stock in the Mallet Land and Cattle Company. Helen's husband Tom Jones took it upon himself to pursue a possible sale of DeVitt interests, perhaps in the best interests of his wife, but also for the commission. In December 1945, he sent from California a secret letter to Neely G. Landrum of Dallas. "Neely, I don't want you to think that this is a sales letter I am writing to you," Tom wrote. "And, it is a most confidential letter for at this time the DeVitt interests are facing the situation of getting as low valuation on their stock as possible, if a settlement has to be made with the government in case they did not sell their stock."[11]

Apparently, nothing developed from Tom's quiet negotiations with Neely, but less than three years later, Tom was still pricing Helen's stock for sale. He continued to believe that the best thing for Helen to do would be to cash in her stock in the Mallet Land and Cattle Company. Because Florence's death forced Helen and Christine to pay nearly a million dollars in inheritance taxes, it became apparent, at least to Tom, that another death in the family would compel the survivor to liquidate just to pay the taxes. Perhaps he believed also that Helen needed just to have lots of cash.

Tom then tried something else. In 1948, he discussed with Lubbock businessman George Etz a proposal that Etz buy Helen's entire interest in the ranch, 266 1/8 shares of the Mallet Land and Cattle Company, for nearly four million dollars, or $1,500 per share.[12] Apparently, this price derived from his estimation that the ranch itself was worth approximately one and a half million dollars, plus royalty income. Tom calculated that with shares totaling 1,000, the value of the ranch in 1948, including minerals, would have been fifteen million dollars. For unknown reasons, the deal never materialized.

Meanwhile, as settlement of inheritance taxes approached, Tom intensified his efforts to raise cash by selling family property other than the ranch. He put on the market DeVitt holdings in Lamb County, city lots in Amherst, and scores of city lots in San Angelo.

The Amherst city lots and two Lamb County farms had been acquired by Mr. DeVitt in 1923 when he was in the city one day closing a cattle deal with the Halsells. Tom had no problem disposing of the farms, but the Amherst lots moved slowly, and several remained unsold for many years. The San Angelo property, which had been in the DeVitt family since the 1890s, was sold to Roscoe Graham of San Angelo in 1949.[13]

Finally, Miss Christine and Helen were able to settle their mother's California estate in late 1948, paying approximately one million dollars in federal and California inheritance taxes.[14] The experience introduced them to a sharp Dallas tax attorney, Wright Matthews, who, with Tom Jones's encouragement, began to encourage the Mallet owners to consider dissolution of the ranch, an idea first offered several years before by David Murphy and J. E. Vickers.

In November 1948, the directors met to listen to Matthews's proposal and tentatively agreed to consider a full or partial dissolution of the company. They hired Matthews to draw up the necessary papers.[15] Within a month, he was ready, and the directors gathered in Kansas City on December 20, 1948, for what would become the final meeting of the Mallet Land and Cattle Company.

With assets totaling more than eleven million dollars, carving up the pie was not going to be an easy matter. How does one divide 53,137.7 acres of land, several oil leases, 703 oil wells, and three million dollars in cash among eighteen stockholders? But Matthews produced a plan, and over three days, the directors slowly hashed out the advantages, disadvantages, and other details of dissolution. The advantages were clear—by doing away with the corporation, the federal corporate income tax of thirty-eight percent would be eliminated. Moreover, each former stockholder would then be able to apply the oil depletion allowance against his or her own personal income. Matthews demonstrated that, because of the tax savings, dissolution would increase Helen's annual income by $220,000, and that she would receive also an after-tax lump sum payment of assets distribution of more than $219,000.[16] He estimated that the overall annual tax savings for all the stockholders would be nearly $800,000. Although each stockholder would have to pay a capital gains tax of twenty-five percent, Matthews reasoned that the money would be recouped in tax savings by each stockholder within three years.

Unlike those of many past meetings, the directors' discussions of the issue were substantive and constructive. As Miss DeVitt reminded the group, "We are undoing in two days what has taken fifty years or more to develop this company to what it is."[17] Most of the discussion focused on the concerns of R. B. Hewitt, longtime trust officer for the Union National Bank of Kansas City, who represented the interests of the W. D. Johnson family. Opposed to the breakup, Hewitt argued that his clients needed the protection that corporate laws offered. When it came time for a vote, the decision was approved by a vote of 80 percent of the shares, with only Hewitt voting his stock against it.

In effect, the dissolution divided the land surface, improvements, and royalty interest of the Mallet Land and Cattle Company into percentages relative to the amount of stock each owner held. For example, both Christine and Helen held 266 and 1/8th shares of Mallet stock. Under the terms of the dissolution, each received 26.6125-percent interest in the surface and royalties. The remaining 46.775 percent was divided among the other stockholders, W. D. Johnson, the W. D. Johnson Trust, William Jewell College, and thirteen descendants of J. Lee Johnson, Sr.

After the vote to dissolve, the Mallet directors still faced the question of how to operate the surface. The Board discussed three possibilities: one would be to create a new corporation that would operate the ranch and farms; another proposed a formal limited partnership arrangement that would be governed by set regulations; still a third option was to operate the surface simply as informal partners.

Already the meeting had taken three days, and Christmas was rapidly approaching. Anxious to get home for the holidays, the directors chose to operate as informal partners. Although the Board recognized that any future action, such as approval of oil leases, would require the approval of all the partners, it probably opted to go with the partnership plan because it was the course of least resistance. Never did they dream that their decision would last for decades.

The meeting was characterized also by a surprisingly congenial relationship between Miss DeVitt and Lee Johnson. Apparently, both of them saw dissolution working to their advantage. For Johnson, it may have promised an end of years of hassling with Christine; for Miss DeVitt, it meant that she had gained considerable control because she knew that any future business deal would require her signature. She had finally gained the control she had wanted since her father's death.

One other question remained: what was to be the name of the new partnership? Wright Matthews, who had orchestrated the dissolution, proposed Mallet Farm and Ranch. But Miss Christine quickly opposed, stating that the Mallet was never intended to be a farm. Thus the directors simply shortened the title to Mallet Ranch, and the Mallet Land and Cattle Company ceased to exist.

After the dissolution meeting had closed late in the afternoon of December 23, 1948, Tom Jones and Wright Matthews discussed their success over dinner. "Thank goodness, we have this road to Kansas City blocked now," Tom expressed during their conversation.[18] Matthews likewise was delighted; not only did he collect a handsome $70,000 fee from the Mallet for accomplishing dissolution, but he also had gained the friendship and confidence of Helen and Tom Jones. "I believe most of your worries are over," Matthews wrote to Helen. "Certainly there will be no more of these very tragic trips to Kansas City."

There were still a few other issues to be resolved. What was to happen to the existing livestock and improvements on the ranch? How was the surface to be operated among the partners? How would the oil companies handle royalty payments? What was to become of the Mallet Land and Cattle Company office employees, especially the company president A. L. Henderson?

The personnel problem was solved within a matter of weeks. A. L. Henderson, who had served the Mallet as president and office manager for four years, suddenly found himself being edged out of his job. By late March, Tom Jones had convinced Christine, Helen, and J. Lee Johnson, Jr. that Mr. Henderson was no longer needed. "As you already know, our business never did run too smoothly,"

Tom noted to Mr. Johnson, "but the time has come now with the setup that we can iron things out to perfection with a little straight thinking."[9] Henderson left the Mallet on May 1, 1949.

To manage the office, the Mallet partners soon found themselves relying heavily on the office secretary, Miss Anne Snyder, who had been hired in June 1948. Anne, who was Tom Jones's niece, was well known in the Lubbock community because her family had been prominent cattle people on the South Plains since the 1880s. Anne brought to the office not only organizational and bookkeeping skills, but also a wealth of patience, a commodity she would soon need in her dealings with Miss DeVitt.

The royalty division was the easiest problem to solve. Because oil companies were accustomed to paying fractions of royalties to multiple parties, it was a simple matter for the Mallet to issue division orders, according each former stockholder a percentage of the royalty income. All of the oil and mineral interests were conveyed directly to the stockholders in proportionate shares according to the amount of stock each held. At the time of dissolution, there were eighteen entities holding interest in Mallet minerals.

Surface ownership and operation was a different story. Under the informal partnership arrangement, the ranchland and cattle held by the former Mallet Land and Cattle Company were owned in the same percentages as those held by the former stockholders, with Helen Jones and Christine DeVitt possessing together the majority interest with 26.6125 percent each. Since there was no stock, nor a formal operating arrangement, there was no such thing as "voting stock." Although the land was divided by the same percentages, (Helen and Christine each held 14,140.35 acres of former Mallet land), the land itself was never subdivided and deeded; that is, each of the eighteen former stockholders held a percentage of the undivided whole.

The one who was most uncomfortable with the new arrangement was R. B. Hewitt, who managed the W. D. Johnson trusts for the Union National Bank in Kansas City. During the dissolution meetings, Hewitt had opposed dissolution; when he had lost, he then insisted that his interests be paid for the cattle and other improvements on the ranch. Moreover, he did not want to operate the farms and ranches under the new informal partnership. As a result, Henderson and Tom Jones began looking for someone to buy the cattle and lease the ranch.

Even before dissolution, Tom Jones had begun searching for someone to lease the entire surface acreage of the ranch. In 1947, he discussed with Tom Coble and J. A. Whittenburg, Jr., of Amarillo the possibility of their leasing the Mallet on a long-term basis. Once dissolution was effected in December 1948, he renewed his search for a lessor. Approaching the Coble interests as facilely as he had Whittenburg's father in 1933, Jones, the experienced real estate man, described the 50,000-acre ranch in very positive terms:

> New wells and windmills have been placed over the ranch at the most advantageous places. The ranch is fenced into twelve pastures, and all are accessible and easy to get over with the exception of some four or five sections in Yoakum County, which are very sandy but which make a splendid winter pasture. Nearly all the country is catclaw and mesquite land with deep soil and a good turf.[20]

Knowing cattlemen's love for rainfall, Tom expertly added, "It has been snowing and raining here steadily for the last ten days. We have had three inches of precipitation during that time, which is the greatest average ever recorded in this area since records have been made. The whole ranch is now muddy, and boggy in places."

In reality, the ranch was an attractive proposition. At dissolution, its twelve pastures contained 49,504 acres (excluding farm land) of grazing land, of which 46,236 acres belonged to the former stockholders and 3,268 acres to the D. M. DeVitt Estate. In addition, the ranch included two sections of leased land, which brought the total of land in grass in a solid block to 50,784 acres. The Mallet farms, which were leased to several Hockley County farmers, comprised an additional five thousand acres.

The ranch also had at its north end private loading pens that had been constructed by Stanolind Oil Company at no cost to the Mallet owners. Branding pens were located in the center of League 53 of

Scurry and Oldham counties school lands. Additional loading and branding pens were situated at the ranch headquarters.

Despite Tom's best efforts to sell or lease the ranch, he kept running into one obstacle, Miss Christine DeVitt. Opposed to the wholesale leasing of the ranch, she had her own ideas and wanted to take her time about deciding what to do.

Thus, the new partnership faced its first challenge—what to do about the Mallet company cattle. All the partners knew that the new arrangement would have its challenges, but none ever guessed that the new partnership would be successful. Indeed, when D. M. DeVitt and F. W. Flato created the Mallet corporation in 1903, probably neither ever dreamed that their hastily created company would last forty-five years. Similarly, in 1948, none of the creators of the new Mallet partnership ever would have believed that their new partnership would last yet another forty-five years.

NOTES

1. Ed Byars to A. L. Henderson, September 4, 1946.

2. J. W. Rice to A. L. Henderson, July 19, 1947.

3. *Kansas City Times*, April 14, 1951, p. 3.

4. A. L. Henderson to J. Lee Johnson, on letter addressed to J. M. North, Jr., July 19, 1947.

5. J. Lee Johnson, Jr., to Christine DeVitt, August 30, 1947.

6. J. Lee Johnson, Jr., to Helen Jones, September 2, 1947.

7. Transcript, Discussion Had Off the Record, December 18, 1947, p. 4.

8. *Ibid.*, pp. 5-6.

9. *Ibid.*, p. 8.

10. Minutes of Special Meeting of the Board of Directors, Mallet Land and Cattle Company, December 17-18, 1947, p. 44, in possession of John Sones.

11. Tom Jones to Neely Landrum, December 26, 1945, Tom Jones Correspondence, Mallet Records.

12. Contract, May 7, 1948, Tom Jones Correspondence, Mallet Records.

13. Christine DeVitt to Sarah Fuller, 11-17-49.

14. Tom Jones to Forrest Monroe, November 11, 1948.

15. John Murphy to A. L. Henderson, November 29, 1948, John Murphy file.

16. Wright Matthews to Helen Jones, December 8. 1948.

17. Transcripts of Special Meeting of the Board of Directors' Meeting, p. 27, December 17-18, 1947.

18. Wright Matthews to Helen Jones, December 23, 1949.

19. Tom Jones to J. Lee Johnson, Jr., March 30, 1949, Stockholder File.

20. Tom Jones to Tom Coble, January 18, 1949.

CHAPTER NINE

A Woman in a Man's World

[Christine] was a woman in a man's
world, and she had figured out a
mode of operation that worked, that
got her respect.
David Fayman, November 12, 1992.

FOR nearly a year after the dissolution of the company, the former Mallet directors continued to wrestle with the question as to what to do about the use and management of the surface property. Most of the stockholders wanted to discontinue cattle ranching entirely and proposed that the ranch's cattle and personal property, such as horses and automobiles, be sold, and that the entire ranch be leased on a long-term basis. Christine was opposed and wanted to give full consideration to taking the ranch herself. No immediate decision could be made; however, the other stockholders insisted that a decision be made within two months of the December 1948 meeting.

Tom Jones tried to persuade Christine to ranch only a small part of the ranch. In February 1949, he suggested to her that she run cattle only on the southeast portion of the ranch, which included five sections that she and Helen owned exclusively and eight sections that she could lease from the other Mallet owners. "You will have a ranch of 9960.8 acres," Tom noted. "This will run some four to five hundred cattle year in and year out and would be plenty big for you to operate and look after. . . . You would need only one good pickup truck, a few horses, and have you a real ranching outfit of your own and have complete control of your own land."[1]

Tom recognized Christine's love for the land and ranching: "There is no doubt in my mind that you seem to have tied yourself to Lubbock, and if you continue to stay there and want to operate a ranching proposition, this is big enough, and ideal for any one person to operate." Yet Christine just could not decide what she wanted to do in such a hurry. Thus, the other owners decided to proceed with selling off the ranch's cattle. Apparently, the decision was made primarily by Tom Jones and J. Lee Johnson, Jr., but with Christine's and Helen's approval.

The Mallet cattle, comprising 414 cows, 152 steers, 307 calves, 134 two-year-old heifers, and 27 registered bulls, sold for $125,020 to Reed and Snyder of Clayton, New Mexico. Branded with either the famous Mallet brand or a "2 bar," the cattle were cleared from the ranch in February 1949, an action that, in effect, finally closed the business of the Mallet Land and Cattle Company. For fifty-four years, Mallet cattle had grazed the pastures along Sulphur Draw, but use of the Mallet brand had come to an end. Recognizing, however, the historical importance of the brand, Tom Jones made note in the contract that the partners were not selling its famous brand.[2]

Meanwhile, Tom continued to hold out for the possibility of leasing the entire ranch long-term. Hoping to get at least fifty cents per acre, Tom looked to his old friends in the Ellwood Estate as the best possibility. Finding no taker, he then negotiated a lease with Kansas cattleman A. E. Smith. Earlier, Smith had leased grass on the north end of the ranch for $1.50 per month per head, and in so doing, established a precedent of leasing by the head, a policy that Mallet partners still follow to this day. Smith's deal with the Mallet was to place 1800 head on the ranch for $1.50 per month per head. The lease was, however, for only one year.

By September 1949, Christine finally made up her mind and proposed to the other Mallet owners that they lease the entire ranch to her, provided that she could sublease all or portions of the ranch as she saw fit. At the same time, she offered Helen the opportunity to join with her in leasing the entire ranch, but Helen declined. The other owners seemed agreeable and apparently asked for the going rate of fifty cents per acre. Christine was unwilling to pay that much, because, as she sharply expressed to R. B. Hewitt, "on account of some 726 oil wells . . ., 75 to 100 oil houses, and possibly 200 miles of roads . . ., my best offer to you for immediate acceptance is 35 cents per acre."[3] In addition, she tendered to the other owners an offer of five thousand dollars for the ranch's stock of fourteen horses, five milk cows, four automobiles and trucks, and related equipment and supplies.

Tom Jones then intervened trying to persuade the other partners to accept Miss DeVitt's offer: "We spent considerable time and effort in getting this contract drawn where it would be fair to all properties concerned," he wrote to J. Lee Johnson, Jr. "Miss DeVitt is taking on quite a responsibility, but I feel like as she lives right here and takes lots of interest in this property, it will be in good hands, or I would have tried my very best to prevent her from making this lease."[4]

Perhaps out of deference to Miss DeVitt, or perhaps not wanting to stretch out negotiations any longer, all of the owners agreed to her terms, and by mid-November, the seventeen partners had signed a lease that gave Christine access to 46,000 acres of Mallet land for $16,000 per year rental. The lease obligated Christine "to take good care" of the improvements on the ranch and at her expense to make "ordinary repairs to fences and windmills" caused by "natural wear and tear only; however, as to any repairs necessary to the windmills, tanks, water troughs, fences, and improvements caused by fire, storm, the elements, or any cause other than natural wear and tear, the necessary repairs or replacements shall be made by Lessors and Lessee and paid for pro rata." In turn, Christine obligated herself to "not overgraze said land but will graze it in a reasonable manner."[5] The three-year lease proved to be an effective agreement remaining in force as written, with an annual rental of $16,000, for more than twenty years.

Helen, more than anyone, was pleased with Christine's decision to become a full-time rancher. "I hope this new lease will make her live longer, don't you?" she wrote to Tom.[6] Christine had a lot to worry with, however. Her ranch, which also included more than three thousand acres of her and Helen's property, comprised a 50,000-acre tract divided into twelve pastures. Included were a total of thirty-five windmills on the ranches and small farms, and 125 miles of outside and cross fences.

For a number of years, Christine subleased portions of the ranch to other cattlemen. Of her tenants, however, she required that they bring only Herefords to the ranch, apparently because her father was a "Hereford" man and always had been. A. E. Smith, who had leased the north end of the ranch in April 1949, remained for four years. But a severe drought, which began in 1951, had taken its toll, and by the summer of 1953, Christine had decided to let the ranch rest for a year.[7] Smith's lease expired October 31, 1953.

Nine inches of rain in the spring of 1954 brightened the picture for Christine's Mallet. She undertook a number of improvements, including replacing seven-and-a-half miles of outside fencing along the east side of the ranch in Hockley County at her own expense. In July 1954, she leased pastures on the south end of the ranch, which had been vacant for four years, to longtime Texas cattleman Ewing Halsell for $2.50 per month per head. Halsell, an old friend of Christine's father, owned a ranch near Venita, Oklahoma, as well as the famous Mashed O in the sand hills of Lamb County and another big ranch along the border in South Texas. Because of the drought, Halsell desperately needed grass and jumped at the chance to lease the Mallet. Beginning in late July, he moved 512 cows and twenty-four bulls to the ranch. In late August 1954, he negotiated with Christine and Tom Jones to take the north end for an annual rental of $30,000, to host 1,200 to 1,500 head of cattle, depending on rainfall.[8] As the drought continued into 1955, Halsell moved his cows from the south end of the Mallet back to their home on the Mashed O Ranch at Springlake, but extended his lease of the north end for another year. Because the drought compelled Halsell to purchase supplemental feed, the lease was reduced from $30,000 to $20,000. In January 1957, Halsell proposed to lease the entire ranch for $25,000, but Christine declined. He continued to lease the north end and portions of the south end for $2.00 per month per head.

Halsell cattle remained on the Mallet for seventeen more years. Ewing Halsell died in December 1965,[9] but his family continued to run cattle on the Mallet Ranch until 1973 when they sold the Mashed O Ranch. When the Halsell lease expired in February 1974, it ended a twenty-year relationship between the two historic families of West Texas ranching.

Christine continued to run cattle herself. For years, she had always kept a few cows on the south end of the ranch, on land that belonged to her and Helen. Since the 1930s, she had spent considerable time at the ranch headquarters. She enjoyed ranch life and the families that lived there. Among the Mallet owners, she was the only one that took a personal interest in the handful of families that had worked on the ranch since the early 1900s.

For much of its early history, the Mallet had only three foremen. Pat Ross, who had worked on the ranch since its beginning, became its foreman in the early 1900s and remained until about 1924. Then, George Green, who had also worked on the ranch since 1903, became foreman, remaining until 1936. To replace him, the Mallet promoted Wadkie Fowler, who had worked on the ranch since 1930.[10]

Fowler and his wife, Ola Mae, became great friends with Christine when she began extensive visits to the ranch after her father's death in 1934. Ola Mae's son, Howard Fowler, who was a small boy when Christine first began coming to the ranch, remembered her love for Coca-Colas, which she would bring to the ranch by the case. She would always give to Howard her empty bottles, so that he could collect the deposits for spending money.[11] Christine would stay for days, riding horseback occasionally in jodhpurs and boots, but more often sitting up until midnight visiting with foreman Wadkie Fowler. Christine loved to talk.

Ola Mae Fowler remembered well one incident in the late 1930s when Dorothy, Christine's niece, paid a rare visit to the ranch with

Christine: "Christine bought some candy and that night all the cowboys and us were at the huge table eating and Christine said, 'The candy almost locked my jaws.' Dorothy said, 'That would be fine for a while.' We all had a big laugh over that."

The Fowlers left the Mallet in April 1943, apparently dismissed by W. D. Johnson, but they remained fast friends with Miss Christine and for many years rented outlying blocks of DeVitt-owned pasture. Charlie Middleton, a friend of Tom Jones, served as foreman of the ranch until 1945. Then Gradon Swanner held the position from 1945 until October 1949, when he apparently had a falling out with Tom Jones and quit abruptly. "He is a good cow hand," Tom evaluated, "but has no executive ability or managing ability whatsoever, and it is difficult, most difficult, to tell him what needs to be done from time to time . . . and [he] will not adjust himself to the change we made when we dissolved the corporation."[12]

After Gradon Swanner departed, Christine was in control of the hiring and firing on the ranch. She chose Gradon Swanner's brother, J. A. Swanner, to serve as foreman, but fired him in late 1951, apparently because he had hired some work done at a price Christine considered exorbitant: "I have tried to make you the best boss you ever had," she wrote to Swanner, "but you have outreached me in your outrageous charges for the services you have employed on my ranch."[13] In a related letter, she warned a Sundown windmill man, "Don't you ever do any more work on the Mallet Ranch again as long as you live without seeing me first."[14] Christine then employed Mallet hand Alfred Dennis as foreman.

Alfred Dennis remained foreman through September 1957. Throughout 1956 and into 1957, he had asked repeatedly that Christine allow him to repair some of the ranch windmills as well as the old house at the Vat Camp residence. Finally exasperated with Christine's reluctance to make some improvements, he resigned. "I was told by *many*, when I took this job, that I could never fulfill it. Being a challenge, I accepted it. Now, to that *many* I shall have to apologize for doubting their word," he wrote to Christine. "Our relationship has proved incompatible to the point where you or I one will have to move. Being of more flexible material than you, I will say I'm to move."[15] Dennis, however, just did not understand Miss Christine's proclivity for procrastination. Had he waited her out, he would have gotten what he wanted. Two years after his resignation, the Vat camp house was replaced with a brand new "ready-built" house at a cost of more than seven thousand dollars.

Joe W. Kirksey, a hand in Dennis's employ, became the new foreman. He remained until early 1964. Then in April 1964, John Sones became the new, and the last, foreman for the Mallet. His tenure was to last more than twenty years.

Even though she had taken a risk by leasing the entire ranch in 1949, Christine was usually able to recover her expenses through subleasing. Making a profit from the ranch was never her motive, simply because oil royalties provided her with a handsome income. During 1950, her first full year to have the whole ranch, the ranch showed an income of nearly $36,000 and expenses totaling $32,000, leaving a $4,000 net profit for her first venture as "the boss."

In 1951, Christine's ranch profits jumped to $16,000, but then began to decline as the drought of the fifties began to worsen. In 1953, her loss totaled $14,000 for the year, and $2,000 for 1954. Throughout the remainder of the 1950s, the ranch managed to show slight profits, only because Christine kept her average annual operating expenses below $25,000.

In December 1960, Christine decided to build her own herd and purchased forty-seven registered cows and three bulls to add to the other few cows she owned. It would be three years, however, before she would make any significant sale of cattle: in 1964, she realized an income of $39,000, including $12,000 from cattle sales; however, expenses had jumped to nearly $38,000. Her herd size had grown to 229 head.

After hiring John Sones as foreman in 1964, Christine allowed him to begin upgrading the Mallet's cattle operation. By the end of 1968, the ranch was able to show a profit of $26,000, its greatest since 1949, owing primarily to sales of the ranch's own cattle. Profits sagged for the remainder of the decade, and by the end of 1971, the ranch lost almost $13,000.

As ranch manager, Christine became well-known for her tight purse strings. As she became older, she also became more reluctant to spend money on improvements. She refused to allow a telephone to be placed at the headquarters. When she would visit the ranch, she would collect discarded shingle nails and other items, and then insist that the foreman use them in repairs. During the early 1950s, Christine complained particularly about the foreman's rising electric bill. For one month in the spring of 1953, the bill for the ranch house and pump totaled $14.22, more than twice the rate for electric bills in town. "[Christine] says this entirely too much," Tom noted to the Mallet foreman Mr. Dennis and asked him to have the utility company check his meter.[16]

The electric bill remained high. Finally in February 1954, Tom Jones fired off a letter to Southwestern Public Service Company complaining about the ranch's high electric bill. The company promptly responded, had the ranch's meter checked, and found it to be running slow rather than fast. "It is our opinion that Mr. Dennis had a chicken brooder on this [meter] during December and January or some other appliance with a high wattage rating," the manager of the utility explained.[17] Whether Miss DeVitt made Dennis remove the brooder is unknown.

While Christine worked hard to prove herself a capable ranch manager, she also made for herself a reputation that became legendary in Lubbock, Levelland, and on the South Plains. People with whom she had personal and business dealings described her with a variety of terms, including obstinate, tough, caring, clever, spend-thrift, generous, smart, savvy, and just plain ornery. And though at one time or another, she perhaps exhibited all of these characteristics, there was a consistency to Christine that only her closest friends and family knew.

Her proclivity for procrastination was her most obvious trait. She took pride in the fact that she weighed every decision carefully; however, the practice annoyed those who had to depend upon her for decisions. She was also in constant trouble with those she owed, but most who dealt with her knew that if she were approached in the right way, the matter could be resolved easily. On one occasion, while Christine was in California tending to her mother's estate, Lubbock attorney Durward Mahon attempted to collect from Christine some money she owed him. When she did not respond to his statements, he sent her a kind letter expressing his sympathy for the loss of Christine's mother and a gentle reminder about the bill.

In her beautiful handwriting, one of the few letters in her own hand to be found among her papers, Christine apologized to Mr. Mahon for her tardiness: "I am unable to locate your letter and statement at present, and therefore am enclosing a signed check made out to you on the Lubbock National Bank and am asking you to please fill out with the correct amount and cash."[18] It was one of the few times, if not the only time, that Christine would ever hand a blank check to her attorney.

DeVitt family members also learned to be as persuasive as possible when trying to get Christine to act. In a 1947 note, in which he attempted to get Christine to return to Lubbock from California to take care of her income tax, Tom Jones wrote, "Now I don't want to see you get scalped, but if you don't come on home and tend to your own income tax business, they're going to scalp you like they did General Custer."[19] Three years later, he was not quite as gentle in a long letter in which he outlined a number of matters to which she needed to attend:

> From time to time when I see you I try to impress upon you the importance of attending to some of these smaller things that come up here in the office. . . . I hope you will pay some attention to this and get these small things behind you. In conclusion, you had better begin to make your plans on the ranch and not wait till the last minute to make them.[20]

There is no evidence that Christine paid him any attention.

Tom Jones believed that Christine was intimidated by anything presented to her in writing. "It is the same old, old story that when anything comes before her in writing she has a mental explosion and blows her top completely," Tom complained to Helen in May 1952. "Anything in writing to her is just the same as flashing a red flag in the face of a wild bull, and it just can't be helped."

Christine's disposition to put things off never changed. Those who needed her cooperation found tact to be the only useful tool. Her longtime attorney, George McCleskey, had to use his best diplomatic skills in getting Christine to take care of her business. One letter is exemplary:

> I hope that in the immediate future you can find time for us to finalize the agreement with . . . Mapco. . . . I recognize that you indicated that you would call me when you were ready to proceed and I do not want to be presumptuous by writing this letter, but it does seem to me that this is a matter that should be taken care of now. I hope it will be convenient for you to let me hear from you promptly.[21]

Others who were not close to Miss DeVitt soon found a formidable foe if they wanted something from her. Because the DeVitt Estate owned a great deal of property in and around Levelland, its citizens found themselves on several occasions at Christine's door with hat in hand in an effort to buy or lease DeVitt property. For example, in 1947, officials of the Levelland Country Club petitioned Christine to sell or lease their organization a tract of land that bordered the city of Levelland for a golf course. After several months of correspondence and meetings, Christine apparently granted their request, but not without expressing her specific reason: she ordered the preparation of an affidavit of affirmation, but concluded it with this statement: "I am not signing this for any loving affection that I may have for the citizens of Hockley County, but I am signing this because I think it is the most prudent thing to do."[22]

Christine was also hard on car salesmen. In August 1950, with the outbreak of the Korean War, which caused her to fear automobile and tire shortages, Christine decided she should get a new car. Tom offered to help her find something suitable and accompanied her to Lubbock's Buick dealer, the Scoggin-Dickey Buick Co. Christine would not have just any car. She told the dealer that she would not have one that had been driven down from Detroit, nor would she have one that had been brought into Lubbock by truck. Fortunately, the dealer's cars had been brought to Lubbock by rail, but, according to Tom, "the battle of words [had] just started:" "To make a long story short," he wrote to Helen, "it was all day into the night that exhausted me entirely. Just picking things to pieces, the car, the Dealer, and everything, although she was wild for the car right along. . . . It was indeed a hard day, but she seems to thrive on it."[23]

While many have attempted to explain Christine's business personality, perhaps no one came closer to understanding her motivations than did David Fayman, a University of Kansas science professor and grandson of W. D. Johnson, who had a number of dealings with her after his grandfather's death. "I think she was just trying to be her old man," he said.

> She was a woman in a man's world, and she had figured out a mode of operation that worked, that got her respect. . . . She had become as difficult as any man to deal with, if not more so. The way she got what she wanted was to never give in. She had found out at an earlier time that that worked. That was not always accompanied by great intelligence [and] she was not giving in on the right stuff; she was not giving in on anything."[24]

By 1950, Christine's reputation for being tough was well known, and oilmen soon found themselves trying to work around her. On one occasion, Lubbock oilman George P. Livermore prepared a lease for signatures, but failed to include a clause about a promised bonus. Apparently, Mr. Livermore thought the lease was fair and asked Tom to get it signed, and offered him $1,500 if he could get Christine's signature. Tom was appalled at the suggestion: "$1,500.00 doesn't mean very much to me. Now if you will take this lease. . . [and] when you get [Christine] to sign this lease that you think is fair and equitable to you, I pledge myself hereby to pay you $1,500.00 out of my own pocket."[25]

George Livermore was not the only oilman who had trouble getting Christine's signature. An agent for the Amoco Petroleum Company, Robert Gaston, found himself negotiating with Christine for many years as he attempted to secure easements and other benefits for his company. He courted Christine at every opportunity, buying her presents and carrying out her every wish. "I got to know Christine so well that I could kiss her on the lips," Gaston recalled, "but for 25 years of working with her, the only thing I got her to sign was a note giving me permission to hunt quail on the ranch!"[26] On the letter she handed to Gaston in November 1971, she noted, in her own hand, that he could bring one guest to hunt game "and also a covey of quail for me."[27]

Another party who found out firsthand how difficult Miss DeVitt could be was the manager of Lubbock's Hilton Hotel, A. G. Griffith, and the hotel's attorney George Dupree. For fourteen years, Miss Christine DeVitt lived in the Hilton Hotel in downtown Lubbock. Even though she had purchased a house in the city, she enjoyed the ambiance of hotel life. The hotel management found it difficult to live with Miss Christine for various reasons. She was often late on her rent and would fill a room with empty coke bottles that she would not return to the store. In 1947, the Hilton raised her rent, but still she would not move from the hotel to her new house. Finally, in 1948, when she was sixty-two years old, the hotel gave her notice that she was to vacate. Miss DeVitt refused, and the hotel brought suit to have her evicted.

The resulting hearing in a Lubbock Justice of the Peace Court became a battle of wits between George Dupree and Miss Christine. A court transcript provides pages of such conversation as follows:

Q: Your name is Miss Christine DeVitt?

A: Yes sir, that is right, it is.

Q: How old are you, Miss DeVitt?

A: I am legal age.

Q: Well, I asked you how old you were?

A: I don't know that I know for sure.

Q: You don't. Well, do you know of anybody in the country that does, so that we can get the information from some source?

A: Must I tell how old I am?

Q: I am asking you to tell this jury how old you are.

A: Well, I am a little over sixty. That is the best I can answer.

Q: Do you have a residence here in Lubbock?

A: No sir, I don't have a residence here in Lubbock.

Q: What?

A: No, I don't have a residence in Lubbock.

At this point, Christine's attorney John Lee Smith objected, noting that the case had nothing to do with whether she owned a house in Lubbock. But Dupree persisted, knowing that she had recently bought a house.

Q: You do own a home out here in Lubbock, don't you?

A: No sir.

Q: Where is that located?

A: What?

Q: You have in your name out here—

A: What is it you are asking me?

Q: I am asking you about your home out here in Lubbock that you have in your name out here?

A: What is a home, Mr. Dupree, may I ask you?

Q: I am asking you whether or not you don't have a home out here in Lubbock?

A: No sir, I don't.

Q: Do you own a residence out there?

A: No sir, I don't.

Q: You don't own a residence anywhere in Lubbock?

A: I will have to have a definition of a residence, Mr. Dupree. What do you mean by a "residence?"

By this time, attorney Dupree was obviously exasperated. "I mean four walls and a yard, just on an ordinary lot like we live [in] out in this country," he sharply replied. But Miss DeVitt remained calm. "I thought a 'residence' meant some place that people were living in," she stated matter of factly.

The judge, weary of the interchange, intervened. "Just answer the question," he charged. Dupree repeated it again. "You do own a residence out here in Lubbock, don't you?" Miss DeVitt calmly replied, "No sir."

"What?" retorted Dupree again, who had just about lost all his patience. Perhaps noting his discomfort, Christine finally gave in to the question, and stated, "I own a house, but I don't own a residence."[28] Despite her semantic skills and her ability to frustrate the prosecuting attorney, Christine lost the case and was evicted from the hotel.[29]

Christine then moved into her house at 3217-21st Street in Lubbock, which was located next door to Tom and Helen Jones's home. Four years later, in June 1952, she bought another house nearby, located at 3223-21st, perhaps with the intention of moving into it. By the end of 1953, she was staying primarily in Tom and Helen's house at 3219-21st. Each move was prompted in part by her need to make more room for her cats, which by 1952 numbered in the hundreds.

Christine's special affection for cats was not lost upon the citizens of Lubbock. Shortly after moving to her house from the Hilton Hotel, she began to adopt every stray cat that came her way. Soon, their care became an obsession with her. "I have just talked to Miss DeVitt," her secretary Anne Snyder reported to Tom and Helen by letter in January, 1950, "and she is trying to get off to the ranch this afternoon, but she has a new crop of cats, which are slowing her up."[30] By May 1950, even her gentle sister Helen was complaining about them. "Why don't all those cats die, and give [Christine] her freedom again?" Helen wrote to Tom.

When she needed more room for her cats, Christine simply bought the house next door so that the cats would have shelter. But the problem became more serious when, in May 1952, Christine fell on one of her litter boxes and injured her leg. "I told her to go and see a doctor immediately," Tom dutifully reported to Helen, "which of course she did not do." Tom finally persuaded her to let him take her to a doctor, who in turn ordered her to stay off the leg and to return in three days, "which, of course," Tom noted, "she did not do."[31]

Instead, Christine tried treating the injury herself, but with no results. Finally, Tom brought another doctor to see her, one who promptly told her to stay off the leg and "get rid of the cats." But Christine would have none of it. Two days after the doctor was there, she removed the bandages, called druggists to ask their advice, and then began treating the wound with her own remedies.

Christine's injury and recovery never dampened her love for cats, but Helen never gave up her insistence that Christine get rid of them. In 1954, the terrible spring sandstorms that smothered the South Plains brought Helen some hope. "My, my," she noted to Tom, "how can anybody take care of cats in such times as this? Isn't it a shame that this weather does not kill them off? It doesn't seem to do anything good for any of us. But what are we going to do, deeds won't avail, 'hot air' is our only weapon against cats."[32]

Christine never apologized to anyone about her love for cats. She once told her ranch foreman John Sones that it stemmed from a terrible accident when she left home for a lengthy period and mistakenly locked a mother cat and kittens in the garage where they starved. When she discovered them, she vowed that she would make up the mistake by caring for cats that came her way.[33] To the mayor of Levelland, R. C. Vaughn, she explained that she liked cats because they were much more loyal and better friends to her than any humans.[34] To longtime friend Nelda Thompson, she explained that she really did not like cats all that much, but because everyone knew that she did like cats, people would simply drop off their unwanted kittens in her neighborhood, and that she had no choice but to take care of them![35]

Cats were indeed family to Christine. Although her sister Helen loved her, Christine and Helen were not close. As the baby of the family, Helen had received the bulk of her parents' attention, which in turn may have caused some strife between the two. In 1956, Helen noted in a letter to her secretary that she "had always felt some guilt that Papa and Mama paid more attention to my birthday than to Christine's." As they grew up, Helen became pretty and petite while Christine was large-boned and frequently overweight. With an age difference of fourteen years, Helen was more like a daughter to Christine than a sister, but when they were together, they fussed constantly with each other, much as children would do.[36]

As a result, Helen, who had no patience with Christine's procrastination and cats, generally kept her distance. But she worried about Christine's being alone and continuing to drive a car. Once she wrote Tom, instructing him not to "let Christine drive any this weekend, and ask her for me not to make the mistake of being mad at the other drivers while she is at the wheel, like she was when I was with her."[37] She worried also, perhaps needlessly, that people were taking advantage of her aging sister. After learning the price that a local department store charged Christine for a new suit, Helen noted to Tom of the seeming tone of Christine's situation: "My!" she noted, "They sure do charge Christine a big price for her suits and things in Lubbock, don't they. I guess she had a time getting fit, too. 'Oil, taxes, and cats,' you say, is the theme of conversation just now."[38] Yet Christine was hardly Helen's only worry. Constantly concerned with her own health and that of her daughter, Dorothy, Helen had many adjustments to make after the death of her mother. It would take years and the loss of her husband before she could finally settle into a life of her own.

NOTES

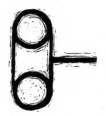

1. Tom Jones to Christine DeVitt, February, 1949, Mallet Records. Unless otherwise noted, all subsequent quotations are from the Records of the Mallet Ranch.

2. Contract with Reed and Snyder, February 19, 1949. Tom Jones to J. Lee Johnson, Jr., February 19, 1949.

3. Christine DeVitt to R. B. Hewitt, September 13, 1949.

4. Tom Jones to J. Lee Johnson, Jr., November 1, 1949.

5. Grazing lease, November 1, 1949.

6. Helen Jones to Tom Jones, November 7, 1949. Unless otherwise noted, all Helen Jones's correspondence is taken from the Helen Jones Correspondence File, Mallet Records.

7. Tom Jones to A. E. Smith, August 5, 1953.

8. Tom Jones had asked for $35,000, but Mr. Halsell talked him down to $30,000 for the period August 1954 through October 1955. Ewing Halsell to Tom Jones, July 25, August 7, 1954.

9. William Curry Holden, *A Ranching Saga: The Lives of William Electious Halsell and Ewing Halsell*, Vol. II (San Antonio: Trinity University Press, 1976), p. 537.

10. Christine DeVitt to Iona Sones, handwritten notes, 1980, in possession of John Sones.

11. Howard Fowler to David Murrah and Lauren Liljistrand, June 18, 1992, tape-recorded interview; Ola Mae Fowler, "The Real Western Frontier: I Was There," typescript, December 1977, in possession of Howard Fowler, Levelland, Texas.

12. Tom Jones to J. Lee Johnson, Jr., October 7, 1949.

13. Christine DeVitt to J. A. Swanner, November 5, 1951.

14. Christine DeVitt to Mike Dominquez, November 5, 1951.

15. Alfred Dennis to Christine DeVitt, June 4, 1957.

16. Tom Jones to Alfred Dennis, July 3, 1953.

17. Harold Roberts to Mallet Ranch, February 10, 1954.

18. Christine DeVitt to Durward Mahon, February 22, 1946.

19. Tom Jones to Christine DeVitt, February 10, 1947.

20. Tom Jones to Christine DeVitt, March 20, 1950.

21. George W. McCleskey to Christine DeVitt, June 5, 1972.

22. "To Whom it May Concern," Levelland Country Club File, undated.

23. Tom Jones to Helen Jones, August 3, 1950.

24. David Fayman to David Murrah, tape-recorded telephone interview, November 12, 1992.

25. Tom Jones to George P. Livermore, November 7, 1950.

26. Robert Gaston to David Murrah and Lauren Liljistrand, tape-recorded interview, September 15, 1992.

27. Christine DeVitt to John Sones, November 15, 1971, Robert Gaston Papers, Southwest Collection, Texas Tech University.

28. Question and Answer Transcript, Justice Court, Lubbock County, No. 894A, *Hilton Hotel Corporation vs. Christine DeVitt*, June 30, 1948, Mallet Records.

29. *Hilton Hotel Corporation vs. Christine DeVitt*, Case No. 5555, Court Records, Lubbock County, Texas.

30. Anne Snyder to Helen and Tom Jones, January 27, 1952.

31. Tom Jones to Helen Jones, June 20, 19 1952.

32. Helen Jones to Tom Jones, March 15, 1954.

33. John Sones to David Murrah, tape-recorded interview, October 2, 1992.

34. R. C. Vaughn to David Murrah, September 14, 1992.

35. Nelda Thompson to David Murrah, tape-recorded interview, November 19, 1992.

36. *Ibid.*

37. Helen Jones to Tom Jones, May 25, 1952.

38. Helen Jones to Tom Jones, undated, c. 1950.

CHAPTER TEN

Oil, Taxes, and Cats

'Oil, taxes, and cats'... is the theme
of conversation just now.
Helen Jones, quoting Tom Jones to
Tom Jones, c. January 1952.

A LTHOUGH Christine DeVitt moved to
Lubbock to stay immediately after the
death of D. M. DeVitt in 1934, it took many
years before her sister Helen could find comfort and happi-ness on
the South Plains.

After her father's death, Helen remained in Los Angeles to be
close to her mother, but she soon sold the little house her father had
bought for her and obtained another on Laurel Avenue, where she
lived until 1939. Her daughter, Dorothy Gail, nicknamed "Teddy"
after a famous radio soap opera character of that day, was thirteen
years old and suffered frequent asthma attacks. Unhappy with both
the climate in the city and the schooling that Dorothy was receiving,
Helen moved to the higher altitude of Altadena. She returned to
her Laurel Avenue house in summer 1942.[1]

With Dorothy finally located in a satisfactory school in Arcadia,
Helen found time for her own interests and soon gave in to a mar-

riage proposal from an old friend of the family, Tom Jones. Because he had been a friend of her father's, Helen had probably known Tom since her mid-twenties, through her summertime visits to the ranch. In one of Helen's few extant letters from that period, she tells her father of an automobile driving lesson given by a willing teacher named Tom on their way to the Zavala Ranch headquarters in April 1925, a few months before she met her first husband, Bill Secrest:

> Tom was ready to drive me to the Havens, where he intended to go anyhow to see Claude Havens about something and from there to go by East Camp. After starting the Hup [Hupmobile] and going a short distance, Tom gave me the wheel and I drove all the way to the Zavala. He is a good teacher, he trusts me to do the harder things.[2]

Helen's marriage to Bill Secrest in September 1925 turned Tom Jones's attention in later years to her older sister Miss Christine, particularly after Christine moved to Lubbock in 1934, but the extent of the romance between Tom and Christine is unknown. When Helen invited Tom to California in spring 1942 to advise her about how to vote her Mallet stock, Tom quickly became interested in the petite, and soon to be rich, Helen DeVitt Secrest. A few months later, on November 9, 1942, Helen married Tom in a ceremony in Austin. She was nearly forty-three, and he was fifty. According to local folklore, Christine became quite angry with her sister for stealing Tom whom she considered to be her boyfriend. If there was a rift between Helen and Christine over Tom, however, it did not last long. After the wedding, Tom and Helen took up residence in the Hilton Hotel in downtown Lubbock, where Christine also lived. Then, in 1943, Helen and Tom purchased a house at 3219 21st in Lubbock. Helen retained her California home to have a base when she would visit her mother. After her mother's death in 1945, Helen sold both the house in Dallas, which she had purchased for her mother, as well as the Laurel Avenue home in Los Angeles.

It was not long, however, before Tom and Helen's marriage became a long-distance relationship. While assisting Christine in the settlement of their mother's estate, Helen found herself virtually confined to Los Angeles, except for a two-month trip to a Battle Creek, Michigan, sanitarium during July and August 1947. Estate matters dragged into 1948. Meanwhile, her daughter Dorothy had enrolled in the University of California at Berkeley, and soon Helen found herself dividing much of her time between Los Angeles and Berkeley. Finally, in late 1948, Helen's and Christine's attorneys were able to bring to closure both the federal and California matters pertaining to their mother's estate.

Owing to Dorothy's continuing battle with asthma, Helen returned to Berkeley in July 1949 and stayed through the fall. By that time, Dorothy had begun to assert her own independence, and her health began to improve. Helen's had not, and she returned to Texas to join Tom, and the two of them went to Florida, where Helen entered the Battle Creek Sanitarium near Miami.

Over the next several years, Helen spent much of her time seeking better health. Always health conscious, she had been plagued from childhood by an enlarged colon that caused digestive problems. Over the course of her life, she sought the help and counsel of one doctor after another and experimented with various diets and remedies. As early as her mid-twenties, her proclivity for being sick had become somewhat of a family amusement as revealed in an explanation she wrote to her father in 1924 when she sent to him her doctor's bill, knowing full well that he would grimace at the thought of seeing his money go "into the no doubt heavy coffers of a sleek-skinned Doc":

> I decided to await the coming of the Grand Bill before mailing it . . . and I have waited until this afternoon to add a few lines of condolence for the unhappy loss you are soon to sustain. Fifty dollars is indeed a sad lot to have to spend 'all in one place.' . . . Of course there are various other points of view which one might take on such a matter, and let me hope that some one of them will justify in a measure at least, the expenditure of these fifty round and shining dollars. I for my part believe that I have received a good many valuable suggestions.[3]

In 1950, twenty-six years later, Helen was still seeking valuable suggestions, some from doctors who were more than willing to accommodate Helen by prescribing extensive, and expensive, treatments. From the Miami Battle Creek Sanitarium, her doctor reported to Tom in late March that "I wish that [Helen] would remain here for another month, but she is anxious to go on home. . . . Helen should not worry too much about the details of housekeeping or any other details for that matter. She should devote her time and energy to getting strong and well."[4]

Throughout the years that followed, Helen continued her search for the right doctor and rarely stayed under the care of one for more than a few months. One of her friends in California wrote to Tom, "The doctor here felt [Helen] should be under one Dr. for six months care. I'm just anxious she should be well and happy. As you said, she's a grand woman. I've not known too many women as intelligent as Helen."[5]

Helen also frequently changed her residency while searching for the right care. In July 1950, she decided to try Dallas again, with the hope that Dorothy would join her there. She purchased a house on Calumet Street and busied herself with decorating and furnishing it. But her condition was little improved. "I have had a hundred [bad days]," she wrote Tom in August, who was himself convalescing after surgery, "and would strongly advise and urge you for your own sake to stay with Lubbock and the house for a very considerable time to come." She added this note, which would have certainly displeased the Dallas Chamber of Commerce, "Choose some other alternative to Dallas, for it is too dull and useless here, and will only make you suffer."[6]

By mid-August, Helen was ready to leave Dallas and return home to Lubbock. Instead, because Dorothy's health was still unsettled, she returned in September to Berkeley, where she remained for much of the fall and winter, as well as most of 1951. During the year, she made frequent trips to Santa Barbara and soon fell in love with the charm and climate of the city's beautiful Bay area. In August Tom visited California and was likewise impressed: "Houses are not as high out here as they are in Lubbock," he wrote to Anne Snyder, the Mallet Ranch secretary, "but we cannot buy one here. It is out of the question."[7]

Buying another house in California was not a question of money, but of residence. Since the early 1940s, the State of California had been pressing Helen to pay California state income tax and had tried to do the same to Tom, even though he had never lived in the state. After Helen and Tom were married, they established legal residence in Lubbock in 1943. California was not satisfied and pursued its tax collecting for many years.

Because California intended to prove that Helen was a legal resident of the Golden State, Helen found herself living in hotels during her California stays. Renting a house was out of the question because Helen had an aversion to renting. Yet the charm of Santa Barbara proved to be too great, and soon she was house-hunting. In October 1951, she found what she wanted and persuaded Christine to buy the house in her own name.[8] Christine obliged her sister, and Helen reimbursed her for the purchase.

Santa Barbara became Helen's home for the winter and spring, and well into the summer 1952. Tom came to visit in March 1952 and liked what he saw: "The flowers are the most beautiful I have ever seen, gorgeous in size and beauty," Tom wrote back to the office in Lubbock. Because television was still a novelty to West Texans, he also noted what Santa Barbara had to offer through the airwaves:

> Our Television is wonderful and I can readily see why people quit the picture shows and stay home to watch the Television. We have seen Amos and Andy . . . and Edgar Bergen and Chas. [Charlie McCarthy]. There are three or four channels that are good here in Santa Barbara and it is especially good after about 8:30 PM.[9]

Meanwhile Christine decided that she wanted to see the house she had bought for Helen and made plans to travel to Santa Barbara. But she backed out of her plan to go during Christmas 1951 and refused to put the house on the market or refund Helen's money. Finally, in July 1952, a big earthquake rocked southern California; Christine decided that she did not want to look at the house after all, and asked Tom to place it on the market for her. Tom pointedly reminded Christine that she had not yet paid Helen for the house, and he would not attempt to sell it until she did. "After some delay, she finally agreed to this, and I made arrangements for the sale," Tom later reported to his wife's attorney.[10] Because the State of California continued to press the issue of residency, Helen apparently decided that she should give up the Santa Barbara venture and returned to Texas in mid-August 1952.

After a very short stay in Lubbock, Helen set her sights on Colorado. Although she stayed only a few months in Colorado Springs in 1952, she soon found the higher climate much to her liking. In December she wrote Tom that among other things about Colorado, she enjoyed the scenic beauty, prime rib beef, buttermilk, Colorado Springs' beautiful Broadmoor Hotel, driving, shopping, and the city's Fine Arts Center, which she described as "being far beyond one's expectation."[11]

Helen was not through looking around. After a short stay in Colorado, she took residence in Phoenix at a resort hotel where Tom later joined her for a winter stay. Although Phoenix and the central Arizona valley offered a dry, hospitable winter climate, Helen's letters to Tom lacked the glowing descriptions of her previous sojourns in other places, and, as the weather became warmer, she was ready to move on. In July 1953, she moved to San Antonio, perhaps hoping to find the charm of Santa Barbara deep in the heart of Texas.

As she had done in Berkeley, Dallas, and Santa Barbara, Helen found a house to buy in San Antonio and plunged into decorating it. She also pursued clinical treatment for her digestive problems, and in May of 1954, about the time she got her new house ready, she entered the Ochsner Clinic in New Orleans.

Because Texas was suffering under terrible drought conditions in 1954, when Helen returned from New Orleans, she decided to abandon San Antonio and try Colorado once again. Her secretary Anne Snyder accompanied her in August on a vacation to Estes Park and Denver. Helen soon tired of Colorado's capital city. "I am tired of being here," she wrote to Tom in late August, "in fact, tired of being in Denver, I guess, but very much wishing I could take 3 or 4 things in Denver and transplant these to Colorado Springs . . . or perhaps Fort Worth."[12]

Obviously, Helen did not mind the physical separation from her husband. She enjoyed being alone, exploring new towns and discovering new restaurants and enclaves of culture. She also enjoyed letter writing and, when she was away, carried on frequent extensive correspondence with Tom. Only rarely did she express any loneliness: "It is one of those times that I wish I were in a small town somewhere," she wrote from Santa Barbara in May of 1952, "or in some live-wire residence district in any town with you and Christine (provided, of course, that all of Christine's cats were damned except about two and maybe one kitten or so to spare). . . . This is no way to say three short words, like 'I am homesick.'"[13]

In the same paragraph, she took her own argument full circle in a rare and poetic expression of her philosophy of life:

> But I guess that either some grandchildren would have to be playing around outside, . . . or somebody we had known a long time. . . . Besides, if one wants neighbors and grandchildren, you have to pay the price in the first place. And even then, you must be ready for any change and keep in the swim. I would rather be just sitting here writing nonsense to you than to be perfunctorily getting in the car and going to look up and down for a picture show, and getting out afterwards to look among the silent empty cars for ours.

Helen's correspondence also reveals her philosophy about the ideal place to live. She enjoyed much of every city in which she lived, but in one letter she noted that Fort Worth seemed attractive because it "must have a feeling of being near-but not-too-near Lubbock."[14]

Helen's aversion to Lubbock was probably rooted in several areas. The continuing drought had turned the South Plains into a new Dust Bowl, which disagreed with Helen's health and temperament. And although she loved her older sister dearly, she had little patience with Christine's cats or her procrastination. She found life to be much more comfortable and rewarding away from the South Plains, especially during the winter and spring.

Helen was probably also uncomfortable with Tom's love for alcohol. A heavy drinker at times, Tom had a reputation well known among the Lubbock business community. When he was seen on Lubbock streets driving his own car, observers knew that he was sober, but if he were being chauffeured by his driver/bodyguard, most people surmised he had been on a binge. Helen tolerated Tom's indulgence, but occasionally chided him in her letters. On one occasion, a business deal appeared to be threatened by Tom's absence from duty, presumably because of his drinking. When Helen mentioned the problem to Tom in a letter, he quickly retorted, "Never in my life was I out of pocket where I could not be contacted for any emergency, drunk or sober."[15]

In her extensive correspondence with Tom, Helen only mentioned the subject one other time. In November 1950, when it appeared that the United States, already embroiled in the Korean War, might also be on the brink of all-out war with Mainland China or the Soviet Union, Helen closed a long letter to Tom with this cryptic note: "By the way, slam the door on that alcohol and keep cool— these are precarious days."[16] There is no evidence that he heeded her advice.

In October 1954, after her short stay in Denver, Helen returned to Colorado Springs, where she had spent a portion of the previous winter. Helen soon found a lovely house and purchased it, this time in Dorothy's name.[17]

Helen dearly loved Colorado Springs, and she soon persuaded Tom and Dorothy to join her there for Christmas 1954. "We had a wonderful Christmas," Tom reported to Anne Snyder by letter. "Everything just right. Dorothy is enjoying her visit here, she is jolly and full of fun. Helen looks better than I have seen her in a long time."[18]

Unfortunately, it was Tom's last letter back to the office. During the early morning of January 12, 1955, shortly after his return to Lubbock, Tom was stricken with a heart attack and died at his home; he was sixty-two.

Helen must have been devastated. Despite Tom's shortcomings, she had depended upon him heavily for advice and leadership. His interest in the ranch and devotion to her and Christine reminded her of her father. In one of her letters to Tom, she recalled fondly some memories of days past: "It is only yesterday after all that he [Papa] was here, and the most wonderful rendezvous that one could have, would be with him, on a fine day, sitting out in a car at some chosen spot in Hockley County. I would like to be in the car listening to you [two] talk."[19]

Tom Jones had few other admirers. Some observers who were close to the family or the Mallet business saw Tom as one trying to take advantage of his wife's business interests. Indeed, a review of his personal and business correspondence reveal a questionable loyalty. On the one hand, in 1950, he castigated Lubbock oilman George P. Livermore who had offered Tom $1,500 to get a Mallet lease closed. "You might have thought that would be a big appeal," Tom wrote, "but I want to impress up on you . . . that the welfare and prosperity of the Mallet owners come first and last with me, and your $1,500 overture means absolutely nothing." Moreover, forgetting that he had more than once tried to sell the ranch for a handsome commission, he hastened to demonstrate to Livermore that his motive was sincere:

> When I came up here in 1943 and saw the laxity and the weakness and the trouble that this company was in, and after I had married my wife, I said to myself that the welfare of this company from there on out had assumed the character of a religion with me in the guidance of my thoughts, and the prosperity of this company came first with me, and I never have in my life tried to make a dollar out of it.[20]

On the other hand, less than two years later, Tom readily accepted a $3,000 commission from another Lubbock oilman Blair Cherry for securing Helen's and Christine's signatures on a lease for Mallet property.[21]

One example of Tom Jones's questionable loyalty about Helen's business and legal affairs had to do with her fight with California over her residency there. For years, the State of California had attempted to collect income tax from Helen for the years 1942 through 1951, even though Helen had owned a Lubbock homestead, paid poll taxes in Texas, and possessed a Texas driver's license since 1943. To represent her, Helen turned to Dallas attorney Wright Matthews, who had handled the settlement of her mother's California estate as well as the dissolution of the Mallet corporation. After months of gathering data, Matthews proposed that Helen try to settle with California. In late 1952, the State seriously considered a proposed settlement from Matthews, which would have required Helen to pay taxes for 1949-1951, but not for 1943 through 1948.[22] Matthews encouraged Helen to settle, but Tom would not hear of it, believing that the law was on his and Helen's side. Moreover, he questioned Matthews's legal fees for the attorney's investigation into California law. Subsequently, Tom told Matthews to have the California authorities communicate with Tom directly and in essence dismissed the attorney:

> Since they [the State of California] are still writing about it, I would suggest that they pick out one of their smartest men and send him here to Lubbock, Texas, and let him make his investigation here of everything we have submitted to them, and I will go all the way to help him get any and all facts which would reveal to him and all the authorities in that state the true and final status of our residence, our home, and our business, both past, present, and future.[23]

Four years later, in 1957, the State of California ordered the California-based Honolulu Oil Corporation, which held a lease on the Mallet Ranch, to garnish Helen's royalty income to make payments to the State until California's claim was satisfied. After Helen gave the oil company assurances that she would hold the company harmless if sued, the company rejected the State's demand.[24] Subsequently, the State of California sued Helen in 1959, demanding payment of $327,000 in taxes for the period 1941 through 1960.

Helen then retained Lubbock attorney Jim Milam to handle the matter. Milam arranged a settlement with the State, much along the lines that Wright Matthews had proposed seven years previously, but that Tom Jones had rejected. The out-of-court settlement amounted to $73,000, the delay of several years costing Helen considerably more than it would have if Matthews had been allowed to settle the case.[25]

The settlement only encouraged Tom's perennial interest in finding a way for Helen to accumulate cash. Having entertained the possibility of selling her Mallet stock outright in the 1940s, Tom led Helen in another direction, in 1950, seeking partial sale of her royalty interest in the Mallet Ranch. Shortly after Helen settled her inheritance taxes in 1949, Tom began to pursue the idea of Helen's selling all or part of her royalties. Past experience with inheritance taxes had demonstrated that Helen or her estate would need ready cash should she, Dorothy, or Christine die prematurely. With the outbreak of the Korean War in 1950, oil prices began to increase, and many investors were attracted to oil properties such as the Mallet.

Adding to the pressure was Wright Matthews, who had become a good friend of Tom's. Matthews encouraged Helen to consider selling all or part of her royalties and place the money in tax-free bonds, so that she could realize tax-free income without loss of principal. Assuming that Helen could sell her royalties for five million dollars, Matthews pointed out to her through Tom that she could realize an annual tax-free income of $112,500, and still have her principal of $4,500,000 intact ($5,000,000 less $500,000 capital gains tax). He noted that it would take twenty-seven years, owing to the tax difference, for the royalty assets to match the sale/bond assets, presuming that taxes and oil prices remained the same. Although he projected that her annual income would be slightly higher if she retained her royalties, the concept of selling offered her freedom from the uncertain future of the oil industry. "In other words," he noted, "if a portion of the royalties is sold we are shifting the burden of a likely change in price, change in days of production, and a possible reduction in rate of depletion."

His final recommendation was that she take half the chance by selling half of the royalties. "In this way, Mrs. Jones will be assuring herself and Dorothy an amount of tax-free money each year more than sufficient to take care of not only the necessities, but also of the luxuries of life."[26]

The deal sounded good and Helen consented. After securing Helen's approval, Wright Matthews approached Southern Methodist University with the deal, offering to sell one-half of Helen's royalty under Mallet lands for $500 per acre, or $2,500,000.[27] In January 1950, Southern Methodist University countered with an offer of $1,750,000. Matthews, in turn, pressed Tom to sell for that price. "I am somewhat skeptical as to whether we should offer this property to anyone else. . . . We are not going to get as much as $1,750,000 from any other purchaser."[28]

Tom thought the offer was too low because of the potential recovery of the field. Reasoning like the real estate man he was, he noted:

> Just last May, seven of the major companies completed the thirty million dollar gasoline plant in the middle of the Mallet ranch. In addition to this expenditure for the plant, they spent some ten million dollars for gathering lines to service this plant. If the life of this field was only for six to eight to ten years, they surely spilled the beans when they built this big plant, and I don't remember of them ever spilling the beans much when they get on top of production.[29]

Perhaps out of a fear of rising taxes under the Truman Administration, and/or perhaps out of a genuine concern for the welfare of Southern Methodist University, Helen, or more likely, Tom decided to sell half of Helen's royalty to the Dallas school, for $1,500,000—$250,000 less than their initial offer. Apparently, the Southern Methodist University negotiators had appealed to Tom's philanthropic interest, his Methodist upbringing, and his fear of the rise of Communism. Tom later admitted to Helen that he "had sold it for a half million . . . or maybe a million dollars less than it was worth, but the only bulwark and the only defense we have against Communism is Christian education."[30]

Meanwhile, word of the potential sale to Southern Methodist University traveled quickly, and soon interests representing Notre

Dame University were inquiring about buying other Mallet mineral interests. Former Mallet president J. E. Vickers reported to Tom that inquiries had been made through Lubbock banker C. E. Maedgen. Tom quickly replied to Mr. Vickers that Helen was not interested, then fired off a note to Anne Snyder, instructing her not to let "Christine discuss any of Helen's business. She has no right to do so. Tell her to concentrate all her business on her cats."[31]

Helen would have been wise to follow through on Matthews's advice to invest the $1,500,000 in tax-free bonds, but Tom apparently recommended to Helen that she hold onto some cash. More than two and a half years after the deal closed, Helen had invested only $500,000 of the funds in treasury bonds. The remainder remained in checking or savings accounts in Lubbock, Dallas, and San Antonio.

Still, Helen worried about her finances and was constantly admonishing Dorothy to be careful how she spent money. Occasionally, Tom had to point out to Helen that her income was more than sufficient for her needs, and in one 1952 letter, noted to her that her income, primarily from royalties, was more than $400 per day, "and is available to spend if you choose."[32] He was pleased to know that, by the end of 1953, he had built her available cash and securities to nearly two million dollars.

Unfortunately for Southern Methodist University, the school held the royalty it had purchased for only nine years, then sold it in 1959 to the Tokay Oil Company of New Mexico, perhaps for $1,700,000.[33] That company immediately mortgaged its holdings to the Republic National Bank of Dallas. Two years later, the bank conveyed half of the Mallet royalty interest to the Pan American Oil Company for an undisclosed amount.

Apparently, the big winner in Helen's royalty sale was Pan American, which subsequently became Amoco Production Company in 1971. The company knew very well the value of the Mallet oil reserves, and because it was about to embark on major secondary recovery efforts in the Slaughter Field, Amoco found it very much to its advantage to have acquired the royalty interest. Of course, neither Tom nor Helen could have foreseen the future and would have never dreamed that oil would rise as high as thirty dollars per barrel.

Shortly after Helen's sale of her interest to Southern Methodist University, Wright Matthews pursued a similar arrangement for Christine. "Would she be willing to sell one-half of her royalty for $1,500,000 in cash retaining say three-fourths of the deep rights?" Matthews inquired of Tom Jones in June 1951. Christine, as usual, put off making a decision, and a month later, Matthews sadly noted to Tom, "I doubt whether Miss Christine will ever make up her mind about this."[34] Once again, Christine's procrastination saved her a fortune.

Although Tom Jones's death may have solved some of Helen's fiscal problems, she had others to face. Her sister Christine turned seventy the year that Tom died and would soon need more attention; her daughter Dorothy, still living in California, was very reluctant to move back to Texas. Moreover, Helen's personal fortune was growing, and she knew that she needed to make some decisions about what to do with her money. Finally, Helen knew that she needed to find herself a permanent home, perhaps a place that would tie together all her loose ends.

After Tom Jones's death in January 1955, Helen remained in Colorado Springs through the spring, but soon found herself on the road again. Because business required her to be in Lubbock, she returned to the Hub City from Colorado Springs—by way of Dallas. "I really don't have to go to [Dallas]," she confessed to Anne Snyder, "It's just that I'd like to ride the Fort Worth & Denver [train] to Dallas, get some meals there at the Baker [hotel] . . . and take plane to Lubbock."[35] Her business completed in Lubbock, she then went to visit Dorothy in San Francisco, where she found her daughter quite ill. She remained a good while before returning to Colorado Springs.

Without Tom's encouragement and prodding, Helen found it difficult to do business, especially when it involved Christine. For example, she found herself with an extra car after his death, and began in the summer of 1955 long-distance discussions with Christine about selling it. For months, she and her secretary Anne Snyder went over and over the car question by letter, debating whether Anne should drive the car out to San Francisco, where either Dorothy would use it or Helen could sell it. Miss Christine vetoed the idea because she felt it too dangerous for a woman to drive the car that far. Finally, after nearly a year of worry, Christine sold the car to former ranch foreman Wadkie Fowler who paid for it with money she had given him. Whether Christine ever reimbursed Helen for the car is unknown.

Although she had sold her house there, Helen remained in Colorado Springs for most of 1956, but by the spring of 1957, she was ready to move again. She returned to Lubbock in April and remained through late June. After securing an appointment at the Mayo Clinic in Rochester, Minnesota, she struck out again on her quest to discover why she was always in ill health. For nearly six months, Helen remained in Rochester consulting with one doctor after another. Shortly after arriving at the Clinic, a psychiatrist interviewed Helen and gently tried to tell her that her problem was more emotional than physical. In one of her letters to Christine, Helen unknowingly confessed to probably what was the root of her problem: "A profound emotional depression had fixated itself upon my intestinal tract, [the doctor] said," Helen explained to Christine.[36] In other words, the doctor politely told Helen that she was making herself sick just by worrying that she was sick.

Although her visit to the Mayo Clinic did not end her health worries, it did build within her a new confidence to concentrate on other matters, particularly her daughter Dorothy. Unlike Helen, Dorothy had spent most of her life in California. In 1942, when her mother married Tom Jones, Dorothy was enrolled in the Flintridge-Anoakia High School for Girls at Arcadia, California, where she graduated in June 1945.[37] Dorothy then planned to enter Mills College at Oakland, but her asthma prevented her admittance. She then decided to attend the University of California at Berkeley, her mother's alma mater, and moved there for the fall term of 1945.

The cold San Francisco climate aggravated Dorothy's asthma, which in turn made school difficult for her. In fall 1947, her mother purchased for her a house at 2251 Virginia Street in Berkeley. Later, Helen tried to persuade Dorothy to abandon the cold climate and come to Texas. Helen enlisted help from her own attorney Wright

Matthews, who lived in Dallas. Matthews played host to Dorothy in December 1950 when she passed through Dallas to see her Secrest aunts in Hamilton, and while Dorothy visited in his home, he tried to persuade her to move to Texas. Matthews reported to Helen that he had tried to impress Dorothy about "the necessity of coming here to Texas to learn something about the interest she will some day inherit." But it did not work, he said. "In my judgment," he told Helen, "the arguments I put before her were not sufficiently strong for her to want to come to Texas."[38]

It would be twenty-five years before Dorothy would change her mind. After the University of California where she majored in romance languages, Dorothy enrolled in nearby San Francisco State, attracted to its courses in psychology. Meanwhile, as most parents, Dorothy's mother worried continually about her daughter's health and well being. Helen could not understand why her daughter would not write her more often. Once, Helen telegraphed her husband Tom Jones, instructing him to "hold the bank's letter for Dorothy; I am simply desperate to find some means to get her to write regularly."[39]

Like any mother, Helen worried about what Dorothy was doing with her money. When Dorothy decided finally to furnish her San Francisco apartment, Helen reported to Tom that she thought Dorothy's taste was a bit lavish for her otherwise humble apartment in San Francisco: "It is all the sort of thing you might expect a young and wealthy girl to buy for her new home on getting married," Helen noted. "It seems strange for her to buy it just for herself in that makeshift apartment, with some kind of an old ugly heater located in the living room. It is furniture that belongs in a beautiful apartment, if such an apartment there be, in a beautiful place."[40]

To her mother's chagrin, Dorothy began to develop a fondness for music other than classical. "I am learning to enjoy popular music to an extent I never dreamed possible," she noted to her mother in March of 1954. "It's like growing in the most incredible way." But she added apologetically, "Not that I don't listen to the Italian Hour."[41]

Dorothy's revolt from her mother's taste in music also coincided with the development of her own financial independence. The sale of her Berkeley house, coupled with income from a lifetime trust established for her by her mother in November 1953, enabled Dorothy to pursue her own interests.[42]

Dorothy also found work as a statistical clerk at a veterans' hospital in San Francisco, but her interest in the growing field of folk music attracted her to other places. "I was drawn into the folk music scene," Dorothy fondly recalled. "I still have lovely memories of that time and a great love for folk music."[43] By 1955, she was ready to follow the developing folk music culture across the country, first to New York City, then to Boston, Chicago, Madison, and then, attracted by flamenco music, to Havana, Cuba.

By 1959, however, Dorothy was ready to settle down and moved to Woodstock, New York, a popular artist colony. The Empire State became home for Dorothy for the next fifteen years. In 1961, at age thirty-four, she married Holley Cantine, Jr., a free-lance writer. Noted primarily for his translation of the Russian history, *The Unknown Revolution* from French to English, Cantine would subsequently get short stories published in *The Saturday Evening Post* and other publications.

While Dorothy pursued the folk music scene in the late 1950s, Helen did the best she could to keep up with her. After spending much of 1958 and part of 1959 in San Francisco trying to improve Dorothy's health, Helen did not want to give up after Dorothy moved to the East Coast. When Dorothy moved to Woodstock late in 1959, Helen stayed for awhile in nearby New York City. For most of 1960, Helen remained on the East Coast, moving about from New York to Cambridge, Massachusetts, to Washington, D.C., and then to Kingston, New York, near Woodstock. She also bought for herself a small house in Bearsville, a village that adjoined Woodstock. Until Dorothy's marriage in 1961, Helen alternated temporary residences between Lubbock, where she had also bought a new house, and New York. After Dorothy had wed, Helen began to spend much more of her time in Lubbock, and by 1965, had begun to feel comfortable with the Hub City as home.

Living in Lubbock also meant living near Christine, and although Christine was getting older, she had not particularly mellowed. Still very much in charge of the Mallet Ranch, Christine also dominated most decisions related to oil development on the ranch. Christine would soon face a formidable challenge from the family interests of her old nemesis, W. D. Johnson, and the attention it would demand would at least keep her from worrying about her sister Helen.

NOTES

1. Helen Jones to Wright Matthews, July 16, 1952, California Income Tax File, Helen Jones Papers, Mallet Records.
2. Helen DeVitt [Jones] to D. M. DeVitt, April 25, 1925, Family Correspondence, Mallet Records.
3. Helen DeVitt to D. M. DeVitt, April 24, 1924, Family Correspondence, Mallet Records.
4. Dr. Estella G. Norman to TJ, March 28, 1950, Mallet Records.
5. Barbara Zadorkin to Tom Jones, June 4, 1951.
6. Helen Jones to Tom Jones, August 1, 1950, Helen Jones Correspondence, Mallet Records. Unless otherwise noted, all correspondence by Helen Jones is from this file.
7. Tom Jones to Anne Snyder, August 13, 1951, Tom Jones Correspondence, Mallet Records. Unless otherwise noted, all correspondence by Tom Jones is from this file.
8. Helen Jones to Tom Jones, October 19, 1951.
9. Tom Jones to Anne Snyder, March 16, 1952.
10. Tom Jones to Wright Matthews, October 24, 1952.
11. Helen Jones to Tom Jones, December 1, 1952.
12. Helen Jones to Tom Jones, August 26, 1954.
13. Helen Jones to Tom Jones, May 9, 1952.
14. *Ibid.*
15. Tom Jones to Helen Jones, March 11, 1949.
16. Tom Jones to Helen Jones, November 3, 1950.
17. Helen Jones to Tom Jones, November 10, 1954.
18. Tom Jones to Anne Snyder, December 27, 1954.
19. Helen Jones to Tom Jones, January 16, 1952.
20. Tom Jones to George P. Livermore, November 7, 1950.
21. Blair Cherry to Tom Jones, May 20, 1952.

22. State of California to Wright Matthews, November 12, 1952.

23. Tom Jones to Wright Matthews, January 8, 1953.

24. Honolulu Oil Corp. to Helen Jones, November 12, 1957.

25. James Milam to Helen Jones, March 8, 1960.

26. Wright Matthews to Tom Jones, October 25, 1949.

27. Wright Matthews to Tom Jones, December 27, 1949.

28. Wright Matthews to Tom Jones, January 6, 1950.

29. Tom Jones to Wright Matthews, January 25, 1950.

30. Tom Jones to Helen Jones, December 8, 1950.

31. Tom Jones to Anne Snyder, February 9, 1950.

32. Tom Jones to Helen Jones, September 12, 1952.

33. Southern Methodist University Royalty Sale File, Mallet Records. This figure is based on Tokay's transfer of the royalty to Republic National Bank of Dallas.

34. Wright Matthews to Tom Jones, June 20, July 3, 1951.

35. Helen Jones to Anne Snyder, July 3, 1955.

36. Helen Jones to Christine DeVitt, July 17, 1957.

37. Helen Jones Affidavit, California Income Tax File, Mallet Records; Dorothy Secrest to David Murrah, personal interview, November 6, 1992.

38. Wright Matthews to Helen Jones, December 20, 1950, California Income Tax File.

39. Helen Jones to Tom Jones, March 13, 1953.

40. Helen Jones to Tom Jones, August 28, 1953.

41. Dorothy Secrest to Helen Jones, March 1954.

42. Trust instrument, November 13, 1953, Mallet Records.

43. Dorothy Secrest to David Murrah, personal interview, November 6, 1992.

CHAPTER ELEVEN

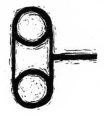

The Prodigal Son Has Returned

*During this period to your great
credit you became the resident keeper
of the key, the son who stayed at home,
the church of the middle ages, you kept
the faith. . . . We now stand at
February 2nd, 1974, as the prodigal
son who has returned . . . but will not
be allowed to speak, contribute, or
even assert what he feels are injustices
that have beset him during his
absence.*
John Archer to Christine DeVitt,
February 2, 1974.

ALTHOUGH Christine DeVitt had taken over
the surface operation of the Mallet Ranch in
1949, her lease did not include the five
thousand acres of Mallet farm land. That operation remained under
the control of all the Mallet owners in an informal partnership,
which in turn had retained Tom Jones as farm manager after dissolution of the corporation was effected in 1948.

After the company had been forced to reclaim much of the land it had sold to farmers in the 1920s, the Mallet Ranch found itself in the farming business. Those lands that lay outside the perimeter of the main Mallet pastures remained farm land, and by the mid-1930s included twelve farms comprising two thousand acres. Mallet rents were structured along traditional practices, with the owner receiving one-fourth of cotton crops and one-third of feed grains. The farmer furnished the seed, labor, and expense of harvesting the crop. Farm income to the Mallet averaged about $23,000 annually in the early 1940s.[1]

J. A. Stroud of Levelland served as farm manager from the late 1920s until 1944, when he was dismissed and replaced by Helen's new husband Tom Jones over the protest of W. D. Johnson.[2] Jones soon persuaded the Mallet owners to put an additional three thousand acres into cultivation. Although the project required extensive grubbing of mesquite roots from the soil, the land was ready for cultivation by spring 1946. "I am sure there never has been eight labors of land on the South Plains of Texas," Jones wrote to Mallet farmer Floyd Hunt, "that has had as much money spent on them to get them in first class farming shape."[3] Initially, because of declining farm prices after World War II, returns from the farms sagged. On 5,481 acres, sixteen Mallet farmers produced crop rents for the year 1946 of $18,289. Income climbed steadily, however, over the next few years as rainfall and prices increased. By the end of 1949, the farms had produced for the Mallet owners $56,000 in rents and averaged a return of $9.75 per acre, probably the highest income ever from the farms.[4]

The 1949 harvest also saw, for the first time, some Mallet farmers using mechanical harvesters instead of migrant labor to gather the cotton crop. Mechanical harvesters, or strippers, had been under development on the South Plains since the 1930s, and by 1948, more than two thousand machines were in use in the region. Strippers accounted for the harvest of 40 percent of the 1949 crop, and, within a few years, hand harvesting would disappear from the South Plains.[5]

But the weather turned dry in the spring of 1950, beginning one of the longest droughts in the history of the South Plains. "We have had no rain in this country for the 1st six or seven months," Tom Jones reported to J. Lee Johnson, Jr. "Right now, the prospects look bad for the 50-51 crop season. The farmers are chiseling their land which means they are cutting the soil one inch to two inches to keep the top soil from blowing."[6]

After the good harvest of the previous year, the harvest in the fall of 1950 proved to be one of the worst ever for the Mallet, with only $19,000 in rent receipts, averaging a return of only $3.29 per acre to the owners. Although some late winter moisture in 1951 improved the 1951-52 harvest significantly, prosperity was short-lived. Farm receipts for the 1951-52 season, which totaled $68,000, or $11.60 per acre, were more than double those for the 1952-53 season.

The worst was yet to come. The 1953-54 season produced less than $6,000 in rents, a return of only $1.02 per acre. Of the Mallet's thirteen tenant farmers, only five showed any return, and one of those farmers, Tom Price, produced half of the Mallet's income because he had put a small irrigation well on his farm. Price had installed the small well on his rented 110 acres in 1951, but because the Mallet owners were reluctant to invest in irrigation, he had to promise that he would bear all related expenses. In his 1951 first season with the well, he produced a return for the owners of $23.02 per acre, exactly double of that of the dry land farmers. The following year, his average return was $24.02 per acre, compared to only $5.12 for the other tenants.

Price's success with irrigation should have been enough incentive for the Mallet partners to consider making major investment in ground water development, but it was not to be. Irrigation on the South Plains from the underground Ogallala aquifer had been demonstrated to be practical in the early 1900s, but it was not until the development of high-speed turbine pumps in the mid-1930s that it became economically feasible. By the mid 1940s, both Lubbock and Hale counties had a large number of irrigated acres, and with the onslaught of the drought of the 1950s, irrigation spread rapidly throughout the region.[7] The irrigation boom in turn boosted the rapid growth of Lubbock and other trade centers of the region.

But Mallet farm manager Tom Jones made no effort to encourage the owners to introduce irrigation. The Mallet tenants continued to struggle with the continuing drought through the mid-fifties. As a result, the Mallet's farm income remained depressed, with a return of $6.29 per acre for 1954, and only $3.38 for 1955.

Tom's death in January 1955 ended his thirty-year influence on the operation of the Mallet interests. As a result, Miss Christine DeVitt assumed the responsibility of finding a suitable replacement, and, uncharacteristically, completed her work by April, only four months after Tom's death.

On April 16, 1955, she reported to J. Lee Johnson, Jr., that she had selected Lee F. York, farm loan manager of Lubbock's First National Bank, to be the new farm manager.[8] Johnson quickly agreed. "Lee York is an excellent choice for this farm managership and I want to congratulate you on being successful in securing the services of such a well qualified man," he noted in response.[9]

York brought to the Mallet nearly twenty years of experience in farm management. A graduate of Texas Tech University, he had served as manager of the Lubbock Production Credit Association office before moving to the bank in 1952. In typical fashion, Miss Christine struck a hard bargain with York: "Since looking after the farms does not require a man's full time," she noted, "I believe Mr. York can do the work required while he continues at the Bank. However, he expects to give the necessary attention to [the farms]. . . [and] is willing to do this for ten percent of the rents." Tom Jones had received 15 percent.

York encouraged Mallet tenants to consider irrigating, but Miss DeVitt apparently was still reluctant to make major investments. In May 1955, Tom Price had a second well drilled on his farm at a cost of $1,761.55 for the hole and casing; he persuaded the Mallet owners to pay $1,000 toward the project, although he paid for the pump and engine himself. The well drew from water-bearing sands only 150 feet deep and produced 560 gallons per minute from a six-inch pipe, an average well by South Plains standards.

Tom Price's additional well, combined with increased rainfall, helped to boost Mallet rents in 1956 by more than 300 percent over the previous year, but without wholesale conversion to irrigation, the farms averaged only $60,000 in rental returns over the next four years. Furthermore, the price for the South Plains short-staple cotton began to fall as competition increased from foreign markets able to deliver long-staple cotton to textile manufacturers. With the end of the drought in the late 1950s, overall production jumped dramatically, driving cotton prices down even more.

Thanks in part to good rains and federal government subsidies, Mallet farmers had their best year ever in 1961 and paid nearly $106,000 in rent, an average return of $17.85 per acre for the owners. Yet, only three of the fifteen Mallet farmers, W. E. Carr, Billy Joe Oliver, and Tom Price, were irrigating their crops.

The early 1960s returned average yields, thanks to adequate rainfall, but drought returned in 1964, reducing Mallet rent income to $34,000, of which half came from government subsidies. Without additional irrigated acreage, the Mallet farms were to gain little over the next few years. Owing to rising costs and a changing economy, the smaller dry-land farmers either retired or were forced to quit. By 1972, the Mallet had only ten tenants, down from fifteen a decade before. Of the 5,915 acres in cultivation, two of the tenants were handling one-third of the acreage.

By the end of the 1960s, much of the South Plains had introduced irrigation, stimulated by the development of hybrid grain sorghum as an alternative cash crop to cotton. Despite the irrigation boom, the Mallet remained largely a dry-land operation. In 1972, only seven hundred of its nearly six thousand acres had any irrigation.

The Mallet's farming situation finally attracted the attention of some of the minority partners, particularly those who were descendants of W. D. Johnson. For nearly thirty years, the Kansas City Johnsons had little to say about the management of their Mallet interests. After W. D. Johnson's death in 1951, the two trustees of his estate, as well as W. D. Johnson, Jr., all of whom were Texas cattlemen, were content to let the Johnson family draw the handsome oil royalties and took little interest in the surface operations of the Mallet Ranch and farms.

In 1971, Johnson's twenty-year trust expired, but most of his heirs chose to reestablish or establish new trusts through Kansas City's Columbia Union National Bank. The bank then assigned the Johnson account to a new trust officer, who eagerly made an appointment to see Miss DeVitt in Lubbock. David Fayman, a Mallet Ranch partner and grandson of W. D. Johnson, recalled the story of the unnamed trust officer's visit with some amusement:

> He went down there and got nowhere [with Miss DeVitt]; his blood pressure went right up, and he came home and had a stroke. It was not a serious one, but it got his attention; he just knew that Miss DeVitt had caused it. He was positive of that. He quit the bank and went to work in a small bank south of Kansas City.[10]

Then in 1971, Columbia Union Bank gave the Johnson account to its newest trust officer, thirty-year-old John Archer. In fall 1971, Archer made his first trip to Texas to visit the Johnson and Mallet properties and had his first meeting with Miss Christine, who had just celebrated her eighty-sixth birthday. "She didn't like me from day one," he recalled. "I was a kid and that was her attitude."[11]

Initially, Archer followed Christine's lead pertaining to the surface operations of the Mallet Ranch.[12] During the first two years of his tenure as trust officer, he directed much of his attention toward redeveloping his clients' control of the Johnson family properties in Loving County, Texas, which comprised ranches W. D. Johnson had acquired in the 1920s. But by the fall of 1973, he was ready to review the Mallet operation and wanted to move beyond business as usual.

The Columbia Union Bank, through its trust arrangements with the W. D. Johnson heirs, controlled 20-percent interest in the Mallet partnership. Soon after he assumed his position with the bank, Archer persuaded William Jewell College, which had been deeded Mallet stock by W. D. Johnson in the 1930s, to vest its 3.2 percent of Mallet ownership with the bank as well. Thus, Archer represented the Mallet's biggest minority partner.

In September 1973, Archer, accompanied by W. D. Johnson's grandsons David Fayman and William Abernathy, both of whom had for years taken an active interest in their family business, made an inspection trip to the Mallet Ranch and farms. "[We] spent many hours just driving in the area, looking at what other landowners are doing, and talking to interested parties, in short doing our homework," Archer later reported to family members.[13] After their extensive inspection, they stopped in Fort Worth to see J. Lee Johnson, Jr., who managed the interests of his family, the descendants of W. D. Johnson's brother, J. Lee Johnson. "We attempted to get a handle as to what was going on," Archer remembered. "The main concern I had was that [the Mallet partners] had a policy of doing nothing, and if any oil company wanted to do anything on the Mallet Ranch, we [meaning, Miss DeVitt] were opposed."

Archer placed the responsibility for the Ranch's lack of flexibility squarely on Christine's shoulders. "Miss DeVitt was firmly in control of the property," he remembered. "[Her attitude] reminded me of the Englishman that was shipwrecked and stumbled ashore on a desert island and announced that 'If there is a law on this island, I'm agin it.' That was the way she operated."[14]

One of Archer's concerns was the surface condition of the ranch, and he had his own ideas as to how it should be managed. "She had way few waterings, and as a result, she had really decimated the ranch as far as excessive grazing around the waterings. Tremendous amounts of invader plants and mesquite had taken the place over, and it wasn't at all effectively managed as a ranch," he recalled, adding, "She was so difficult that nobody would enter into any kind of deal with her, and the oil companies were inclined to . . . take as much as they could take."

Wanting to formulate a new plan for the ranch, Archer refused to sign a new grass lease with Miss DeVitt and continued his efforts to meet with J. Lee Johnson, Jr., but was forced to postpone by Mr. Johnson's illness. In January 1974 he returned to Fort Worth and outlined his findings to Mr. Johnson. Among other things, his report noted: 1) the partners' grass rental at thirty-five cents per acre was far below market rate; 2) the Mallet was declining in value as a working ranch because of its failure to keep up with changing trends; 3) the oil companies were not paying for ground water use;

and 4) some of the Mallet farm lands should have been converted to irrigated row crop production.

J. Lee Johnson, Jr., agreed in principle with the representative of his Kansas City cousins, thus clearing the way for Archer to face his most formidable task, convincing Christine of the need to reform the Mallet Ranch operating policy.

In February 1974, John Archer began his quest by outlining his concerns in a long letter to Miss Christine:

> Your Kansas City partner is concerned that you might not be looking at all the partners in this joint venture as your partners, that you might be looking at your partners as customers, suppliers, lessors, financiers, or other arms length business associates who are to be considered advisory to the ultimate profit objective. This is not the case.
>
> We are all your partners in a Joint Venture, the ownership of the Mallet Ranch. When you hurt, we should hurt, when you prosper, we all should prosper. A fat deal for one owner is a fat deal for all owners, a lean deal for owner number one is a lean deal for all other owners.[15]

Archer also asked Christine several pointed questions about her management of the ranch, including why she had not allowed any development of water resources, why she only allowed one breed—Herefords—on the ranch, and why she had refused to enter into any federal farm and range management programs. He concluded by noting that Christine's twenty-five-year-old rental rate of thirty-five cents per acre for the ranch was far below market price. "[S]imply stated," he noted, "you have not been a fair and open partner."

To soften the tone of his letter, he quickly added, "Please understand we wish to know this ranch like you know it, we certainly love the land like you obviously love it, and that we represent real, live flesh and blood people who like you are extremely proud of the fact they trace their past, their family, and their roots to the high plains of West Texas." He credited her with her steadfastness and loyalty to the land when the other owners seemed to care less about the fate of the Mallet and in turn likened his own position to that of a child gone astray:

> During this period to your great credit you became the resident keeper of the key, the son who stayed at home, the church of the middle ages, you kept the faith. . . . We now stand at February 2nd, 1974, as the prodigal son who has returned . . . but will not be allowed to speak, contribute, or even assert what he feels are injustices that have beset him during his absence.

Christine was not impressed with Mr. Archer's poetic language; while reading his letter, she took pencil in hand, and in bold strokes, underlined his words about not being able to speak or assert himself, then penciled in the margin, "Nobody stopped you, Mr. Partner."

Apparently, after fuming over Archer's letter for several days, Christine finally agreed to a meet with Archer and members of the Johnson family on February 26, 1974. Before the meeting, she launched her own examination of the ranch and dispatched her secretary Anne Snyder, along with Anne's brother Dick Snyder, to check out Archer's complaints. Anne's report confirmed Archer's critique somewhat: the ranch needed at least fourteen new waterings, and twenty miles of fences replaced; she also learned that the Soil Conservation Service would be willing to help in mesquite eradication, and that some of the grass was in bad shape. The report noted also that the waterings and fencing alone would cost $65,000.[16]

Meanwhile, John Archer and Johnson family member David Fayman arrived in Lubbock and before their scheduled meeting with Christine, spent the day reviewing Mallet problems with Hockley County soil conservation officials. Then they discussed between themselves three possible proposals: the first would offer Christine the opportunity to continue leasing the ranch, but for the rate of $1.50 per acre instead of the current rate of thirty-five cents; in turn the Johnsons would agree to allow the expenditure of $200,000 of unspent farm income on capital improvements. The second would allow the Johnson family to have the ranch for $1.50 per acre and for the Johnsons to manage the capital improvement project; their third proposal would allow "free-for-all occupation" by all the owners.

When the appointed time for the meeting came, Miss DeVitt, in typical fashion, postponed it until the afternoon, keeping her Kansas City visitors waiting for four more hours. Finally, she was ready and, accompanied by her attorney George McCleskey, met with Archer and David Fayman until late in the evening.

"Our meeting with Miss DeVitt, while being mixed," John Archer noted in his report to his employers, "could be classified as productive wherein Miss DeVitt seemed to invite an interest in being brought up-to-date on the Ranch and the information she was not aware of regarding current Ranch practices in the area."[17] Apparently to Archer's surprise, he noted that she seemed willing to cooperate, and committed herself to reviewing his information and to responding by April 10.

Miss DeVitt lived up to her promise to cooperate, and with her attorney George McCleskey did her own inspection of the ranch and also visited with Hockley County Soil Conservation officers. Through McCleskey, she pushed Archer to sign the grass lease; at the same time, McCleskey tried to persuade Archer to recognize Miss De-Vitt's accomplishments:

> She is a remarkable person and has done a great job holding that ranch together and taking care of it. The ranch is suffering from a severe drouth. . . . I do not believe the ranch has been mismanaged. Please be assured of our mutual interest in improving the ranch and maintaining it in a proper condition. In the meantime, I suggest that the best interests of all concerned can be best served by refraining from criticism.[18]

McCleskey also persuaded Archer to postpone consideration of ranch improvements until the Soil Conservation Service had made its report. Meanwhile, Miss DeVitt implemented her own improvement program. She began windmill repairs and new fence construction. Archer was quick to praise her work. "You are making sizable progress on the projects we have discussed and I am looking forward to visiting the Ranch property," he wrote to Christine in September, noting that he was beginning now to appreciate her wisdom about ranch and land management.[19]

In October 1974, John Archer returned to the South Plains, this time supported by six members of the Johnson family as well as his boss, C. T. Rafter, vice-president of the Columbia Union Bank. He used the occasion to conduct an extensive orientation about the Mallet for the Johnson heirs, and included tours of the Mallet Ranch and farms and visits with soil conservation officials, ranch manager John Sones, and farm manager Lee York.[20]

Miss DeVitt, who was approaching ninety years of age, could only try to upstage young Mr. Archer during the Johnson family visit. Still miffed at Archer because he had signed an easement granting Hockley County additional acreage for a county road, she turned to David Fayman, grandson of W. D. Johnson, during one of the meetings and pointedly asked, "Mr. Fayman, you've been a professor at the University of Kansas, and you look like a person who's mature, and responsible. Why do you let this young whippersnapper run your business?"

Somewhat surprised at Miss DeVitt's pointed query, Fayman responded, "What's the matter [with Mr. Archer]?"

Miss DeVitt fired back, "He's so proud of the fact that he can sign his name that he will put it on anything anyone puts in front of him!"[21]

But Miss DeVitt had her soft side, too, David Fayman remembers. "Before the day was over and the meeting ended, I took Miss DeVitt over to the window that looked to the west, and there was a beautiful Texas sunset; I put my arm around Miss DeVitt and said, 'We're so lucky to be able to stand here and see this beautiful sunset.' I think that touched her. . . . She had a nice side to her, but she was determined to be a tough lady."

The Johnson heirs' visit to Texas seemed to impress Miss Christine and she reluctantly expressed willingness to concede some points, provided that John Archer would agree to a new lease on the ranch. She accepted his proposal that her rental of the ranch be raised from the original thirty-five cents to $1.50 per acre.[22] She also conceded to "give due consideration" to recommendations made by the Soil Conservation Service and the Texas A&M Experiment Station for improving the ranch and farm lands. In exchange for her concessions, she insisted that the Kansas City bank sign her new lease for the ranch's grassland.

Still John Archer delayed because he could not get Miss DeVitt to commit to a consistent, working capital improvements program. In an effort to establish a policy that required immediate and consistent decisions, he wrote out in mid-November 1974 a long proposal for funding major and minor ongoing capital improvements. Exasperated and perhaps realizing the futility of his effort, he could not help but note:

> Miss DeVitt, in the last several years, I have come to grow quite fond of you and respect very much your character and initiative. I have also noticed that you are well blessed with another characteristic that could be a problem in this regard. It is a characteristic I also suffer from on many occasions. That is the inclination to procrastinate.[23]

There is no recorded response from Miss DeVitt's to Archer's evaluation because she never received the letter. Apparently having second thoughts about his statement and also wanting to further clarify his proposal, Archer pulled the letter from the mail, but overlooked the copy made for Miss DeVitt's attorney George McCleskey. In his subsequent redraft, written a week later on November 27, Archer eliminated his reference to Miss DeVitt's procrastination. Although Archer's statement was certainly true, no one will ever know what Miss DeVitt's reaction would have been.

She did choose to ignore Archer's counterproposal of November 27 and instructed George McCleskey to insist that the Kansas City interests sign the lease. "Miss DeVitt has shown good faith in dealing with needed improvements on the ranch, and I know you are aware of this fact because you have said so," McCleskey wrote to Archer. "The cattle business has suffered severe reverses since this lease was first submitted to you more than a year ago, and any further delay in accepting this proposal from her could result in a decrease in the proposed rental."[24]

Meanwhile, presuming that the dispute was near resolution, Miss DeVitt forwarded her lease payments to the other partners, with a promise that, "Within the next few days you will receive another letter from me regarding the ranch and some matters in connection with it that I consider highly important." Then in her own hand she added, "So please do not make any agreements with anybody until you receive it."[25]

Finally, perhaps bowing to Miss DeVitt's counter tactics and procrastination, Archer signed the lease in January 1975, and returned it by mail to Lubbock. Apparently still miffed at the young trust officer, Miss DeVitt refused to issue his grass lease checks until well into the spring of 1975.[26]

Meanwhile, a bumper year for Mallet farmers encouraged Archer to continue his efforts to persuade Miss DeVitt to make major changes on the Mallet farms. The year 1973 proved memorable and exceptional on the South Plains as economic and weather conditions combined for the best farming return since the World War I years. The Arab oil embargo drove cotton and grain prices skyward, and heavy winter moisture and ideal summer growing conditions meant a record harvest, a rare "double the price, double the yield" year. Mallet farm rent for the 1973 season totaled more than $132,000.

This situation only made John Archer feel that the return could be much greater with improved utilization of the Mallet lands. Since 1973, he had advocated that the Mallet partners convert more of their ranch pastures to irrigated farm land. He suggested that by raising grain sorghum, owners should be able to realize a return of $80 per acre. According to a report prepared by farm manager Lee York, the cost to convert to irrigation would require an investment of only $50 per acre. Recognizing quickly the potential to increase farm profits from $2.50 an acre to $30 per acre, Archer mused that it "sure makes one question the continuation of a commitment to the present grazing programs."[27]

But Archer was unable to make any major changes in the surface operation of the ranch and farm. Needing to turn his attention to other Johnson-owned interests, he decided changing Miss DeVitt's mind was not worth the trouble, or, as David Fayman surmised, "John just could not get anywhere, and he didn't want to have a stroke either."

Moreover, by the mid-1970s, the water level of the Ogallala aquifer, from which South Plains farmers had been drawing millions of gallons annually for agriculture, had dropped significantly. Some wells were going dry, and the cost of fuel to pump water and fertilizer prices were both rising dramatically, causing many farmers to abandon irrigation. With irrigated farming suddenly losing its economic appeal, the Mallet partnership had missed, in effect, its chance to be a major farm operation; however, damages paid by oil companies somewhat offset the loss of surface income.

The 1974 crop year proved to be as disastrous as the 1973 crop had been profitable. Rent returns were barely $7,000 for the year. Still, the Mallet owners could not agree to an equitable capital improvements program. Although some money was spent on windmills, fencing, and housing, nothing was done to improve farm yields. Moreover, because of the disagreement of expenditures, the owners refused to draw a dividend. The income from the farms, coupled with a steady flow of surface-damage money from oil companies, left the Mallet owners with more than $400,000 in their farm account by the end of the 1970s but with no improvements program in place. With a rapidly growing royalty income providing all the money they needed, the partners had little choice but to leave the money alone.

On the ranch, it was a different story. Archer's prodding Christine to increase her rent dramatically improved the ranch's income, and within the next few years would increase nearly five-fold. Ranch profits for 1973 totaled only $20,000 on a gross income of $58,000. But in 1974, receipts jumped to $88,000, thanks to the sale of 248 head of steers and heifers. Still, Christine faced a $20,000 loss as ranch expenses topped $107,000 for the first time in its history, owing primarily to the increase in her grass lease payment from the 1949 level of thirty-five cents per acre to the new price of $1.50.

By 1977, the Mallet partners had spent some money for capital improvements on the ranch. With the upgrade of her own herds, instituted by ranch foreman John Sones, Christine's ranch income increased dramatically. By 1978, her cattle numbered nearly 700 head, with a calf crop of 247 head. By 1981, Christine had rebuilt the Mallet herd to its largest number since 1949. As a result, the ranch produced a gross cattle income in 1981 of more than $200,000 for the first time in its history, and in 1982, cattle income topped a quarter of a million dollars. With expenses of approximately $135,000, Christine's cattle operation showed a nice profit of approximately $120,000, excluding any expense before taxes.

Despite her unwillingness to put all of John Archer's suggestions into place, Miss Christine found herself with an improved ranch and increased income. And although her cattle income paled in comparison to her oil income, which by the 1970s was more in one month than the annual gross income of the ranch, she was much more proud of her success on the ranch than she ever was of all those oil wells.

NOTES

1. Mallet Farm Reports, 1943, 1944, Mallet Records.
2. W. D. Johnson to J. E. Vickers, June 17, 1944.
3. Tom Jones to Floyd Hunt, May 6, 1946.
4. Tom Jones to J. Lee Johnson, Jr., May 28, 1950.
5. Richard Mason, "The Cotton Kingdom and the City of Lubbock: South Plains Agriculture in the Post-War Era," in L. L. Graves, ed., *Lubbock: From Town to City* (Lubbock: West Texas Museum Association, 1986), p. 23.
6. Tom Jones to J. Lee Johnson, Jr., 1950.
7. Mason, "The Cotton Kingdom and the City of Lubbock," pp. 7-8.
8. Christine DeVitt to J. Lee Johnson, Jr., April 16, 1955.
9. J. Lee Johnson, Jr. to Christine DeVitt, April 19, 1955.
10. David Fayman to David Murrah, November 12, 1992, tape-recorded interview.
11. John Archer to David Murrah, July 17, 1992, tape-recorded interview.
12. John T. Archer to J. Roy McCoy, March 14, 1972, John Archer File, Mallet Records. Unless otherwise noted, all John Archer citations are from the John Archer File.
13. Untitled typescript, undated, c. 1974, John Archer File.
14. John Archer to David Murrah, July 17, 1992.
15. John Archer to Christine DeVitt, February 2, 1974.
16. Memorandum to Miss Christine DeVitt, February 20, 1974, Christine DeVitt Files, Mallet Records.
17. John Archer, Report, attached to letter, John Archer to Christine DeVitt, March 1, 1974.
18. George McCleskey to John Archer, April 1, 1974, Mallet Records.
19. John Archer to Christine DeVitt, September 11, 1974.
20. Itinerary, October 1974, John Archer File.

21. John Archer to David Murrah, tape-recorded telephone interview, July 17, 1992; David Fayman to David Murrah, tape-recorded interview, November 12, 1992.

22. John Archer, typescript, undated, c. 1974.

23. John Archer to Christine DeVitt, November 18, 1974.

24. George W. McCleskey to John Archer, November 4, 1974.

25. Christine DeVitt to Mallet Ranch owners, November 18, 1974, Christine DeVitt file.

26. George W. McCleskey to Christine DeVitt, March 11, 1975.

27. Archer, typescript, c. 1974.

CHAPTER TWELVE

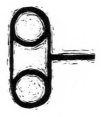

Even Greater Contributions

*Frankly, I talked to Miss DeVitt this morn-
ing and she asked me to be sure to tell you
that she is most thankful to her parents for
the selection of the land on which the
Mallet Ranch and Cattle Company was
founded. She's very appreciative to the oil
company and to the oil industry which
helped develop that land and which
provided the funding. And she's very
appreciative of Uncle Sam's magnani-
mous tax structure which has prevented
even greater contributions on her part.*
Dr. Grover E. Murray, Dedication of the
David M. DeVitt and Mallet Ranch
Building, Ranching Heritage Center,
Texas Tech University, July 2, 1976.

F OR the first half-century of the Mallet Ranch,
its business was cattle; for the second fifty years,
it has been oil. Because the oil field beneath the
Mallet proved one of the richest in Texas, it would inevitably provide
great wealth for the Mallet partners, especially the DeVitt family.

In the very early years that followed the discovery of the great Slaughter Field in 1937, no one ever dreamed that it possessed such potential. By 1943, geologists had come to recognize the field as the one of the largest in size in the state, second only to the rich East Texas field near Longview. Because the surface was surveyed in 177.3-acre labors rather than by sections, the Texas Railroad Commission in 1946 altered its forty-acre spacing requirement for the Slaughter Field to allow as many as five wells per labor.[1] As a result, the oil companies that held leases on the Mallet redoubled their efforts to find additional oil and increased the number of producing Mallet wells from 675 in 1945 to 759 in 1952, for an allowable production of more than 17,000 barrels per day.[2]

Because of such extensive drilling activity, the Mallet owners also reaped profits from surface damages paid by the oil companies. Moreover, Stanolind Petroleum, later to become Pan American, and now Amoco Production Company, leased Mallet acreage for a large gasoline plant. Initially slated for construction in 1947, the project was delayed for a time by Miss DeVitt, who was holding out for a better lease.[3] The multi-million dollar plant, located near the middle of the Mallet Ranch, finally opened in May 1949.

New drilling on the Mallet slowed after 1952 and came to a halt two years later. Discouraged by flat oil prices and declining production, oil companies turned elsewhere for exploration. By the end of 1959, Mallet daily production had dropped to 14,432 barrels, down three thousand barrels from 1953 allowables. As a result, the major operators of the Mallet leases began to consider undertaking secondary recovery methods in an effort to extract more oil from the field. In the late 1950s, Stanolind organized a recovery project for the central area of Hockley County, joining with all the operators in the field to inject water into the underground reservoir, which forced more oil to the surface. This process required that the entire area be operated as a single lease, or unit, regardless of surface lease or mineral ownership.[4]

The Mallet soon became a target for unitization, but the process took several years to implement, partly because of a dispute between the ranch and the oil companies over water rights. By the mid-1960s, however, most of the problems had been settled, and the Mallet leases were eventually organized into six waterflood units. This waterflooding, or secondary recovery program, produced astounding results on the Mallet. In 1964, daily production on the ranch was 12,956 barrels, but after waterflooding began, production quadrupled within three years to more than 48,000 barrels per day.[5]

After unitization of the Mallet leases began, oil companies renewed their drilling efforts, and by 1971 had added 178 wells, bringing the ranch's inventory to 978 wells. In January 1972, the Mallet's daily allowable production topped more than 55,000 barrels, never again to reach such a figure. Despite dramatically rising oil prices that followed the 1973 Arab embargo, increased drilling, and even the introduction of more sophisticated carbon-dioxide recovery techniques, Mallet oil production began after 1972 a long slide that continues to this day. By the end of 1980, the ranch boasted 1,267 producing wells, but daily allowable production had dropped to less than 30,000 barrels. Yet, because oil prices climbed to more than $21 dollars a barrel in 1980 and then jumped to $34 in 1981, the Mallet's declining production was more than offset by unparalleled royalty income, which in turn made several of its owners multimillionaires.[6]

Because Miss Christine DeVitt owned more than one-fourth of the minerals under the Mallet Ranch, oil made her probably the wealthiest woman in Lubbock, and in turn encouraged her to become one of the city's great philanthropists. For many years, Miss DeVitt was reluctant to make donations. When she did, she refused to accept any recognition. In 1958 she made her first significant gift, a $10,000 donation to the Methodist Hospital School of Nursing in Lubbock, the first of many major contributions to Methodist. In 1959, she doubled her annual giving through similar contributions to the then-new Lubbock Christian College and to Texas Tech University.

Subsequently, Texas Tech University became the object of many of Christine's major philanthropic gifts. After her 1959 donation of $10,000 to the school, she matched that amount in 1960, doubled it in 1961, and then tripled it in 1962. In 1966, she gave her first $100,000 gift to Tech, and over the next few years, steadily increased her annual giving level, which by 1971, had reached $500,000, then probably the largest cash gift to the University's endowment from a single donor.[7]

Miss DeVitt also gave more than a million dollars to the Museum and the Ranching Heritage Center at Texas Tech. Because of her historic interest in ranching, she was elected to the first Board of Overseers of the Ranch Headquarters Association (later to become the Ranching Heritage Association), and her support ensured longterm success for the fledgling organization. Her gifts persuaded Texas Tech to name the Ranching Heritage Center's main building in honor of her father, David M. DeVitt, and the Mallet Ranch, and to design the structure along the lines of the old Mallet headquarters in Hockley County. Similarly, Texas Tech named the west wing of its new museum building in honor of David M. and Florence A. DeVitt because of Christine's and Helen's generous support of the Museum's construction and endowment programs.[8]

Miss Christine also made major donations to Texas Tech University's Department of Music and the College of Arts and Sciences, and provided $30,000 toward the construction of Texas Tech's new library, which opened in 1963. She established at Texas Tech the DeVitt Endowment for the Fine Arts with gifts totaling $300,000 in 1979 and 1981. Before her death in 1983, Christine had given to Texas Tech more than two-and-a-half million dollars.

Christine contributed significantly also to Lubbock Christian College, later renamed Lubbock Christian University, as well as to South Plains College in Levelland. In 1964, she gave $10,000 to William Jewell College, a small Baptist school near Kansas City, Missouri, primarily because of the College's long association with the Mallet Ranch. In the 1930s, W. D. Johnson had given the College stock in the Mallet Land and Cattle Company, and even after dissolution, the school retained its small interest in the Mallet partnership. Considering Christine's long dispute with the W. D. Johnson interests, her gift to William Jewell College was not insignificant.[9]

As Miss DeVitt grew older and her income continued to rise, she began to give generously to Lubbock medical causes. In 1966, she made her first major medical-related gift, $50,000 to St. Mary of the

Plains Hospital. By the mid-1970s, she had doubled that amount in annual gifts to both St. Mary and Methodist hospitals, and by her death in 1983, she had made several $300,000 gifts to Lubbock medical institutions.

Miss DeVitt also expected something in return. In 1976, she spent several weeks in Methodist Hospital, after which the hospital sent her a bill, even though she had given the institution a $100,000 gift that year. She was not pleased and apparently let Methodist administrator George Brewer know her feelings. Brewer responded quickly: "It is extremely difficult for us to understand how this happened," he wrote apologetically. "Perhaps one of the best explanations would be to say that computers sometimes replace the personal touch in some areas. . . . We do ask that you forgive our error, and assure you we have taken steps to prevent a future occurrence."[10] Apparently, she did forgive him; during the last few years of her life, she gave Methodist Hospital nearly one million dollars.

Christine expressed her philanthropy in other ways as well. For example, she made generous gifts to former ranch foreman Wadkie Fowler and his family until her death, even though the Fowlers had not lived on the ranch since the early 1940s. Moreover, Wadkie rented a small DeVitt pasture and would annually send Christine rent money, but she would never cash his checks. Christine was generous also to Mallet farm tenants and ranch hands. Usually at Christmas, and occasionally at Easter, she would send checks to each of the farm tenants and others associated with the ranch. These gifts were made from her own personal account rather than from that of the DeVitt estate or from the Mallet Ranch partners.[11] She also gave handsome cash gifts to close family and friends. For Christmas of 1973, for example, she gave $104,000 to forty-three individuals, many of whom were children of former ranch employees.

Miss DeVitt apparently received a great deal of pleasure from giving, and she particularly enjoyed having college and university presidents or hospital administrators wait for their annual donation until near the midnight hour every December 31. Perhaps for that reason, she delayed consideration of establishing a charitable foundation. In the 1960s, she began to discuss the idea with her attorneys and friends, and in December 1969 applied for and obtained a charter for a foundation, which she named The CH Foundation.[12] Because CH was the brand her father first used to indicate the ownership of cattle belonging to his two oldest children, Christine and Harold, the brand was always special for Christine. After Harold's accidental death in 1901, the brand was used to designate the ownership of Christine's and Helen's cattle. She also named herself, her sister Helen, and Jack Gray Johnson of Dallas to be the Foundation's incorporators and trustees.

In 1970, Christine first documented her thoughts on the purpose of such a foundation in a draft of her will:

> I am interested in caring for and advancing the cause of the West Texas Museum at Texas Tech University in connection with the establishment and expansion of the ranch complex . . . and scholarships for worthy students of high scholarship and character, specifically those who are interested in art, literature, music, and drama. I am also interested in the Lubbock Symphony and other music and educational organizations . . . [and] in the care of animals, since it has always been my practice to aid and assist stray cats and other animals in the neighborhood.[13]

In a draft of a 1976 will, she noted, "My primary purpose is to dedicate as a memorial to my family a substantial portion of my estate which shall be held solely for charitable, educational, religious, scientific, literary, and public uses and purposes."[14] Later that year, she finally formalized her plans and set aside $10,000 in a Lubbock bank under the name of The CH Foundation. She also convened the first meeting of the Foundation, at which she and Helen elected Helen's daughter Dorothy to serve as a trustee in place of Jack Gray Johnson, who had resigned.[15]

In September 1975, Miss DeVitt celebrated her ninetieth birthday, and with the assistance of longtime Mallet Ranch bookkeeper and secretary Anne Snyder, continued to handle her own affairs. But in July 1976, she became ill and spent two months in the hospital. She returned for another six-week stay in late January 1978. Then in February 1979, she returned once again, this time to remain for more than four years until her death.[16] Her lengthy residence at Methodist became as legendary in Lubbock as her cats. She maintained an office in her room and received oil company employees, her own ranch hands, and a constant stream of friends and well-wishers daily.

Dramatic increases in oil prices in the early 1980s steadily pushed the total monthly income of the Mallet Ranch owners to nearly two million dollars, of which Christine received more than one-fourth. Her income tax payments mushroomed as well. On the back of one check, written to the Internal Revenue Service in January 1980 for more than a quarter of a million dollars, Miss Christine scribbled a cryptic message for the federal government before allowing it to be mailed: "Who are you to take our money from us?" she demanded. "This is tyranny not democracy. You are a bunch of thieves under the protection of the law, worse than the common thief."[17]

Determined not to let the government have any more of her money than necessary, Miss DeVitt decided in June 1983 to rewrite her will. Under the provisions of a will she had filed in 1977, in which she had bequeathed a sizable portion of her estate to her sister Helen, Christine's estate would have been required to pay more than fifteen million dollars in taxes to the state and federal governments. Under the terms of her 1983 will, she placed a greater portion of her estate in trust for her sister and for her niece Dorothy, thereby engineering a tax savings of more than four million dollars for her estate, a move that would be of direct benefit to her CH Foundation.[18]

Shortly after signing the new will, Miss DeVitt convened the second meeting of The CH Foundation in August 1983. Knowing that she was approaching death, she wanted to finalize her plans for the Foundation by adding two more trustees. But while she, Helen, and Dorothy agreed to add to the board Christine's longtime attorney George McCleskey, the three could not agree as to who should be the fifth member and postponed naming the additional person.[19]

Three weeks later, Christine's ninety-eighth birthday passed quietly. Her ninety-seventh in September 1982 had been a gala affair at Methodist Hospital, with many of her friends, hospital staff employees, and well-wishers stopping by to greet her. On her ninety-eighth birthday, however, she was too weak to receive visitors. As Helen recalled, "She barely had the strength . . . to ask one of us nearby . . . to step out into the hall and thank you finally for coming over to wish her well on her last birthday."[20]

Less than a month later, on October 12, 1983, Christine DeVitt quietly passed away as a resident of Methodist Hospital. Funeral services were held on Saturday, October 15, 1983 in the Chapel at the Resthaven Funeral Home in Lubbock, a place Christine had passed many times on her treks to the ranch during her long association with Lubbock and the South Plains. The men her family chose to be pallbearers represented the broad spectrum of Miss DeVitt's associations and included an attorney, a doctor, a banker, a farmer, an oilman, a hospital administrator, a university president, and two cowboys. Burial was in the Resthaven Mausoleum.[21] Christine's death left a vast estate, estimated by some to be worth as much as forty-four million dollars. It meant also that her sister Helen and niece Dorothy would become central figures in the legal struggles that followed.

Oil made wealthy individuals of both Helen Jones and her daughter Dorothy Secrest, also. Although Helen had not been involved in much of the day-to-day business of the Mallet, she watched carefully over her own financial affairs. Even after she had sold part of her royalties in 1950 for a large amount of cash, she worried about her personal finances and often admonished Dorothy to be careful how she spent money. Occasionally, before his death, her husband Tom would have to remind Helen that her income was more than sufficient for her needs.

After Tom's death in 1955, Helen began to realize that she would never have to worry about her finances and began to develop interest in philanthropic giving. During that year, she gave her first major gift, a $10,000 donation to the San Antonio Children's Hospital, a contribution that heralded her giving of millions of dollars to charitable causes. By 1958, Helen was ready to give in a significant way. "I am very serious about disposing of something during my life which will benefit a chosen cause," she reported to her secretary Anne Snyder in February 1958. "The chosen cause is the Menninger Foundation so far."[22] She subsequently gave several large gifts to

The Villages, a children's home operated by the Menninger Foundation, in Topeka, Kansas, which later honored her by naming one of its buildings the Helen DeVitt Jones Cottage.[23]

As the years passed, there would be many more chosen causes. Helen's philanthropy included both local and national charities. Local Lubbock favorites included the YWCA, United Way, Methodist Hospital, St. Mary of the Plains Hospital, the Lubbock Civic Ballet, South Plains College, the Ranching Heritage Center, NAACP, Planned Parenthood, Boy Scouts of America, League of Women Voters, Contact Lubbock, and Texas Tech's music and art departments, and College of Education. She also made a single one-million-dollar gift to the National Committee for Citizens Information.

One of the most visible beneficiaries of Helen's charity was the Museum of Texas Tech University. In April 1955, a brochure published by the West Texas Museum Association in Lubbock caught her eye because it asked for the donation of paintings to then small West Texas Museum located on the Texas Tech campus. Already inspired by the art collecting of her doctor in Colorado Springs, Helen purchased two paintings, one for the benefit of Colorado College in her adopted home of Colorado Springs, and the other for the West Texas Museum. "I thought of them as a memorial . . . to Tom's interest in Lubbock and his friendship with two or three of the men who teach there at Tech," Helen explained to Anne Snyder.[24]

After 1965, Helen began to spend the majority of her time in Lubbock and quickly became interested in the development of Lubbock's cultural base and the West Texas Museum. Encouraged by the longtime director of the Museum, W. C. Holden and his wife Frances, Helen subsequently played an integral part in the development of a new museum building for Texas Tech. In December 1966, at the annual meeting of the West Texas Museum Association, the new president of Texas Tech, Grover E. Murray, dramatically announced a $500,000 challenge grant from Helen Jones, which was intended to be seed money to "make the proposed museum a reality very soon."[25] The gift produced the desired effect. Texas Tech subsequently raised two-and-a-half million dollars for a new museum complex, which opened in 1970.[26] In the years that followed, Helen would give to the Texas Tech Museum and many other departments and colleges in the University an additional three million dollars.[27] Christine's death in 1983 made Helen probably the wealthiest woman in Lubbock; it also left her with an enormous business burden at age eighty-four. For nearly thirty-five years, most of Christine's and Helen's business affairs had been handled by Miss Anne Snyder. Hired in 1948 as the Mallet Ranch's bookkeeper and secretary, Anne subsequently assumed much of the responsibility for the day-to-day operation of the Mallet Ranch as well as its office, especially after Tom Jones's death in 1955. As the years passed, she became the principal contact and negotiator for the Mallet operation and continued to maintain its accounts as well as those of Christine and Helen. As Miss DeVitt grew older, Anne also assumed much of the responsibility for her personal care, arranging for valets, chauffeurs, nurses, and food provision.

After Helen's return to Lubbock in 1965, Anne also assisted Helen with much of her personal business. But in the spring of 1983, Anne suffered a severe stroke. Helen turned for help to her close friend Louise Willson Arnold. Louise, who had served with Helen on the Texas Tech Foundation Board and shared with her a common love for art and museum activities, began to assist Helen with her business affairs until Anne Snyder could return to work. But Miss Snyder never recovered from her stroke and died in 1984.

Meanwhile, Helen, in anticipation of the settlement of Christine's estate, activated The <u>CH</u> Foundation. Its trustees met in May 1984 and made plans for securing office space, hiring a staff, and establishing guidelines and procedures. They also added to the Foundation's Board two trustees, Louise Arnold and Dorothy's new husband, Theodore Klein.[28] In May 1985, the Foundation added two other trustees, Christine's friend and former Lubbock United Way director Nelda Thompson, and longtime DeVitt family accountant L. Edwin Smith.[29]

Christine's vast estate would not be settled quickly. Unhappy with some of the provisions of Christine's will, and at the insistence of her husband, Theo, Dorothy had filed an Opposition to Probate of Will in August 1984, which put her in direct conflict with her mother Helen, who, along with attorney George McCleskey, was co-executor of Christine's estate.[30] The legal maneuverings that followed would last more than six years.

First, Dorothy's attorneys suggested that she and her husband withdraw from the deliberations of The CH Foundation meeting in May 1985; subsequently, they resigned in March 1986.[31] The attorneys also pressed Dorothy's challenge of Christine's will, but in March 1986, a Lubbock court issued a summary judgment that, in effect, declared that Dorothy had no the right to challenge the will.[32] But Dorothy's principal attorney, State Senator John Montford, appealed the decision to the Texas Court of Appeals in Amarillo and won a reversal of the Lubbock court's decision in late May 1988.[33] Then, the Christine DeVitt Estate attorneys appealed to the Texas Supreme Court, which, in July 1989, initially agreed to hear the case. The Supreme Court, in a rare instance, changed its mind in October and refused to hear the dispute, declaring that its July order to grant the applications was "improvidently granted," and consequently remanded the case back to Lubbock for trial.[34]

Both sides then began extensive preparations for the will contest trial. Before the issue could be taken up in court, a second major conflict had developed that overshadowed the will contest. In December 1985, Helen had filed a Designation of Guardianship of Person and Estate, in which she named Louise Arnold to be her guardian if such action should be necessary.[35] At the time, Helen was eighty-six.

During the four years that followed her designation of a guardian, Helen tried to continue to manage her own affairs. First, perhaps realizing that settlement of Christine's estate might require many years, she set aside her plans to fund The CH Foundation and decided to establish her own. For many years, she had given consideration to establishing such a foundation. Although she had been funding many projects through outright gifts, particularly to her fellowship program in public education at Texas Tech, it had become apparent to her also that she needed to ensure continued support of certain projects if she should die before they were completed.

In March 1984, Helen organized the Helen Jones Foundation and named herself president and treasurer; Louise Arnold, a director and vice president; and her accountant L. Edwin Smith, a director and financial advisor.[36] Her attorney John Crews obtained a charter for the Helen Jones Foundation in October 1984, and Helen funded it promptly with a $5,300,000 gift. Within a month after obtaining the charter, the new foundation had made grants of nearly $200,000.[37] Because she had so many projects she wanted to fund, Helen soon realized that the interest earned from her initial gift was not going to be enough. Over the next several years, she continued to make large contributions to her Foundation including a three-million dollar gift in 1987, and by 1990, had built its assets to more than twelve million dollars.

Although she finally had a charitable foundation in place, Helen still found herself besieged with requests for personal gifts and donations. Moreover, as she approached her ninetieth birthday, she was experiencing memory loss and, by late 1989, it had become apparent to herself and those close to her that she needed to be placed under the supervision of a guardian. After a January 1990 hearing, the Lubbock County Court agreed and named Louise Arnold Helen's temporary guardian.

Dorothy also applied to the court to be made guardian of her mother. As a result, the stage was set for a lengthy trial to determine whether Helen needed a guardian, who that guardian should be, and, in effect, who would control the management of Helen's affairs as well as the destinies of both The <u>CH</u> and the Helen Jones foundations.

With the guardianship contested, Lubbock County Judge Rod Shaw sent the case to the County Court at Law Number 3, presided over by Judge Mackey Hancock. The hearing began July 23, 1990, but, two days later, a juror recalled that he had once been represented by one of the contending law firms. As a result, Judge Hancock declared a mistrial and the case was postponed until August 13.

With a new jury, the case began again. No fewer than seven attorneys participated, creating, in effect, a scene of the magnitude played out in Lubbock nearly fifty years before when eight attorneys represented the DeVitt and Johnson contestants in the Mallet's receivership controversy. Representing Louise Arnold were Lubbock attorneys Don Graf and Frank E. "Dirk" Murchison. Bill Sowder of Lubbock was appointed by the court as attorney *ad litum*. The attorney for Dorothy was Senator Montford, assisted by Larry York, John McLeod, and Mark Roebeck from the prestigious Austin firm Baker and Botts. From August 13 until August 22, the jurors heard testimony from fifteen witnesses and arguments from five of the seven attorneys, which produced more than fifteen hundred pages of transcribed testimony. Finally, in the late afternoon of August 22, 1990, after three hours of deliberation, the jury returned its verdict in favor of Louise Arnold. As a result, Mrs. Arnold was named permanent guardian of both the person and estate of Helen DeVitt Jones.[38]

With the guardianship issue settled, both sides began to prepare once again for the postponed will contest, which had been scheduled for trial for September 17, 1990. Neither side relished the fight. After learning that she could settle the matter independently of her husband, Theo Klein, Dorothy asked her attorney to seek a settlement. Five days before the trial was to begin, Senator Montford offered a proposal to the directors of The CH Foundation and the other interested parties. The Foundation directors agreed in principle with the proposal and instructed its attorneys to proceed with negotiations. By the court date, all parties had agreed to a complex twenty-page settlement proposal, thus saving both the rigor and expense of another long trial.[39]

Although it would take more than a year to work out the complex settlement, by the end of 1991, all of the details of the partitioning were completed, thereby clearing the way for the full implementation of Christine's 1983 will. On December 31, 1992, more than nine years after Miss Christine's death, her estate was officially closed when the final accounting was filed with the probate records.[40]

With the six-year legal battle resolved, Christine's CH Foundation, although it had been in existence for more than thirteen years, finally became a viable charitable organization. In 1988, its five directors, which included Helen Jones, Louise Arnold, George McCleskey,

L. Edwin Smith, and Nelda Thompson, revised the Foundation's by-laws to note that its gifts would be dedicated to "medical, educational, and public charities located in West Texas."[41] Helen Jones continued to serve as The CH president until 1990, when her health would no longer allow her to continue. The directors then made her honorary chairman and elevated L. Edwin Smith to become the Foundation's second president.[32] In March 1991, the Foundation directors named Nelda Thompson The CH's first executive director. Later that year, it awarded its first significant grants, almost one-half million dollars, to area causes.[43]

Meanwhile, the Helen Jones Foundation has been conducting extensive grant reviews and awards since its establishment in 1984. Louise Arnold continues to serve as its executive secretary, a position she has held since the Foundation's beginning. In July 1989, its directors elected her husband, retired Lubbock physician Dr. Robert Arnold, as a new trustee. Both Helen Jones and Ed Smith continue to serve as directors, although Helen resigned as president in 1990, and Louise Arnold was elected in her place.[44] Among the largest gifts of the Helen Jones Foundation has been an $800,000 four-year commitment to fund the Center for Human Interdependence at Chapman College in Orange County, California. With a scope more national than that of The CH Foundation, the Helen Jones Foundation has focused its support primarily on education and medical causes.

Since the settlement of Miss DeVitt's will, a third DeVitt family foundation has also been established. After receiving a sizable inheritance under the terms of her Aunt Christine's will settlement, Dorothy (who was divorced from Theodore Klein in 1991) decided to establish her own foundation. To direct it, she chose, in addition to herself, her attorney Senator John Montford, and longtime friends Emily Maupin, William Baldridge, and Dr. Robert N. Wolfe. Named the Plum Foundation and based in Dorothy's home state of California, the organization's Board of Directors held its first meeting on September 23, 1991, to establish guidelines and elect officers. Dorothy Secrest was elected Chairman of the Board; Senator Montford, President; and Emily Maupin, Secretary. At the same time, the directors established the following areas of interest for the Foundation's support: medical and scientific research, health and human services, education, visual and performing arts, and environment and animal protection.[45]

Today, as it has done for more than a half-century, the Mallet Ranch continues to produce oil, cattle, cotton, and grain sorghum. It is still operated in much the same way as it was when oil was first discovered. A Lubbock-based land manager, Carter Williams, oversees the farms and keeps a close eye on the oil companies' activity on the ranch. The ranch's surface is leased to former Texas Tech football star Fred Brown and his partner, Ellwood Keeney of Lubbock. On pastures that bear the same names given them nearly one hundred years before, Brown maintains approximately 1,200 cows. Although most of the current owners have changed in name, nearly all are direct descendants of David DeVitt, W. D. Johnson, or J. Lee Johnson.

Yet the Mallet has wrought profound change, especially for the descendants of its founder David DeVitt. He probably never dreamed that his 1895 venture onto the then-isolated prairies of the western Llano Estacado would prove to be a legacy that would last for a century. As an eastern, urbane, sophisticated entrepreneur, he certainly would not have visualized his daughters making Lubbock and the South Plains their permanent home.

Yet as the dutiful elder child, Miss Christine DeVitt did her best to assume control of her father's business, despite the worsening Depression and the gauntlet of legal problems. For Miss Christine, Lubbock became home after a few years. Through the Mallet, she fulfilled her dream of being a powerful Texan and found purpose in life. For the last thirty-five years of her long life, she was the Mallet Ranch.

Her sister Helen took the longer road to finding a home and happiness. Unlike Christine, who had grown up on the West Texas ranches, Helen was enchanted with the sophistication of cities. Content to let Christine, and later, her husband Tom, handle the rigors of business affairs, Helen pursued her cultural interests across the country. By the time she chose Lubbock to be her home, the

Mallet was providing her an income that enabled her to support substantially those aspects of education and culture to which she had devoted a lifetime of interest.

David DeVitt never dreamed that the ranch that he established on the remote Llano Estacado would someday make millionaires of his two daughters and granddaughter. Whether he would have been pleased to know that each would find a way to donate millions of dollars to charitable causes is a matter for conjecture.

His legacy, sustained by Miss Christine DeVitt's persistence that the family keep the ranch and nurtured by Helen DeVitt Jones's life-long interest in intellect, health, and culture, continues to improve the quality of life for thousands of people who benefit from the generosity of The <u>CH</u>, Helen Jones, and Plum foundations.

NOTES

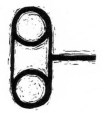

1. Myres, *The Permian Basin*, Vol. II, p. 241.
2. Compiled from monthly oil production reports, Mallet Records.
3. A. L. Henderson to Christine DeVitt, February 19, 1947, Christine DeVitt Stockholder File, Mallet Records.
4. "Secondary Recovery of Oil Through Waterflooding," brochure, undated, Mallet Records.
5. Compiled from oil production records, Mallet Records.
6. *Texas Almanac, 1990-91* (Dallas: *Dallas Morning News*, 1989), p. 548.
7. Christine DeVitt Gift History, January 28 1993, compiled by Texas Tech University Development Office. Notes in possession of author; "Texas Tech University Foundation, History of Donations by Christine DeVitt," typescript, undated, Christine DeVitt File, Mallet Records.
8. *Lubbock Avalanche-Journal*, October 13, 1983.
9. A. Guy Moore to Christine DeVitt, January 3, 1964, Stockholder file, Mallet Records.
10. George Brewer to Christine DeVitt, October 11, 1976.
11. Lee York to Paul McCulloch, April 28, 1972, Mallet Records.
12. Articles of Incorporation, December 30, 1969, Minute Book, CH Foundation, in possession of law firm of McCleskey, Harriger, Brazill, and Graf, Lubbock, Texas (hereinafter cited as CH Minute Book).
13. Christine DeVitt, Will, 1970, unsigned, Christine DeVitt File, Mallet Records.
14. Christine DeVitt, Will, 1976, unsigned, Christine DeVitt File, Mallet Records.
15. CH Minute Book, August 31, 1978.
16. Dr. Myron D. Mattison, February 8, 1985, Deposition, Estate of Christine DeVitt File, in possession of law firm of McCleskey, Harriger,

Brazill, and Graf, Lubbock, Texas (hereinafter cited as Estate of Christine DeVitt).

17. Photocopy of canceled check, Mallet Records.

18. Exhibits Transcript, p. 427, Estate of Christine DeVitt.

19. CH Minute Book, August 26, 1983.

20. Helen Jones, Speech to Lubbock Women's Club.

21. *Lubbock Avalanche-Journal*, October 13, 1983.

22. Helen Jones to Anne Snyder, February 9, 1958, Helen Jones File, Mallet Records.

23. "A Tribute to the Mallet Ranch and Helen DeVitt Jones, " *Benefactor* Vol. 1, No. 1 Summer 1991, pp. 5-7.

24. Helen Jones to Anne Snyder, April 20, 1955.

25. Draft News Release, undated, Helen Jones File, Mallet Records.

26. Lawrence L. Graves, "The Expansion and Deepening of Cultural Life," in Graves, ed., *Lubbock: From Town to City*, pp. 359-360.

27. Helen DeVitt Jones, Gift History, January 1993, compiled by Texas Tech University Development Office. Notes in possession of author.

28. CH Minute Book, May 10, 1984.

29. *Ibid.* , May 10, 1985.

30. "Opposition to Probate of Will," The Estate of Christine DeVitt, Deceased, No. 83-768,049, Vol. 426, p. 535, Lubbock County Court Records.

31. CH Minute Book, May 10, 1985; Theodore Klein to Helen Jones, March 17, 1986, and Dorothy Klein to Helen Jones, March 17, 1986, CH Minute Book.

32. "Motion for Summary Judgment of Executors Helen DeVitt Jones and George W. McCleskey," No. 83-768,049, Vol. 432, p. 932; "Order Granting Motion for Summary Judgment, March 19, 1986, Vol. 454, p. 391, Lubbock County Court Records.

33. "Estate of DeVitt," *Southwestern Reporter*, 758 W. W. 2d 601, pp. 601-707.

34. "Orders of the Supreme Court of Texas Pronounced October 25, 1989, *Texas Supreme Court Journal*, Vol. 33, No. 4 (October 28, 1989), p. 2.

35. "Designation of Guardian," Vol. X, Transcript Exhibits, Guardianship of Person and Estate of Helen DeVitt Jones, No. 90-775,642, case files in possession of law firm of McCleskey, Harriger, Brazill, and Graf, Lubbock, Texas.

36. Minutes of the Organizational Meeting of the Helen Jones Foundation, Minute Book, Helen Jones Foundation, March 5, 1984, Records, Helen Jones Foundation (hereinafter cited as Jones Foundation Minute Book).

37. *Ibid.*, November 10, 1984.

38. *Lubbock Avalanche-Journal*, August 23, 1990, p. 1.

39. Settlement Agreement, September 17, 1990, Records, <u>CH</u> Foundation.

40. Frank Ratliff to <u>CH</u> Foundation, January 7, 1993, Records, <u>CH</u> Foundation.

41. <u>CH</u> Minute Book, May 4, 1988.

42. *Ibid.*, May 10, 1990.

43. *Ibid.*, March 8, 1991, December 31, 1991.

44. Helen Jones Foundation Minute Book, July 6, 1990.

45. Dorothy Secrest to David Murrah, November 6, 1992, personal interview.

INDEX

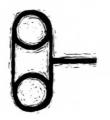

Oil, Taxes, and Cats:
A History of the DeVitt Family and the Mallet Ranch
was supported generously by The <u>CH</u> Foundation
and the Helen Jones Foundation through grants
to Texas Tech University.

JAN - - 1995